D1693212

The Enterprise Engineering Series

Series Editors

Jan Dietz
Erik Proper
José Tribolet

Editorial Board

Terry Halpin
Jan Hoogervorst
Martin Op 't Land
Ronald G. Ross
Robert Winter

For further volumes:
http://www.springer.com/series/8371

Marc Lankhorst
Editor

Agile Service Development

Combining Adaptive Methods
and Flexible Solutions

Springer

Editor
Marc Lankhorst
Novay
Enschede
The Netherlands

ISBN 978-3-642-28187-7   ISBN 978-3-642-28188-4 (eBook)
DOI 10.1007/978-3-642-28188-4
Springer Heidelberg New York Dordrecht London

Library of Congress Control Number: 2012936072

ACM Codes: J.1, H.4, D.2, H.1, K.6

© Springer-Verlag Berlin Heidelberg 2012

This work is subject to copyright. All rights are reserved by the Publisher, whether the whole or part of the material is concerned, specifically the rights of translation, reprinting, reuse of illustrations, recitation, broadcasting, reproduction on microfilms or in any other physical way, and transmission or information storage and retrieval, electronic adaptation, computer software, or by similar or dissimilar methodology now known or hereafter developed. Exempted from this legal reservation are brief excerpts in connection with reviews or scholarly analysis or material supplied specifically for the purpose of being entered and executed on a computer system, for exclusive use by the purchaser of the work. Duplication of this publication or parts thereof is permitted only under the provisions of the Copyright Law of the Publisher's location, in its current version, and permission for use must always be obtained from Springer. Permissions for use may be obtained through RightsLink at the Copyright Clearance Center. Violations are liable to prosecution under the respective Copyright Law.

The use of general descriptive names, registered names, trademarks, service marks, etc. in this publication does not imply, even in the absence of a specific statement, that such names are exempt from the relevant protective laws and regulations and therefore free for general use.

While the advice and information in this book are believed to be true and accurate at the date of publication, neither the authors nor the editors nor the publisher can accept any legal responsibility for any errors or omissions that may be made. The publisher makes no warranty, express or implied, with respect to the material contained herein.

Printed on acid-free paper

Springer is part of Springer Science+Business Media (www.springer.com)

Foreword

Business Stakeholder: *'We have a vastly different economic environment. One that is more volatile, more uncertain, more complex, and simply structurally different. The complexity our organization must master over the next five years is off the charts. Today's complexity foreshadows an even more complex future. The inflexibility of our current application landscape and system development hinders our ability to be agile. We need help. Describe how you or your organization can help us navigate this mess, be more agile?'*

Consultant, Architect or Software Engineer: *'That's very interesting, can you describe what has been done to date to address these issues if anything? An assessment of your current system development state may be warranted to pinpoint next steps and chart a course of action'*.

C-Level Business Stakeholder: *'Frankly, we are disillusioned with assessments as we have done a number of them over the years. We have implemented the recommendations from several of these assessments. However, looking back we find our systems still lack the necessary flexibility and agility we require. We continue to successfully apply agile development approaches; yet, we would not describe ourselves as agile. Nor would we describe the systems we created with such approaches as agile. In fact, we would describe them as just the opposite. Such systems built with agile approaches hinder our business and have become legacy systems. They are difficult to reconfigure and adapt to our changing business needs. We want to know how to build agile systems that are easy to change in the future, based on requirements we cannot articulate today. How can you help?'*

Consultant, Architect or Software Engineer: *'We'll have to spend some time together figuring out what you need and how we should proceed, we recommend a workshop as a next step'*.

Conversations like this occur all the time. Ever found yourself in such a conversation? Did you stumble or have that awkward moment and then suggest assessments, workshops, and reviews as the next step? The kind of problem being presented is as old as software engineering. The problem is the ever-elusive goal of achieving agility, where dealing with uncertainty, volatility, complexity, that is change, is a part of your business strategy. This conversation illustrates the 'elephant in the room.' Everyone wants agility and everyone knows agility matters, but no one is prepared to define what is agility, how is it measured, how it creates business outcomes, how it influences innovation, or how an organization makes its system development agile and creates agile systems. This book provides one-stop shopping in defining and achieving agility in areas of business, process, and system agility. This book substantially contributes to the state of practice in systems development where agility is a desired attribute of business processes, architecture, organizational dexterity, and building adaptable applications.

Agility comes with a cost and as a result not all aspects of an organization, its business operations, processes, systems, or people may need to be agile. Herein lies the rub, how do you know which aspects of the business should be more agile? Agility is not binary; it lies on a continuum and stakeholders must understand the business drivers for agility and chart a course accordingly for enterprise agility where both agile practices and agile systems are necessary. The authors make this point abundantly clear and provide a blueprint for charting a path where agility becomes an outcome and attribute of system development.

The approach described in this book focuses on the notion of a service, where a service is a piece of functionality that offers value to its environments and its constituents, that is, its customers, citizens, or society. Instead of solely looking at agility in the context of system development or software development, agility is approached in a broader context. For example, instead of just trying to create applications faster, it is equally important to provide for system agility by creating systems that are easy to reconfigure, adapt, and change as the environment demands and as business demands. Instead of making business processes more efficient it is just as important to make them more effective, where achieving business process agility is tightly coupled to system agility. Instead of talking about agility as a goal or platitude in c-level conversations, business agility is when managing change is something organizations do as part of implementing their business strategy. If you struggled with providing a crisp answer to anyone asking the questions in the earlier conversation this book is a must read.

Our industry is faced with a myriad of challenges and what can be described as 'wicked problems': problems that are difficult to solve because of incomplete, conflicting, or changing requirements, often too difficult to even recognize. Add interdependencies, cost, and effort and the problem just gets more wicked. Agility is such a wicked problem. The authors illustrate three kinds of agility that can be found in an agile enterprise: business, process, and system agility. These three types of agility reinforce each other and establish the foundation for the agile enterprise. The content herein provides illustrative and prescriptive guidance for understanding how to approach achieving agility in the context of service development and building agile systems or applications.

Architecture, patterns, models, and all of the best practices in system development contribute to agile service development and building agile applications. Looking at ways of working that are focused in rapid delivery of business outcomes, working with all necessary stakeholders and an ever-changing and volatile business landscape is discussed. Taking a holistic approach is required for agility to become a key ability of an enterprise. Such an approach requires services, business processes, workforce, and applications that can easily adapt to a less predictable, multi-faceted, interconnected, more volatile, and the new economic environment of the twenty-first century.

Companies are challenged to close the complexity gap and use complexity to their advantage. Embracing ambiguity, continually tweaking, and piloting radical innovations will be the earmarks of successful twenty-first century enterprises. Borrowing from the success of others and leveraging best practices, tried and true approaches will be necessary. Software engineers, architects, business architects, and business stakeholders seeking to make agility a key ability of their enterprise will find this book invaluable. Agile enterprise engineering has arrived and this book is a primer.

San Francisco, CA, USA

Kerrie Holley
IBM Fellow and CTO Global Business Services,
Application Innovation Services

Preface

Economies around the globe have evolved to become largely service economies. Consumers no longer just want a printer or a car. They rather ask for a *printing service* or a *mobility service*. Many types of services are provided (initiated and/or delivered) by way of the Internet. As a result, services-oriented organizations increasingly exploit new devices, technologies, and infrastructures.

Despite its importance, the level of professionalism in developing services cannot match the level of expertise in product development. Business cases, user studies, design alternatives, and actual development are not really linked, and information and knowledge is lost en route. Especially in the case of IT-based services, initial requirements are underspecified, leading to change requests in the process, with higher cost, longer time to market, and increased risk of disappointing customers. While this shift towards a service economy happened, organizations have also seen their pace of change accelerate steadily.

Enterprises must deal with this and adapt their way of working to increase their capabilities in anticipating and responding to such developments. *Agility* is the ability to deal easily with such changing requirements and environments. Agile ways of working embrace change as a positive force and harness it for the organization's competitive advantage.

In this book, we address the interplay of three different sources of agility for service development:

- *Business agility*: using change as an essential part of your enterprise strategy, outmaneuvering competitors with shorter time-to-market, smarter partnering strategies, lower development costs, and higher customer satisfaction.
- *Process agility*: using agile practices for design and development, focused on people, rapid value delivery, and responsiveness to change.
- *System agility*: having organizational and technical systems that are easy to reconfigure, adapt, and extend when the need arises.

These different types of agility reinforce each other: if an enterprise's infrastructure, applications, or business processes are more flexible, an iterative and incremental development process can more quickly and easily add value, and strategy execution is facilitated. Thus, these three kinds of agility are the foundation for the agile enterprise.

Our Innovations

With this book, we aim to contribute to the state of practice and the scientific background of agility in service development. The main innovations and contributions we present here are the following. First of all, the current and desired agility of an enterprise should be regarded from the perspective of its business drivers. Why do you want to be agile? An analysis of common business drivers is the starting point for our approach.

To facilitate enterprise agility, we need both agile practices and agile systems. We do not only address the 'traditional' notion of agility, i.e. agile development processes, but we also focus on the realization of agile systems.

Moreover, an agile process should in itself be adaptable. To this end, we describe a method engineering approach with agile practices as method fragments, which are selected based on business drivers, goals, and situational factors, and assembled to create an agile way of working.

To achieve agility in service systems, we focus on the role of architectures that promote agility by using declarative, rule-based, and executable models instead of software code. In particular, our attention goes to the integration of different aspect models to provide a coherent, holistic approach to service development, starting from high-level business goals and requirements, via the design of the business operations, and down to the actual implementation and execution.

Another architectural aspect is the use of architecture and design patterns. The use of patterns is a common technique for sharing generic solutions to common design problems. As such, patterns already contribute to agility of the development process. Moreover, patterns can be used to provide specific contributions to different aspects of system agility. We have categorized a large collection of patterns to this end, in order to support design decisions that require such agility.

Models also serve other purposes in our approach. In particular, (views on) these models are a means for facilitating communication between the various stakeholders in service development, and hence of fostering mutual understanding, coherence, and consistency within the enterprise. This strong focus on communication between all those involved in agile service development (architects, developers, customers, users, managers,etc.) is also an important aspect of this book.

Finally, our agile model-driven approach focuses on uncertainty reduction via an incremental and iterative evolution of the entire collection of artefacts that constitute a service, as opposed to daisy-chaining these artefacts in classical waterfall fashion, from requirements specification, via functional and technical design to implementation, testing, and deployment.

Audience

This book is targeted at two audiences. On the one hand, it is intended for agile and architecture practitioners, especially those who are looking for more agile ways of

Preface

working in designing and building business services, and those who are interested in extending and improving their agile methods by using models and model-based architectures. On the other hand, it is aimed at students of (enterprise) architecture and software or service development courses, both in computer science and in business administration.

Overview of the Book

The structure of this book is as follows. Chapter 1 provides an introduction to the subject of *services* and service development. It outlines what we mean by 'service' and it explains why service-based enterprises in particular need to be agile. Moreover, it argues why we need an agile *engineering* approach to service development.

Chapter 2 is the place to start if you want to know more about what *agility* means and what its role in enterprises is. We first look at commonly used agile methods and then go deeper into the definition and foundation of agility, its relations with organization strategy, social and operational aspects, ways of working, and the various structures of the enterprise. Most importantly, we look at various *business drivers* for agility: why does an enterprise want to be agile, and in which aspects do these different drivers require agility? This chapter also introduces AgiSurance, our fictitious but realistic company that is used as a running example throughout the book.

In Chap. 3, we go deeper into the agility of the enterprise's structures such as business processes and software applications. We describe how the use of *architecture* can help you to improve agility: on the one hand, it helps to explicitly design agile systems; on the other hand, it helps an organization to keep a balance between stability and change.

Building on this use of architecture, in Chap. 4 we describe the use of *models* for the development and operation of various aspects of the enterprise. Models can play a crucial role in managing the coherence between the different aspects of service design, and in facilitating and accelerating changes. To this end, we propose a comprehensive framework and method for service modelling that takes all the aspects of services into consideration. Use of a coherent set of models enables a shorter path between requirements and execution by feeding models directly to runtime execution engines, fast validation at the model level, support for communication with stakeholders, and the integration of different aspects, domains, and expertises to promote consistency across the enterprise.

The use of *patterns*—general solutions for common design problems—is an important practice in the architecture and software development communities. This is the topic of Chap. 5. Specific patterns may help to improve the agility in various aspects of the enterprise. We therefore examine several pattern collections and explore their contributions to agility.

The next main question is: how do we create all these models, architectures, and other artefacts needed in service development? In Chap. 6, we go deeper into the agile *ways of working* that are focused on rapidly delivering business value, in close contact with all relevant stakeholders, and open to changing requirements and circumstances. In particular, our focus is on the construction and adaptation of agile ways of working that uses various practices as building blocks and aims to fit the particular needs and circumstances of an organization, programme, or project.

Because of the highly iterative and interactive character of agile development processes, the role of *stakeholders* is even more important than in traditional processes. In agile projects, stakeholders are continuously involved. Moreover, in our field of service development, the set of stakeholders is even larger than in software development. This requires particular attention to stakeholder communication, which is the topic of Chap. 7. The prominent role of models in our approach is a basis for various communication guidelines and instruments.

Finally, in Chap. 8 we describe how the various parts of our agile service development approach can be combined and how the relevant *capabilities* of the enterprise may develop. The core premise of our approach is that you need agility in both your way of working and your organizational and technical systems. This chapter provides a development path for both of these. To this end, we outline a capability model that positions the elements of our approach in a series of stages or levels, based on commonly known capability maturity models. In conclusion, we give our outlook on this field of agile and architectural, model-based service development and engineering.

Enschede, The Netherlands   Marc Lankhorst

Acknowledgements

This book results from the Agile Service Development project (http://asd.novay.nl), a collaborative research initiative focused on methods, techniques, and tools for the agile development of business services. We want to thank all organizations involved in the project consortium: Be Informed, BiZZdesign, CRP Henri Tudor, Everest, HU University of Applied Sciences Utrecht, IBM, Novay, O&i, PGGM, RuleManagement Group, Radboud University Nijmegen, TNO, Twente University, Utrecht University, and Voogd & Voogd.

The project was part of the programme Service Innovation & ICT of the Dutch Ministry of Economic Affairs, Agriculture and Innovation. Some of the authors where partially supported by the FNR (Fonds National de la Recherche Luxembourg) funded ASINE PEARL Programme.

We would like to thank our fellow project members for all the inspiring discussions and feedback: Hanri Batavier, Marcel Brouwer, Wiel Bruls, Hugo ter Doest, Jeroen van Grondelle, Arian Jacobs, Philip de Lang, Richard Lugtigheid, Wouter Prinsen, Dick Quartel, Eelco Rombouts, and Sjaak Spiegels.

We are also grateful to the editors of the Enterprise Engineering series in which this book appears for their valuable comments on our book proposal, giving us a better insight into the contribution and position of our work in a larger context.

Contents

1 Introducing Agile Service Development 1
  1.1 Introduction 1
  1.2 Services and Service Thinking 3
      1.2.1 Service Definitions and Properties 5
      1.2.2 Our Definition of Service 6
      1.2.3 Service Development as a Wicked Problem 7
      1.2.4 The Need for Agility 9
  1.3 Agile Enterprise Engineering 10
      1.3.1 Limits to an Engineering Approach 11
      1.3.2 The Enterprise Engineering Manifesto 12
  1.4 Towards an Engineering Approach to Agile Service
      Development 13

2 Agility 17
  2.1 Introduction 17
  2.2 Common Agile Methods 19
  2.3 Operationalizing Agility 21
      2.3.1 Business Agility 23
      2.3.2 Process Agility 25
      2.3.3 System Agility 27
  2.4 Business Drivers for Agility 29
      2.4.1 Describing Agility Drivers 31
      2.4.2 Product and Service Dynamics 32
      2.4.3 Revenue Dynamics 34
      2.4.4 Volume Dynamics 35
      2.4.5 Channel Flexibility 35
      2.4.6 Supply Chain Flexibility 37
      2.4.7 Continuous Compliance 38
      2.4.8 Technology Adoption 39

3	**Agile Architecture**	41
	3.1 Introduction	41
	3.2 Architecture to Manage Agility	44
	3.2.1 Agility Aspects	46
	3.2.2 Operating Models	49
	3.2.3 Standardization and Variation	50
	3.2.4 Model-Based Development	52
	3.3 Architecture Processes in an Agile Context	53
	3.3.1 A Risk-Driven Approach	54
	3.3.2 Refactoring and Technical Debt	55
	3.3.3 An Agile Architecture Process	56
4	**Service Modelling**	59
	4.1 Introduction	59
	4.2 The Role of Models in Agile Service Development	60
	4.3 Adoption Levels of Modelling	63
	4.4 The ASD Framework	64
	4.4.1 Service Aspects	66
	4.4.2 Abstraction Levels	68
	4.4.3 Overview and Use of the Framework	70
	4.4.4 Modelling AgiSurance	71
	4.5 The ASD Conceptual Model	72
	4.5.1 The Context Domain	73
	4.5.2 Requirements Modelling	75
	4.5.3 Interaction Modelling	77
	4.5.4 Structure Modelling	79
	4.5.5 Function Modelling	81
	4.5.6 Coordination Modelling	82
	4.5.7 Decision Modelling	85
	4.5.8 Product Modelling	88
	4.5.9 Integrated Service Metamodel	90
	4.6 Model Integration	90
	4.7 Requirements for Tool Support	93
5	**Patterns for Agility**	95
	5.1 Introduction	95
	5.2 Conceptual Model	97
	5.3 Pattern Classification	98
	5.3.1 Activities	98
	5.3.2 Problem Type	99
	5.3.3 Role	100
	5.3.4 Contribution to Agility	100
	5.4 Pattern Catalogue	101
	5.5 Example: Multichannel Management Patterns	102
	5.6 Patterns at Work	107

Contents

6 An Agile Way of Working 111
   6.1 Introduction 111
   6.2 A Situational Approach to an Agile Way of Working 113
   6.3 Practices, Goals, and Stakeholders 114
      6.3.1 Practices as Method Fragments 114
      6.3.2 Identifying Practices 116
      6.3.3 Situational Factors 116
      6.3.4 Stakeholder and Goals 120
   6.4 Constructing a Situational Way of Working 121
   6.5 Step 1: Identify Situational Factors, Goals, and Practices 123
      6.5.1 Setting Goals 123
      6.5.2 Situational Factors: Strategy and Business Drivers 124
      6.5.3 Situational Factors: Service 126
      6.5.4 Situational Factors: The Process 128
   6.6 Step 2: Select Agile Practices 129
   6.7 Step 3: Combine Practices 129
      6.7.1 Assembly Through Activities 130
      6.7.2 Assembly Through Artefacts 131
      6.7.3 Assembly Through Conditions 131
      6.7.4 Assembly Through Process Increments 132
      6.7.5 Assembly Through Iteration Matching 133
      6.7.6 Activity Planning 134
      6.7.7 Tool Support 138
   6.8 Step 4: Execute the Way of Working 138
   6.9 Step 5: Reflect on the Way of Working 139

7 Stakeholder Communication 141
   7.1 Introduction 141
   7.2 Communication Situations 146
   7.3 Communication Set-Ups 152
      7.3.1 Artefact Creation Patterns and Communication Practices 152
      7.3.2 Structures, Languages, Representations; Topics 154
      7.3.3 Participants and Facilitation 156
      7.3.4 Space and Time; Media, Tools, and Technologies 157
   7.4 Communication Needs and Capabilities of Stakeholders 158
      7.4.1 Measuring the Meaning of Concepts 159
      7.4.2 Abstraction Skills in Talking About Models 161
   7.5 Model Visualization Guidelines 164
      7.5.1 Semiotic Clarity 165
      7.5.2 Symbol/Edge Overlap 166
      7.5.3 Minimize Edge Bends 167
      7.5.4 Semantic Transparency 168
      7.5.5 Complexity Management 168
      7.5.6 Visual Expressiveness 169

7.6 Communication Practices 170
  7.6.1 Apply Focused Conversations 170
  7.6.2 If a Problem Cannot Be Modelled, Do Not Model
        the Problem 171
  7.6.3 Do Not Communicate the Model, Communicate
        the Effects of the Model 171
  7.6.4 Collaboratively Model, But Not Just for the Model 172
  7.6.5 Respect Stakeholders Perspectives During Modelling 172
  7.6.6 Do Not Organize Stakeholder Interaction Sessions Without
        a Concrete Purpose of the Model 173
  7.6.7 Avoid Collaborative Sessions with Polarized Stakeholders . 173
  7.6.8 Communication Does Not Stop After the Service
        Has Been Created 174
  7.6.9 Be Aware of Power and Hierarchies That Might
        Affect the Outcome 174
  7.6.10 Apply User Involvement with Care, Not by Default 175
  7.6.11 Do Not Always Publish a Model Publicly 175
  7.6.12 Use Visualization Wisely 175
  7.6.13 Take into Account the Limitations of Your
         Domain Experts 175

8 Adopting Agile Service Development 177
  8.1 Barriers to Agility 177
    8.1.1 Technical Barriers 177
    8.1.2 Organizational Barriers 178
  8.2 Scaling Up Agile Processes 180
  8.3 A Capability Model for Agile Service Development 181
    8.3.1 System Agility Capabilities 182
    8.3.2 Business and Process Agility Capabilities 184
    8.3.3 Investing in Agility 188
  8.4 Concluding Remarks 188

References 193

Index 201

List of Contributors

Chintan Amrit University of Twente, Enschede, The Netherlands

Leon G.J. Debije O&i, Utrecht, The Netherlands

Wilco Engelsman BiZZdesign, Enschede, The Netherlands

Khaled Gaaloul CRP Henri Tudor, Luxembourg, Luxembourg

A.W. (Lex) Heerink Novay, Enschede, The Netherlands

Stijn J.B.A. Hoppenbrouwers Radboud University Nijmegen, Nijmegen, The Netherlands

Maria-Eugenia Iacob University of Twente, Enschede, The Netherlands

Wil P.M. Janssen Novay, Enschede, The Netherlands

Henk Jonkers BiZZdesign, Enschede, The Netherlands

Maarten Joosen Everest, 's-Hertogenbosch, The Netherlands

Marc M. Lankhorst Novay, Enschede, The Netherlands

Dirk J.T.van der Linden CRP Henri Tudor, Luxembourg, Luxembourg

Wolfgang A. Molnar CRP Henri Tudor, Luxembourg, Luxembourg

H.A. (Erik) Proper CRP Henri Tudor, Luxembourg, Luxembourg; Radboud University Nijmegen, Nijmegen, The Netherlands

Ad Schrier TNO, Enschede, The Netherlands

Maarten W.A. Steen Novay, Enschede, The Netherlands

Wim van Stokkum Everest's-Hertogenbosch, The Netherlands

Johan Versendaal Utrecht University and University of Applied Sciences Utrecht, Utrecht, The Netherlands

Ilona Wilmont Radboud University Nijmegen, Nijmegen, The Netherlands

Martijn M. Zoet University of Applied Sciences Utrecht and Utrecht University, Utrecht, The Netherlands

Chapter 1
Introducing Agile Service Development

M.M. Lankhorst, W.P.M. Janssen, H.A. Proper, and M.W.A. Steen

This chapter introduces the topic of our book: agile service development. It describes the economic importance of services, defines the service concept, and shows how it may provide a handle on several management issues. Furthermore, it introduces the notion of agility, applied at organizations, at their service development processes, and at the services themselves. Finally, this chapter positions our work in the context of enterprise engineering and explains what its core contributions are.

1.1 Introduction

Economies around the globe have evolved to become *service economies*. This is in particular the case for Europe and the USA, but emerging markets are expanding in this direction as well. Service sectors are responsible for about 73% of the GDP in Europe (CIA 2011), 55% in India, and 43% in China. As the Europe 2020 strategy (European Commission 2010) makes clear, Europe's future wealth and well-being of its citizens depend on how effectively its businesses can innovate and respond to changing markets, technologies, and consumer preferences. We therefore need a better understanding of how innovation is changing and how the traditional divide between manufacturing and services is blurring.

Organizations (including companies, government agencies, etc.) that were traditionally production oriented are now also adopting new service-focused business models. Consumers no longer just want a printer or a car. They rather ask for a *printing service* or a *mobility service*. Many types of services are provided (initiated and/or delivered) through the Internet. As a result, services-oriented organizations increasingly exploit new devices, technologies, and infrastructures, such as smartphones, tablets, or interactive televisions, to improve their customers' experiences. Innovation is no longer the preserve of research and development laboratories but has become more of a distributed, cultural phenomenon, where the processes for developing new goods and services, channels to market, and revenue models are evolving in response to new technical opportunities, increased customer engagement in innovation, and changing organizational structures.

Despite its importance, the level of professionalism in developing services cannot match the level of expertise in product development. Business cases, user studies, design alternatives, and actual development are not really linked, and information and knowledge is lost en route. Especially in the case of IT-based services, initial requirements are underspecified, leading to change requests in the process, with higher cost, longer time to market, and increased risk of disappointing customers. While this shift towards a service economy happened, organizations have also seen their pace of change accelerate steadily. This correlates with the increasing speed of development in IT, exemplified by Moore's law and the rapid rise of the Internet and mobile Internet, which in turn have driven customer demands and expectations. Organizations need to deal with this and adapt their way of working to increase their capabilities in anticipating and responding to such developments. *Agility* is the ability to deal easily with such changing requirements and environments. Agile ways of working embrace change as a positive force and harness it for the organization's competitive advantage.

At the same time, many organizations find themselves bogged down by a legacy of large, inert, complex systems and business processes. Often, traditional 'waterfall' development processes have been used to create these systems. These systems, and their development processes, cannot cope with the speed of change required by the modern day environment of the organization. Moreover, traditional software development projects have a dismally low success rate, due to both poor project planning and poor execution. The often quoted Chaos reports (Standish Group 2011) are a well-known source of this observation, but there are many more indicators. For example, there is a strong correlation between project size and failure rate (Verhoef 2002). In general, we struggle to successfully manage large IT projects and ensure they finish on time and within budget.

So-called agile methods for software development, such as Scrum and Extreme Programming, have become very popular in the software engineering community; according to a recent study by Forrester, 35% of the organizations surveyed already have mature agile methods in place and 33% were implementing agile (Forrester 2009). This popularity is not only because these methods feel less of a straitjacket to engineers but also because they are of help in realizing software systems that are better aligned with business and user needs, with a smaller risk of cost and time overruns.

Another way of managing large-scale IT-related projects and programmes is through the use of architecture (Zachman 1987, The Open Group 2011). This used to be the domain of IT experts only but nowadays includes the design of an enterprise as a whole. This is, for example, reflected by a definition of enterprise architecture as submitted to a survey of The Open Group by the Enterprise Architecture Research Forum (2010): '*The continuous practice of describing the essential elements of a socio-technical organization, their relationships to each other and to the environment, in order to understand complexity and manage change'*. Empirical support for the business value of architecture has also been shown, for example, in the work of Slot (2010).

Given the observation that agile methods and enterprise architecture both can contribute to effective agility, it seems logical that agile methods and architecture should be combined. Until now, however, this has been a somewhat awkward marriage. Many agile practitioners tend to see architecture as 'Big Design Up Front', a big no-no in agile development. However, as we will describe later, agile and architectural approaches can be combined in a fruitful manner.

1.2 Services and Service Thinking

As we have outlined in the introduction of this chapter, service sectors have become a mainstay of the economy. But the service concept also serves an important purpose in business and IT management. This encompasses different aspects, ranging from determining the strategic orientation of the organization and its IT to management and control of delivery and operations. Furthermore, the information systems' landscape itself, especially of large, information-intensive organizations, has become a complex field that combines all kinds of concepts, paradigms, building blocks, and instruments. How can we get a grip on this multifaceted landscape?

It is impossible to manage all these different elements individually. Some of these are too fine grained, such as business rules or events; some are too IT-centric, such as business objects or components; some are too large and serve too many purposes to manage them as a single functional element, such as complete business applications like ERP systems; and some of these, such as business processes, are too business specific to provide a management handle on more generic IT functionality. We need a concept that is in between these other notions and captures the essence of what an organization does or means for its surroundings: *service*.

In short, a service is a piece of functionality that offers value to its environment. By concentrating on service development, we focus on the value that organizations provide to their environment (customers, citizens, society). Of course, these services are realized by all kinds of business processes, software applications, and technical infrastructure. However, these are subordinate to the services they deliver. Traditionally, agile methods are strongly focused on software development; here we take a much broader scope, applying agile principles and practices to more than just software.

Using the notion of service as core concept in guiding the development of organizations, both for business and for IT design, has several advantages. First, services provide a clean separation of the 'what' and 'how'. A service provides a clear interface to its functionality, without disclosing how this functionality is realized internally. As such, a service is self-contained and has a clear purpose and function from the perspective of its environment. Its internal behaviour, on the other hand, represents what is required to realize this functionality. For the 'consumers' or users of a service, the internal behaviour of a system or organization is usually irrelevant: they are only interested in the functionality and quality that will be provided.

In this way, services also facilitate interoperability, minimizing the necessary shared understanding: a service description and a protocol of collaboration and negotiation are the primary requirements for shared understanding between a provider and user of some service. Therefore, services may be used by parties different from the ones originally conceived or used by invoking processes at various aggregation levels.

This also points to the second advantage of the service notion: a service is independently useful and therefore has a manageable level of granularity. Since it delivers a concrete business contribution, it is the subject of service-level agreements, its performance can be monitored separately, and it can be combined with other services to provide new functionality, while its delivery can be bought from and sold to other organizations.

Finally, the service concept provides a potential bridge between business and IT vocabulary. In business terms, 'service' signifies what the organization does for its customers; more recently, IT has started to use the word 'service' for concrete, independent units of business functionality delivered via a software interface. Both uses of the word are based on the concrete contribution to the environment and the relatively self-contained character of a service.

This is of course not really new. Organizations have long been thinking in terms of the services provided to customers, and internal business processes are designed to provide these services. Software engineers think in terms of functional interfaces, information hiding, and encapsulation. Service thinking, however, can also be applied to, for example, internal business processes and software applications, rendering them into 'service networks': services become the core building block of the entire information ecosystem.

Service orientation also stimulates new ways of thinking. Traditionally, applications are considered to support a specific business process, which in turn realizes a specific business service. Service orientation also allows us to adopt a bottom-up strategy, where the business processes are just a mechanism of instantiating and commercially exploiting the lower-level services in a collective offering to the outside world. In this view, the most valuable assets are the capabilities to execute the lower-level services, and the business processes are merely a means of exploitation.

Hence, by concentrating on agile development of business and software services, we focus on the *value* that organizations provide to their environment. Of course, these services are realized by all kinds of business processes, software applications, and technical infrastructure. However, these are subordinate to the services they deliver. Traditionally, agile methods are strongly focused on software development; here we take a much broader scope, applying agile principles and practices to more than just software.

1.2.1 Service Definitions and Properties

Let us be more clear about what we mean by the elusive notion of 'service'. The service concept is widely used in economics, business science, innovation, business process engineering, and IT. However, the concept is used in several ways across these fields. An extensive number of interpretations from the literature have been reviewed by Quartel et al. (2007). They list the following types of definition for the term 'service':

- *Value creation*. In economics and business science, a service is seen as the nonmaterial equivalent of a good, creating value for the service consumer, for example, by Quinn et al. (1987).
- *Exchange*. Many definitions focus on the exchange between the provider and consumer of a service, such as the definitions of Spohrer et al. (2007) and Papazoglou and van den Heuvel (2007).
- *Capability*. Often the service concept is defined as an abstract resource that represents some capability, for example, by the W3C (2004) and the OASIS SOA Reference Architecture (OASIS 2006, 2011).
- *Application*. Web services, but also services in general, are commonly seen as applications (pieces of software) that can be accessed over the Web, for example, in W3C (2004).
- *Observable behaviour*. In data communication, a service is traditionally defined as the observable, or external, behaviour of a system, for example, by Vissers and Logrippo (1986).
- *Operation*. In object-oriented and component-based software design, each operation or method defined on an object or component is usually seen as a service of that object or component.
- *Feature*. In the telecommunications domain, the term service is used to refer to a feature that can be provided on top of the basic telephony service, such as call forwarding, call back when busy, and calling line identification.

Generalizing the definitions listed above, Quartel et al. (2007) identify four defining characteristics of services:

- **Services involve interaction**. A service involves one or more interactions between a *service user* and some system that provides the service, also called *service provider* or *service system*.
- **Services provide value**. The execution of a service provides some value to the user and the provider. In case of IT services, this value may only involve 'intangible benefits', such as the change in possession of goods and money. For services in general, the value may also involve 'tangible things', such as the actual exchange of parcels using a parcel delivery service.
- **Services define units of composition**. Services are units of composition. Business processes and supporting applications are composed from services, which define smaller business process or application pieces that may be reused when chosen properly.

- **Services are a broad-spectrum concept.** The service concept is meant to be applied at successive abstraction levels along a broad spectrum of the design process, i.e. from specification to implementation.

1.2.2 Our Definition of Service

The definitions and characteristics above lead us to our own definition of service, which aims to be both concise and generally applicable to different kinds of services.

> A *service* is a unit of functionality that a system exposes to its environment, while hiding internal operations, which provides a certain value (monetary or otherwise).

This definition, reused from the ArchiMate 2.0 standard (The Open Group 2012), is generic enough to encompass most of the business-oriented definitions above. It focuses on the functionality and value inherent in a service and stresses that a service should hide its internal operations, i.e. its users should perceive it as an integrated whole that can be used on its own. The definition does not specifically speak about a 'consumer' or 'provider' of a service, unlike some of the definitions reviewed above. Although a service must of course be provided and consumed, we do not wish to limit ourselves a priori to an implied one-on-one relation between a provider and a consumer, since services may be used and produced by more complex groups, networks, or other structures of actors. Furthermore, the same service may be offered by different parties, and we do not want to suggest that the service is tied to a specific provider. Hence, our definition simply speaks of a service establishing value to its environment.

A service represents only the 'externally visible' behaviour of a 'service system' (see below), as it is experienced by the users of the service. A service should not be confused with the interface or channel at which clients can obtain that service; for example, an organization may offer the same information service via its website, call centre, or front desk. Also, a service offer need not be targeted at a pre-existing, specific demand; it may also be used to *create* such a demand: 'if you build it, they will come', as the famous movie quote from Field of Dreams put it. Hence, the value established by a service may only become clear *after* it has been created and used.

We can distinguish different types of services:

- A *business service* is a service that is provided by an organization to its environment or by an organizational unit to the organization.
- An *application service* is a service that is provided by a software component to its environment (both users and other software components).

- An *infrastructure service* is a service that is provided by some infrastructure element (e.g. a hardware device) to its environment.

These services may be viewed as ordered in layers that support each other: business services may be delivered in part or completely by way of software and infrastructure services. All these services are realized by service systems, which in turn may rely upon other services.

> A *service system* is a value-coproduction configuration of people, technology, other internal and external service systems, and shared information (such as language, processes, metrics, prices, policies, and laws).

This recursive definition, taken from (Spohrer et al. 2007), highlights the fact that service systems have an internal structure and may be part of an external service network. A single application may be a service system, realizing a specific software service; individuals and organizations are service systems, and at the extreme end of the spectrum, so are entire nations and economies.

Even though we define the general concept of service as a self-contained unit of functionality that establishes a meaningful value to its environment, it sometimes is necessary to be more specific about the fact whether we refer to a service consumer or producer, or to a service request or offering, or to a service delivery as a whole. In particular, the following concepts are useful:

> *Service delivery*: the combination of a service offering, execution, and completion as conducted by the service producer
>
> *Service consumption*: the combination of a service request to a service producer and the associated acceptance of its completion

These concepts also resonate well with the generic transaction pattern as for instance described by Dietz (2006) and with the definition of service as suggested by Albani et al. (2009) and elaborated by Terlouw (2011).

1.2.3 Service Development as a Wicked Problem

The development of new services is likely to take place in situations where technology platforms evolve rapidly, introducing several technological uncertainties, while at the same time, several stakeholders with conflicting stakes are involved. This confronts service designers with major challenges. To add more spice to the challenges, it may not even be clear what the business model will be for a new service. Competitors struggle with the same challenges and potential benefits; hence, doing nothing is not an option.

As Hevner et al. pointed out, this type of design problems is 'wicked', i.e. no optimal solution can be found in reasonable time (Hevner et al. 2004, p 89):

> Given the wicked nature of many information system design problems, however, it may not be possible to determine, let alone explicitly describe, the relevant means, ends, or laws. Even when it is possible to do so, the sheer size and complexity of the solution space will often render the problem computationally infeasible [...] In such situations, the search is for satisfactory solutions, i.e., satisficing (Simon 1996), without explicitly specifying all possible solutions. The design task involves the creation, utilization, and assessment of heuristic search strategies. That is, constructing an artifact that 'works' well for the specified class of problems.

The concept of 'wicked problem' was first coined by Rittel and Webber (1973). They characterize this wickedness as follows:

1. You do not understand the problem until you have developed a solution.
2. Solutions to wicked problems are not right or wrong.
3. Every wicked problem is essentially unique and novel.
4. Wicked problems have no stopping rule.
5. Every solution to a wicked problem is a one-shot operation.
6. Wicked problems have no given alternative solutions.

Jeff Conklin (2005) complements the notion of wickedness with the concept of social complexity, stating that:

> Social complexity means that a project team works in a social network, a network of controllers and influencers including individual stakeholders, other project teams, and other organizations. These relationships, whether they are with direct stakeholders or those more peripherally involved, must be included in the project. For it is not whether the project team comes up with the right answer, but whose buy-in they have that really matters. To put it more starkly, without being included in the thinking and decision-making process, members of the social network may seek to undermine or even sabotage the project if their needs are not considered. Social complexity can be can be understood and used effectively, but it can be ignored only at great peril.

Social complexity exacerbates a problem's wickedness. In terms of Conklin: 'Fragmentation = wickedness × social complexity'. For such wicked and socially complex problems, top-down, waterfall-style design approaches fail. This requires us to look for different ways of thinking and working.

Moreover, as Ciborra (1992) argued, 'bricolage', emergence and local improvisation, instead of central control and top-down design, may lead to strategic advantages: the bottom-up evolution of socio-technical systems will lead to something that is deeply rooted in an enterprise's organizational culture, and hence much more difficult to imitate by others. Such bottom-up tinkering may also lead to much quicker responses to a changing environment than a highly structured and formalized design process; this speed itself may be a strategic advantage over competitors, and as we have argued before, the increasing speed of change in the environment requires organizations to be evermore responsive.

A similar line of reasoning is followed in the design thinking approach, as introduced by Rowe (1987) and made popular by Brown and Kelley at the design company IDEO (Brown, 2009). Design thinking emphasizes the role of iterative design and strong user involvement to tackle the social complexity of many design problems. Iterative design here involves early prototyping and user feedback not only for objects to be designed but also for services. Design thinking is not so much process oriented but distinguishes three overlapping design spaces: inspiration, ideation, and implementation. In these spaces, desirability, viability, and feasibility of a service or product are balanced.

1.2.4 The Need for Agility

Wickedness and social complexity are not only a challenge to service development. They are, for example, a challenge to software development as well. In the context of software development processes, this has, over the last decade, given rise to the notion of 'agility', with popular software development methods, such as Extreme Programming and Scrum, and with the well-known Agile Manifesto (Beck et al. 2001) as a kick-starter. Agile methods, with short iterations, close customer contact, continuous adaptation, self-organization, and cross-functional teams, have been adopted by an increasing number of organizations.

In battling wickedness and social complexity in the context of service development, we look at agility as a means to deal with the complexity and dynamicity. However, the traditional agile approaches only concern the agility within the development process. The object of that development, a service system, comprising both IT and business elements, should itself also be flexible and adaptable, to accommodate future changes. This is where we see an important role for architecture: designing service systems in such a way that they are flexible in the areas that may undergo rapid changes and on the other hand offer a stable infrastructure for these services. This may seem paradoxical: agility and flexibility often arise from the use of a set of standardized 'building blocks' and interfaces. Lego is a good example: you can build almost anything from these standardized blocks with their fixed studs. Agile architectures also consist of stable elements that are easily configured and combined. We therefore address different kinds of agility:

> *Business agility*: using change as an essential part of your enterprise strategy, outmanoeuvring competitors with shorter time-to-market, smarter partnering strategies, lower development costs, and higher customer satisfaction
>
> *Process agility*: using agile practices for design and development, focused on people, rapid value delivery, and responsiveness to change
> *System agility*: having organizational and technical systems that are easy to reconfigure, adapt, and extend when the need arises

These different types of agility reinforce each other: if an enterprise's infrastructure, applications, or business processes are more flexible, an iterative and incremental development process can more quickly and easily add value, and strategy execution is facilitated. Thus, these three kinds of agility are the foundation for the agile enterprise.

The core of all three kinds is that *uncertainty* is given an explicit and prominent place. Whereas traditional management, design processes, and architectures plan for fixed goals and situations, agile methods and systems are aware of the uncertainties of their environment and know that they are aiming at a moving and often ill-defined target. Later on in this book, we will see how we give this uncertainty an explicit place in our way of working and in the artefacts we design.

The notion of agile systems also leads us to define agile services, based on our previous definition of the service notion:

> An *agile service* is a service (i.e. a self-contained unit of functionality that establishes a meaningful value to its environment) that has the ability to accommodate expected or unexpected changes rapidly.

The definitions of business, application, and infrastructure services can be augmented likewise.

An integrated approach for agile methods, architectures, and services, based on sound engineering principles, is not yet available. Some organizations have practical experiences with elements of such a new way of working; others have only just embarked on such a trajectory or first want to gain more insight into its potential benefits and pitfalls. This book aims to fulfil that need.

1.3 Agile Enterprise Engineering

Management science and organizational science have long aimed to take a science-based approach to the design and evolution of enterprises. However, the complexities of modern day society where organizations, business, and IT 'fuse' to a complex whole require a powerful instrument that enables effective and evidence-based decision-making. In our view, now more than ever, there is an evident need to complement the existing social sciences-based views on the development of organizations with a model-oriented perspective on the design of enterprises, inherited from the engineering sciences. This will help us to create an evidence-based approach to the design, and associated decision making, of these complex and open socio-technical systems. Such a model-oriented and evidence-based approach will enable senior management to make better founded decisions, based on actual insight.

1.3 Agile Enterprise Engineering

The core idea is to provide a model-based stream as *part of* change efforts, enabling evidence-based decision-making on the future direction of the enterprise. Models provide a good way of understanding where an enterprise is 'at', where it is currently moving 'towards', analyse the desirability of these, and articulate where it should ideally be moving 'towards'.

Complementing the development of organizations with a model-based engineering perspective is comparable to the evolution of other engineering disciplines in the past, such as mechanical engineering, electrical engineering, or civil engineering. Initially, the intuition and experience of a craftsman was leading, but increasingly, this expertise was objectified and founded on scientific knowledge. Nowadays, all mature engineering disciplines are firmly rooted in the use of formal, mathematical models for predicting the various properties of their design artefacts in order to make the right decisions. The increased use of formalized business models, architecture models, risk assessment models, or valuation models also clearly points towards the increased use of a model-based approach to the design of enterprises.

Another development indicates the same process of maturation: the increased use of standards not just on a technological level but also in methods and techniques. IT management uses well-established frameworks such as COBIT (ITGI 2009), ITIL (2011), and ASL (Pols and Backer 2007). Similarly, the increased popularity of architecture standards such as The Open Group Architecture Framework (TOGAF) (The Open Group 2011) and ArchiMate (The Open Group 2012) also demonstrates this maturation in the realm of enterprise architecture.

The Oxford English Dictionary (OED 2009) defines engineering as 'the branch of science and technology concerned with the design, building, and use of engines, machines, and structures'. This definition, especially the 'structures' part, also applies to (the structural parts of) enterprises and enterprise networks. Designing and operating business models, organizational hierarchies, work processes, information systems, and other parts of the various structures of enterprises can be done with an engineering approach.

1.3.1 Limits to an Engineering Approach

While adding an engineering approach to the development of organizations makes sense, we should at the same time also recognize its limits. As already suggested above, we see an engineering approach as being complementary to existing approaches originating from management science and organizational science.

It would be a mistake to think that the use of formalized models and methods means that the design of organizations and their information systems becomes a deterministic exercise: drawing up plans and then faithfully executing them. The traditional engineering mindset presumes that there is a predefined problem worthy of a solution; however, in social and socio-technical systems such as the service systems we consider here, problems and solutions co-evolve in a closely connected way. The social stream in change is crucial in ensuring that the models of the enterprise's design are indeed aligned what is actually established in the real social-technical system that makes up the enterprise. We should avoid using a 'blueprinting-only' (in terms of the change management 'colours' of De Caluwé and Vermaak (2008)) style of change management, i.e. not approaching organizational problems with a top-down blueprinting approach, while ignoring the softer, social, and political aspects of organizations. A classical engineering approach to social systems may invite such a way of working, but social issues, for example, cultural differences between partners in a merger, cannot be 'engineered' in a top-down, command-and-control-like fashion. Furthermore, the rapidly changing environment of enterprises necessitates a flexible response, which cannot be provided by classical engineering methods only, as an enterprise is first and foremost a *social* construct.

1.3.2 The Enterprise Engineering Manifesto

Taking an engineering approach to the design of enterprises is also one of the key points made by the *Enterprise Engineering (EE) Manifesto* (Dietz 2011). We regard this Manifesto as a laudable attempt to formulate the goal of evolving the development of enterprises into a proper engineering discipline. While we support the goals of the Manifesto, our discussions above on the agile and socio-technical aspects of the development enterprises do suggest several improvements.

While the manifesto justifiably focuses on enterprises as being essentially social-technical systems, its current wording suggests a rather traditional and linear view on the development of enterprises. Its first postulate states: 'In order to perform optimally and to implement changes successfully, enterprises must operate as a unified and integrated whole. Unity and integration can only be achieved through deliberate enterprise development (comprising design, engineering, and implementation) and governance'. This postulate presupposes that there is one optimum to strive for. However, different stakeholders are more than likely to differ in what they consider to be optimal, just take the different perspectives of a customer, shareholder, or employee, for example. Agile methods explicitly take this multi-stakeholder view. They are aware of the wickedness and social complexity of the design problem at hand and try to find solutions that are sufficiently good from these different perspectives, instead of striving for an optimum, thus applying a satisficing approach (Simon 1996).

Nevertheless, in this context service development, with many different stakeholders and an uncertain and changeable environment, some level of guidance and control may be needed to keep local optimization and variation within bounds and to balance the needs of the various stakeholders. The Manifesto rightly emphasizes the role of architecture as an important instrument to provide such guidance. Architecture can serve a prominent role in explicitly designing for uncertainty: not by rigidly planning for a predetermined future but by providing mechanisms for adaptation in those places where future changes may be expected.

In conclusion, we think that the Enterprise Engineering paradigm provides an important step forward in the design and operation of organizations. Once again, however, it would be a mistake to think that the use of formalized models and methods means that the design of organizations and their information systems becomes a deterministic exercise: drawing up plans and then faithfully executing them. The traditional engineering mindset presumes that there is a predefined problem worthy of a solution; however, in social and socio-technical systems such as the service systems we consider here, problems and solutions co-evolve in a closely connected way. To address this complex and evolving web of relations and perspectives, we think that important lessons can be learned from the iterative and interactive ways of working of the agile movement. An Agile Enterprise Engineering Manifesto may therefore be in order.

1.4 Towards an Engineering Approach to Agile Service Development

A new perspective on service design processes is needed, providing development teams with the means to tailor their way of working to specific circumstances and deal with multiple stakeholder perspectives, bottom-up innovation, and co-evolution of different service aspects. This book aims to provide steps in this direction. We advocate that agile development processes are much better suited to accommodate these needs than classical linear, top-down design processes, in which individual aspects are often developed separately and sequentially. The iterative character of agile processes, with a focus on people and interactions, close contact with customers, and cross-functional teams that tackle different aspects of development at the same time, is a much better fit with the complex and multidimensional nature of service development.

Development processes should also be explicitly focused on observing changes in their environment and acting upon these. As we have argued before, the speed of change that organizations have to deal with keeps increasing, and processes must be responsive and even predictive in character to accommodate these changes. These properties should be designed into the development processes, which should be treated as systems in their own right. Such a systemic approach also requires the use of development processes that are self-aware, i.e. that use mechanisms and practices to observe their own performance and, if necessary, change their own operation accordingly. This use of reflection is a common characteristic of agile methods. Scrum, for example, uses the 'sprint retrospective' meeting in which after each iteration, the way of working of the team is evaluated and adapted. In fact, this closed-loop, adaptive character is perhaps the most important factor in the success of agile processes compared to the traditional open-loop, linear type of development.

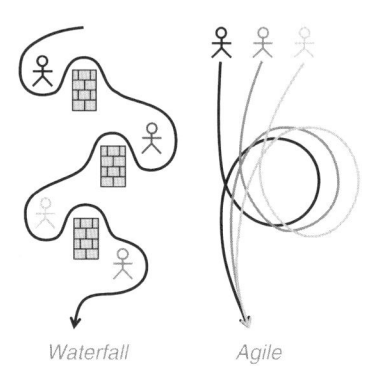

Fig. 1.1 Waterfall vs. agile process

This adaptive character of development processes does not mean that change knows no bounds. The complex nature of service design necessitates the use of sound engineering principles and techniques. External dependencies, technological complexity, regulatory compliance, risk management, and other factors all require an approach of bounded or controlled variation. Architecture is a core discipline to provide such managed variation. It specifies the high-level, strategic, or otherwise important principles and decisions that together span the design space, like a vector space in algebra.

Another important use of architecture is to explicitly design mechanisms in the operational processes and systems that support change. Not only should development processes be agile and adaptive but the results they create should also be flexible and amenable to change. Various kinds of architecture and design models, ranging from domain, requirements, and architecture models to detailed artefacts describing the inner workings of business processes and IT systems, play an important role in both controlling complexity and fostering change. Such models make business knowledge visible across the enterprise, which promotes coherence and consistency across the enterprise.

Moreover, a flexible infrastructure that can be configured with such models, instead of laboriously writing software code, may greatly enhance the agility of the organization and its systems for those specific aspects of agility that are captured by these models. Models can be changed more easily than code, and the effects of changes may be evaluated at the model level before processes and systems are changed, thus avoiding costly errors and re-implementations.

In agile development, the role of these models is not the same as in traditional design processes, however, where specialists each work on their own aspect models and then hand them over to the next person in the design chain. Rather, different models need to be evolved iteratively and in parallel, while guarding their mutual coherence and consistency. This is illustrated in Fig. 1.1.

1.4 Towards an Engineering Approach to Agile Service Development

This way of working with models has at least three important advantages:

1. Developing these models and other artefacts concurrently within a cross-functional team and in close cooperation with business stakeholders helps aligning the results with each other.
2. Using models and model-based views to discuss aspects of the service helps in aligning the result with stakeholder expectations in a very early stage, avoiding costly rework later.
3. Similarly, errors and misinterpretations can be detected early, by verification and testing at the model level, thus improving the quality and lowering the costs of the resulting services.

Next to this, the obvious advantages of iterative processes apply, such as early delivery of value and the possibility of changing course when circumstances change.

Our approach is different in another aspect as well: whereas traditional development processes try to reduce uncertainty as early as possible, for example, by having an extensive requirements engineering phase before starting the design, then writing complete functional specifications, technical designs, etc., we only reduce uncertainty when it is needed, but no sooner. And at that time, we use information from sources that may offer certainty from *all* directions, not just the 'flow of the waterfall'. This information may, for example, come from decisions already taken on the business network of the service, models that have been worked out further, available building blocks, interface standards, available infrastructure elements, processes that are fixed because of regulatory compliance, and more. In this way, the collection of artefacts that jointly constitute the entire service, from abstract models of the value network to specific infrastructural components and detailed work instructions for employees, evolves as a whole, gradually and iteratively converging on the final result.

This approach requires that various models of service aspects can inform each other. To this end, we have defined a framework and set of basic concepts to which these models are mapped to capture their relationships. This will be discussed in Chap. 4 of this book.

Chapter 2
Agility

M.M. Lankhorst, M.M. Zoet, W.P.M. Janssen, and W.A. Molnar

In this chapter, we elaborate on the concept of agility. Where does this notion come from, what does it mean, and how can it be applied? We look at the definition and foundation of agility, its relations with enterprise strategy, social and operational aspects, and commonly used agile methods. Specifically, the chapter describes how agility is related to the field of service development and how agile systems and agile processes together provide the foundation for agile organizations. Attention is paid to the assessment of an organization's agility, focusing on strategic drivers and the barriers to change that determine its current and desired agility.

2.1 Introduction

The agile movement in software development has received much attention over the last 2 decades. Lightweight iterative methods have gradually taken over much of the software development community; in 2009, some 35% of organizations already had mature agile methods in place, and another third were implementing them, according to Forrester (2009). On the one hand, these methods provide better results than linear waterfall-like methods in many types of projects, and on the other hand, they provide a more stimulating work environment for developers. Since the 1990s, evidence has been mounting that agile ways of working, using short iterations and close customer contact, have a higher success rate than traditional methods for software development, at least for many types of software projects.

Already in the 1980s, with methods like James Martin's Rapid Application Development (Martin 1991), the focus in software development started to shift towards iterative and interactive approaches. In the 1990s, the three most important agile methods arose: Extreme Programming (Beck 1999), DSDM (Stapleton 1997), and Scrum (Schwaber and Beedle 2002). In 2001, representatives from these and other agile methods joined forces and wrote the Manifesto for Agile Development (Beck et al. 2001) that describes the common ground of these methods in a simple set of statements and principles:

> **Manifesto for Agile Development**
> We are uncovering better ways of developing software by doing it and helping others do it. Through this work we have come to value:
>
> - Individuals and interactions over processes and tools
> - Working software over comprehensive documentation
> - Customer collaboration over contract negotiation
> - Responding to change over following a plan
>
> That is, while there is value in the items on the right, we value the items on the left more.

Although the origins of this manifesto are within the software engineering community, its principles are widely applicable to any kind of development in a dynamic environment. Moreover, the notion of agility has other and older roots. The Iacocca Institute (1991) introduced the term 'agility' in an effort to define a new paradigm for enterprise strategy, which the authors called agile manufacturing. Indeed, agility is a paradigm shift, not only in day-to-day development practice but as the core of an organization's strategy. As is the case in software development, the focus in agile manufacturing is on responding quickly to customer needs and market changes while still controlling costs and quality.

A useful definition of agility consistent with the above is given by Qumer and Henderson-Sellers (2008):

> *Agility* is a persistent behaviour or ability of an entity that exhibits flexibility to accommodate expected or unexpected changes rapidly, follows the shortest time span, and uses economical, simple, and quality instruments in a dynamic environment.

Of course, many different aspects of an organization are subject to this notion of agility, ranging from the organizational culture and competencies of the workforce to the modifiability of the technical infrastructure. In this book, we are concerned with the development of enterprise services and their supporting IT services and systems; this limits our scope. In particular, we focus on organizational and technological aspects and the associated practices, methods, models, and tools that provide agility in these aspects.

Agile approaches have also gained the attention of the academic community, who have investigated their foundations and effects from a scientific point of view. The rigour and volume of research into the effects of agile methods still need improvement (Dybå and Dingsøyr 2008). However, recent studies provide theoretical and empirical evidence for the effectiveness of agile methods; see, for example, the extensive overview and research by Lee and Xia (2010).

2.2 Common Agile Methods

There are many agile methods in particular for software development. This book is not the place to provide an in-depth comparison of these; for such a comparison, see Abrahamsson et al. (2003) and Qumer and Henderson-Sellers (2008). Nevertheless, we want to provide an overview of some of the most common methods and in particular of the ideas, principles, and approaches they all share.

Perhaps the first software development method to use the 'agile' moniker is Extreme Programming (XP) (Beck 1999). The two focal points of XP are customer satisfaction and teamwork. The focus on customer satisfaction is stressed by having an iterative work process that delivers valuable working solutions early and often; in this process, the customer is required to be continuously available, for example, to decide on functionality and priorities. Teamwork is stressed by having the team self-organize: developers, customers, and managers are equal partners in the team and are collectively responsible for its success. XP also has specific practices to foster quality and teamwork. For example, test-driven design, where test code is written first and functionality later, is one such practice. Another is pair programming, in which two developers share a workstation and together develop code, thereby increasing product quality and improving knowledge transfer between team members. A third is that the team measures their 'velocity', the amount of work that is getting done, in order to improve the forecasts for coming iterations.

Another, more structured agile method is the Dynamic Systems Development Method (DSDM) (Stapleton 1997; DSDM Consortium 2008). Like XP, DSDM is an iterative and incremental approach, originally based on Martin's Rapid Application Development (Martin 1991). DSDM was designed as an iterative method that would fit with management and process frameworks such as Prince2 and ISO 9000. It is based on eight principles:

1. Focus on the business need
2. Deliver on time
3. Collaborate
4. Never compromise quality
5. Build incrementally from firm foundations
6. Develop iteratively
7. Communicate continuously and clearly
8. Demonstrate control

DSDM takes a phased and iterative approach. This starts with a pre-project phase and a feasibility study, then continues with foundations, exploration, and engineering and deployment phases, and ends with a post-project phase. Within each phase, results are delivered iteratively and incrementally, based on a MoSCoW (Must, Should, Could, Won't have) prioritization of requirements by the stakeholders. This phased approach is similar to that of the Unified Process (Kendall 2002), with its inception, elaboration, construction, and transition phases.

DSDM pays explicit attention to measuring progress, ensuring quality, and mitigating project risks. It also provides quite an extensive definition of roles, from project manager to business ambassador and from workshop facilitator to solution tester. Most other agile methods defer a large part of the responsibility for defining and assigning roles to the self-organizing, collaborative team. Among agile methods, DSDM is considered relatively heavyweight.

Possibly the most popular agile method nowadays is Scrum (Schwaber and Beedle 2002). The name 'Scrum' derives from rugby and is also used for the daily stand-up meeting of all the team members, one of the important practices of the method. Scrum is a relatively lightweight framework that identifies only three roles:

1. The Scrum Master, who maintains the processes and removes impediments
2. The Product Owner, who represents all stakeholders and decides on features and priorities
3. The Team, a cross-functional, self-organizing group who do the actual analysis, design, implementation, testing, and deployment

Crucially, Scrum does not have a project manager, with command-and-control authority over the team. The Scrum Master is a facilitator, but the Team are responsible for how they organize their work; planning is a collaborative effort between Team and Product Owner, based on the priorities set by the latter and the effort needed as estimated by the former.

Scrum's time boxes are called 'sprints' and typically take 2–4 weeks. Each sprint should deliver a working product increment, however minimal in functionality. Scrum works with a 'product backlog', a list of desired features ('user stories') owned by the Product Owner, from which a 'sprint backlog', the work items for the current sprint, is taken. No new requirements may be added during a sprint; this keeps the team focused, but is criticized by some as not being agile enough.

Scrum identifies four basic types of meetings. The aforementioned daily stand-up or scrum; the sprint planning meeting, to decide upon the sprint backlog; the sprint review meeting, where the results from a sprint are reviewed; and the sprint retrospective, where the team reflects on what went well and what could be improved for the next sprint.

The latter is very interesting, because this provides an explicit learning cycle, which is perhaps one of the main success factors of agile methods. Due to the closed-loop character of these methods, teams both learn from and improve their own work as well as create results that are better aligned with the changeable and often underspecified needs of stakeholders.

If we look at these and other agile methods, we can observe at least the following commonalities:

1. Cross-functional, empowered teams with a strong focus on team communication
2. Close interaction with stakeholders, who are constantly kept in the loop and play an active role in prioritizing requirements and reviewing (intermediate) results

3. The use of iteration cycles and time boxes, in which partial but working results are delivered early and often in order to continuously add value for these stakeholders
4. Incremental development, where these results are shaped gradually and the direction can be changed if new circumstances or stakeholders' needs arise
5. Continuous integration and testing, to ensure high-quality results
6. A closed-loop learning cycle, where the team measures its velocity and performance, reflects upon its way of working, and adapts this if needed

These attributes of agile methods are not confined to software development. In fact, methods like Scrum are increasingly used in other contexts. As an example, the research project from which this book is a result also adopted agile working practices.

Agile methods are usable in many different circumstances. Service development has an even broader scope than software development, requires more disciplines and stakeholders to be involved, and has to deal with an even more changeable environment. For this complex discipline, we think that agile methods, with their focus on iterative and incremental development, cross-functional teams, and close stakeholder involvement, are ideally suited. But these adaptive ways of working alone are not enough for an organization to achieve true agility. In the next chapter, we will describe in more detail how well-chosen architectures can help to build flexible systems that contribute to agile enterprises.

2.3 Operationalizing Agility

In the context of information technology, the notion of agility is mostly associated with software development processes, as outlined in the previous section. But we should also pay attention to the products of that development process. True agility of an organization also requires that the workforce, services, business processes, systems, infrastructure, and other elements that make up the enterprise can easily adapt to changing circumstances. Hence, we recognize three main sources or providers of enterprise agility, which fit within the previous definition and conceptual model of agility:

- *Business agility*: using change as an essential part of your business strategy. True enterprise agility starts at the top of the organization. Management is focused on rapid recognition of changes in the environment, speed in responding, and value delivery. It recognizes the value of agility and strategically uses shorter time to market, smarter partnering strategies, lower development costs, and higher customer satisfaction to stay ahead of the competition.
- *Process agility*: organizations and processes focused on people, value delivery, and responsiveness to change. They have an iterative, incremental way of working, involving all relevant stakeholders, and span the entire service delivery chain, from infrastructure and software to business processes and value

propositions. Also, they are adaptable to changing circumstances: if the goals of the organization, the environment of the system, or the situation of the project change, you can change the development process accordingly. Furthermore, if the current process does not achieve the envisaged goals, this can also be a reason to change that process.
- *System agility*: systems (both technical and organizational) that are easy to change. Business knowledge should be made visible, accessible, and adaptable, instead of hidden in software applications or administrative handbooks. This requires new architectures, in which business knowledge is described and enacted using models, for example, for business processes or business rules. This makes this knowledge accessible to business experts and other stakeholders, reduces the effort in system changes, and facilitates offline simulation and testing to forecast the effects of changes.

These different types of agility reinforce each other: if an enterprise's infrastructure or business processes are more flexible, an iterative and incremental development process can more quickly and easily add value. Together, they result in agile enterprises: nimble organizations that strategically use change to their advantage, outmanoeuvring competitors with shorter time to market, smarter partnering strategies, lower development costs, and higher customer satisfaction.

Sherehiy et al. (2007) provide a broad overview of the aspects and concepts that play a role in enterprise agility. In their extensive literature review, the core characteristics they identify are flexibility, responsiveness, culture of change, speed, integration and low complexity, high-quality and customized products, and mobilization of core competences. These core characteristics should be reflected in the strategy, organization, and workforce of the enterprise. For each of these, they provide a further subdivision of the important characteristics. For example, an agile organization exhibits such attributes as decentralized knowledge and control, few formalized rules and procedures, fluid role definitions, informal and personal coordination, employee empowerment, and cross-functional teams.

In a study on agile manufacturing organizations, Sharifi and Zhang (1999) define a conceptual model of agility that fits with the above definition of agility and is also applicable to our context. Figure 2.1 summarizes this model. On the left hand, we see the drivers for agility, that is, the reasons why an organization has to become (more) agile. In the middle, we see agile capabilities, that is, how agile the organization actually is, decomposed in a set of four aspects that align with the definition above. On the right, we see the providers or sources of agility, that is, the practices, methods, and tools for establishing or improving agility in the organization, its technology and people, and the innovations it produces.

The focus on change as the driving factor means that agility is not a *state* to strive for or obtain, since the increased uncertainty and unpredictability in the business environment means that the way in which enterprises respond to their environment needs to be adaptive itself. Rather, agility is an *attitude* of embracing change as an opportunity and to harness it for the organization's competitive advantage.

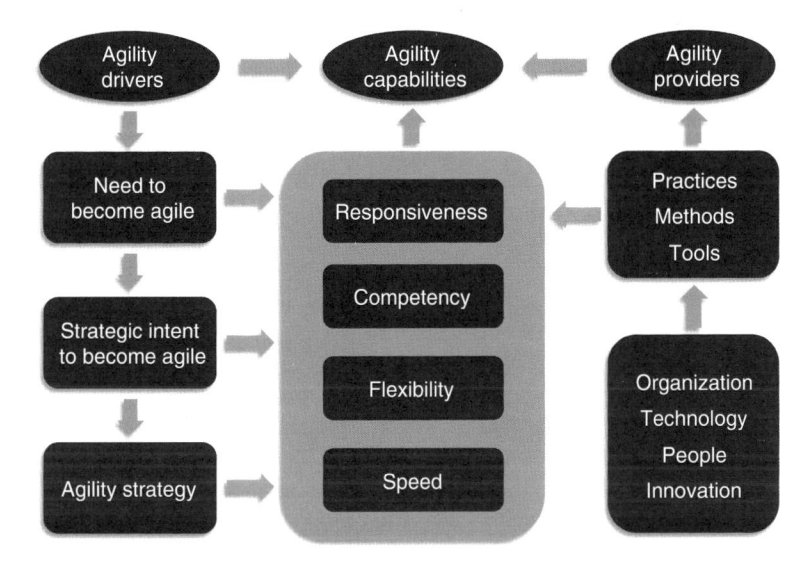

Fig. 2.1 Conceptual model of agility (Sharifi and Zhang 1999)

2.3.1 Business Agility

Agility has become a key ability of enterprises. The pace at which customers demand changes, laws and regulations are introduced that affect services and processes, and competitors can copy services, leads to tremendous pressure. Pressure to change, adopt, scale up, or reduce cost. So in many organizations, being agile is as crucial as being able to innovate. Nowadays, innovation and agility are both crucial competences for a sustainable business, albeit that they are often tackled separately. Innovation does not require agility, but agility can greatly leverage innovation capabilities.

Agility does not come for free; you often need to make a considerable effort to create flexible organizations and IT systems, from renovating or replacing legacy systems to perhaps even changing the organizational culture. Hence, organizations need to choose where to focus their efforts in becoming more agile. Every organization needs to think strategically about where it needs agility as a core competence and to develop its processes and structures accordingly. Only then the time to market of new or changing services can match or exceed the expectations of customers.

There is a strong connection between the IT competences of an enterprise, the options this creates, the agility resulting from these options, and the competitive actions the enterprise can take. And all of these crucially depend on entrepreneurial alertness: strategic and systemic insight used to profit from opportunities when they arise.

Also important for most enterprises is cost reduction or, more generally, a change in cost and revenue structure. In recent years, public and private service organizations have been confronted with the largest budget cuts in decades. These cuts are often so severe that they require these organizations to rethink their entire business model. An interesting example of a sector that has had to reinvent itself, and will continue to have to do so, is publishing. Under pressure of the wide availability of free content, they have been frantically searching for new business models and new services, even moving into cross-selling of wine through web shops. Also, sharing services and information between newspapers has become a necessity. The struggle over free or 'freemium' business models is still going on.

Focusing on customers and costs may come at a price: reduced intrinsic innovation capabilities. An organization needs to be able to innovate constantly and therefore needs skills to collaborate with external partners as well as combine operational excellence with new product development. The latter requires a so-called *ambidextrous organization* (O'Reilly and Tushman 2004). This means that an organization should take care to invest in the right portfolio of projects, serving a combination of short-term goals and longer-term objectives, leading to a mixed set of competences in the organization. It should be agile in its portfolio of services and not only in the way it can deliver or produce services.

The outcomes of these efforts are inherently difficult to predict. Moreover, agility cannot be discussed from the perspective of a single organization alone. Many aspects of agility require taking the network of collaborating organizations, or sometimes even competitors, into account. This implies that agility transcends the individual enterprise. Popular informal approaches such as the Business Model Canvas (Osterwalder and Pigneur 2009) illustrate this, using concepts such as key partners, revenue models, and customer segments. We look this issue in more detail when we elaborate on the business drivers for agility in Sect. 2.4.

Example: AgiSurance, A Medium-Sized Insurance Company

To illustrate our approach, we will use a common case throughout this book. This case describes AgiSurance, a fictitious but realistic medium-sized insurance company; the content and scenarios of the case are based on our own experience with similar companies.

AgiSurance is the result of a recent merger of three previously independent insurance companies:

- Home & Away, specializing in homeowner's insurance and travel
- PRO-FIT, specializing in car insurance
- LegallyYours, specializing in legal expense insurance

The company now consists of three divisions with the same names and headquarters as their independent predecessors. AgiSurance was formed to take advantage of numerous synergies between the three organizations. While the three pre-merger companies sold different types of insurance, they had similar business models. All three sold directly to consumers and small businesses through the web, e-mail, telephone, and postal mail channels.

Each had loyal customer bases and strong reputations for integrity, value, service, and financial stability.

They realized that only a larger, combined company could simultaneously control its costs, maintain its customer satisfaction, invest in new technology, and take advantage of emerging markets with high growth potential. In particular, AgiSurance's strategy is to become the product leader in specialist insurances for niche markets. Such niches often demand rapid response to sudden market demand and require the combination of different insurance components from multiple product divisions. By combining and configuring modular elements of different insurance types, AgiSurance wants to be fast and efficient in delivering such niche products.

For example, recent mishaps at pop festivals have generated a market demand from festival attendees for insurance packages that comprise elements from cancellation, travel, sports, and accident insurance. Policy elements include, for example, the right to get a refund in case of bad weather or changes to the festival line-up, property insurance for damages incurred while crowd-surfing, etc. This insurance product is sold via a marketing and sales strategy targeted at students, exploiting social media channels and smartphone apps. Cooperation with festival organizers and ticket resellers is an essential element in the business model. Similar 'event insurance' products are targeted at companies to insure their employees during company social events and trips; although the products themselves are comparable, the business model, channels, and partners are radically different here.

2.3.2 Process Agility

Core capabilities of agile organizations are responsiveness, speed, competency, and flexibility (Sharifi and Zhang 1999). As applied to development processes for services, we think that the following quality attributes of such a process are important:

1. The *responsiveness* to business needs. By being in close and continuous contact with users and other stakeholders, agile processes are better attuned to their needs than waterfall-like ways of working and hence are more effective at delivering value. Note that seemingly technical qualities such as the extensibility or scalability of a system are in the end also based on a business need.
2. The *speed* of delivering business value through working results, that is, the response time to new requirements. Agile processes deliver early and often, in an iterative fashion, and 'always' have partial but working results available.
3. The *competency* of the organization, that is, delivering optimal results, in terms of both quantity and quality, with limited resources. Agile processes work with

fixed budgets and resources, but optimize the business-relevant results that can be delivered within these bounds.
4. The *flexibility* of the process, that is, its adaptability to changing circumstances, learning experiences of team members, etc. Agility not only manifests itself in the services that are developed and the way in which the process is able to deal with, for example, changing requirements, but also in the working process itself, for example, scaling it up for a growing project. This should be able to adapt to different circumstances, and double-loop learning should be employed to improve the process based on previous experience.
5. The *sustainability* of the way of working, for example, whether it can be applied in the long run without resulting in demotivated employees or strained customer relationships. Agile processes focus on a steady workload for team members instead of demanding peak performance just before a deadline. This issue is not addressed by Sharifi and Zhang, but important nonetheless.

The qualities listed above are *external* process properties. They are related to the principles of the Agile Manifesto. There are other internal aspects that contribute to these qualities. Many agile practices aim to capture such contributing aspects. In Chap. 6, we will go deeper into these practices and their contribution to agility.

Agility in development processes requires an appropriate organizational foundation, which supports agile ways of working. This may be achieved through appropriate authorities, rules, coordination guidelines, structure, and human resources management (HRM) practices. For example, decentralized knowledge and control may support agile processes better than a central command-and-control authority. Particularly, HRM is supported by the principles of the Agile Manifesto (build projects around motivated individuals, give them the environment and support they need, and trust them to get the job done).

In classical organizations, there is often a strong distinction between the standing organization and the change or project organization. Larger changes are defined and designed 'offline', in projects, and once they are ready, they are deployed in the standing organization. In agile organizations, however, this distinction is less clear. Short iterations and direct feedback from practice make the interplay between standing and change organization much tighter. Moreover, the delay induced by a strong separation of these is also unwanted from an agility perspective; agile organizations should be able to handle larger changes without the need for separate projects, in order to provide a fast response to drivers from the environment.

As described previously, another common characteristic of agile processes is their use of feedback loops and learning. In classical waterfall processes, you define your requirements in detail at the start of a project and only use a feed-forward approach in realizing these. In agile processes, however, the partial results are continuously evaluated with users and other stakeholders, and their response is used in refining these results and prioritizing the next work items. This is the first feedback loop of agility. Moreover, agile processes reflect on themselves and use double-loop learning to improve the process based upon past experience. This constitutes the second feedback loop of agility. These feedback loops require support by an agile workforce. Participants of teams with agile processes need to be proactive, adaptive, and resilient.

Cockburn and Highsmith (2001) focus on this people factor. They state that a principal idea in agile environments is that the team can be more effective in responding to change if it can improve the distribution of information between people. For example, the agile team works to place people physically closer, replace documents with face-to-face communication and whiteboards, and involve user experts in the team. In addition, agility requires responsive people and organizations, so that they can focus on the talents and skills of individuals and cast processes to specific people and teams, not the other way around. Agile processes are intended to take advantage of each individual's and each team's particular skills. Therefore, we should select, tailor, and adapt every process to the individuals in a particular team. This attention to people and their talent, skills, and knowledge is a key element of social and organizational aspects of agility (Cockburn and Highsmith 2001).

Misra et al. (2009) identified some important success factors in adopting agile software development practices: customer-centric issues (satisfaction, collaboration, and commitment), decision time, corporate culture, personal characteristics, societal culture, and training and learning. Customer-centric issues are important, because the whole idea of agility is trying to satisfy the customers. Therefore, this requires that the customers are dedicated to the project and they participate in agile development projects. Decision time is critical to reduce the requirements and partition the whole time into short periods, which leads to higher efficiency of the decision-making process. Another important success factor in adopting agile practices is corporate culture, as noted by, for example, Lindvall et al. (2002) and Bossavit (2002). For example, organizations with a welcoming culture of dynamic communication and trusting people may adopt agility easier.

Furthermore, personal characteristics have a significant impact in adopting agile practices. Various characteristics are considered as important for agility, and Lindvall et al. list some of those attributes, such as having honesty, a collaborative attitude, a sense of responsibility, readiness to learn, and work with other people. An additional influence in adopting agile practices is the societal culture, since the culture of the society in which the organization operates is critical. Besides cultural attributes, training and learning readiness also influence the adoption of agile practices. Lindvall et al. (2002) state that the emphasis on continuous learning in agile projects needs to be supported by the social aspects of an organization.

2.3.3 System Agility

The various qualities of a system or service can be expressed in many forms and attributes. Some of these attributes provide a contribution to the agility of the system and may help us in operationalizing what this elusive notion of agility really means. In the IT domain, there is a well-known set of such 'non-functional' or quality attributes, the so-called -ilities described by the ISO/IEC 9126 standard for software product quality (ISO/IEC 1991; now part of the ISO/IEC 25000:2005 standard). This defines six main qualities: functionality, usability, efficiency, reliability, maintainability, and portability, each decomposed in a number of subqualities. Although these are properties pertaining to aspects of software quality, they also extend beyond the realm of software development to the general kind of systems that provide services as defined in this book. The Extended ISO model (Van Zeist and Hendriks 1996) adds a number of relevant aspects and also provides various indicators that can be used to measure these qualities.

Based on this, we have defined the agility of systems to consist of the following five aspects, each comprising the relevant and related -ilities from these standards:

1. The ease of *making changes* to a system: customizability (by users), adaptability (by system management), analysability (by designers) and changeability (by developers), and also scalability (e.g. to accommodate higher volumes). Of course, the ease of adapting or changing a system is a core element of agility.
2. The ease of rapidly *deploying* changes: learnability, installability, testability, and manageability. Particularly important in iterative development, where a system and its parts have to be tested, installed, and used many times over.
3. The ease of minimizing and dealing with *effects* of changes: stability, fault tolerance, and recoverability. If something goes wrong during a change, the effects should be minimal and easily corrected to minimize disruption of and risk to the day-to-day operations. The more and the more often a system changes, the more important this becomes.
4. The ease of *integrating* a system with its environment: interoperability and conformance to standards. These make it easier to use the system in its environment and connect it to other systems.
5. The ease of *decoupling* a system from its environment: replaceability and reusability. How dependent is the environment on the particularities of the system, and how dependent are the system and its components on their particular environment? The more independence between system and environment, the more agile the organization who owns it becomes.

These five aspects may serve as guidelines in the development of agile systems. Later on in this book, we will see how we pay attention to these aspects in developing agile services and architectures. Of course, other qualities than those mentioned above are also important in service development, as agility is not the only design concern. Furthermore, the -ilities listed above are *external* system properties. Other, internal properties contribute to these. A prominent example is modularity. Modularity is a way of achieving some of the above-mentioned -ilities, in particular maintainability and portability (analyzability, changeability, adaptability). So it is an important design principle, but it is not a system quality like the ISO 9126 -ilities. Like other good (and related) design principles, for example, high cohesion, low coupling, and separation of concerns, modularity only pays off indirectly because it positively influences some of these -ilities, but it has no direct return for users or customers. As such, it is never an end-user requirement, whereas the -ilities are.

Specifically for software-based systems, more detailed agility assessments can be applied, by examining their design and code. Lagerström et al. (2010) have developed a method for maintainability analysis based on architecture models and Bayesian statistics based on a large number of real-life cases. The Software Improvement Group uses a method for determining the maintainability of software products using automated source code analysis (Heitlager et al. 2007). They derive qualitative scores for the maintainability sub-characteristics as defined in the ISO/IEC 9126 quality model by calculating several properties of the software, such as unit size and complexity, fan-in and fan-out, duplication and modularization, and mapping them to the quality characteristics of analysability, changeability, stability, and testability. Similar properties could be calculated for other aspects such as portability, and for other domains such as business processes. Furthermore, the online version of the Extended ISO model (Zeist and Hendriks 1996; http://complexitymap.com/quint2/) describes a number of concrete metrics for measuring the -ilities mentioned above. However, many of these measures only assess aspects of quality (or agility) after the fact. One measure of changeability, for example, is 'modification effort per unit volume'. Such measures do not provide guidance in achieving agility in newly built systems or services and need to be supplemented by predictive, forward-looking assessments.

2.4 Business Drivers for Agility

We have seen that agility can have many forms and aspects, and organizations may be agile in many different areas of operation. Whether it is useful or necessary to be agile in a specific domain depends on the one hand on the organization's *environment* and, in particular, on the events and changes in this context and, on the other hand, on the organization's *strategy*. For example, an insurance company that has an operational excellence strategy may aim for low cost and high efficiency by standardizing processes and IT platforms. If this company lives in an environment that demands frequent changes to its service parameters (e.g. insurance coverage, premium calculations, and legal compliance), this may require an IT platform that can be (re)configured rapidly and inexpensively, but does not need to differentiate between customer types. If the organization has a customer intimacy strategy, differences in customer segment (their expectations, their value to the company, etc.) may instead be the driving factor for agility, requiring frequent changes to, for example, channels and customer interaction based on these differences.

As explained by Sharifi and Zhang (1999), a method for becoming more agile could comprise the following steps:

1. Determining the agility drivers of the organization, that is, which changes in the environment affect the organization
2. Assessing how agile the organization needs to be
3. Determining its current agility

4. Analysing the gap between current and desired agility
5. Defining a course of action to close this gap by using the right agile practices to improve the organization's agility capabilities

To assist organizations in assessing their current and desired agility, we must first address the business drivers for agility. To this end, we have developed an analysis instrument, which is described in Chap. 6. Based on our practical experiences with this instrument, we have observed the following common business drivers for agility:

1. *Product/service dynamics*: introducing new services, phasing out services, or changing service parameters, rules, or other aspects, as a response to market demands or new opportunities
2. *Revenue dynamics*: coping with changes in pricing strategies and other aspects that influence your revenue stream
3. *Volume dynamics*: dealing with changes in demand and supply, requiring, for example, resource scaling
4. *Channel flexibility*: changing the use of different channels to deliver services, add new channels, drop expensive ones, and move to new technologies
5. *Supply chain flexibility*: involving different partners in realizing or delivering your services
6. *Continuous compliance*: complying with applicable rules and regulations
7. *Technology adoption*: applying new technology to lower costs or gain an advantage over competitors

> **Example: AgiSurance Business Drivers**
>
> Quickly setting up such insurance products in cooperation with relevant partners and using the right channels requires a great deal of agility. The main business drivers for agility in case of AgiSurance are product and service dynamics, to deal with the specifics of these niche products; volume dynamics, to cope with sudden changes in demand; and channel flexibility, to use the right channels and partners to target these niche markets.

Next, we need to relate the business drivers to the specific parts of the organization where flexibility is required to accommodate such changes. This provides a basis for determining the needs for agility. Below, we will describe these drivers in more detail.

Secondly, we need to investigate the effects of such changes and possible barriers for accommodating them, addressing various aspects of the enterprise, its business processes, and its IT systems. This results in an assessment of the enterprise's current agility. Combining the desired agility with these barriers provides us with insight into the 'hotspots' of an organization: where is flexibility needed, but lacking? This is where our attention should be focused.

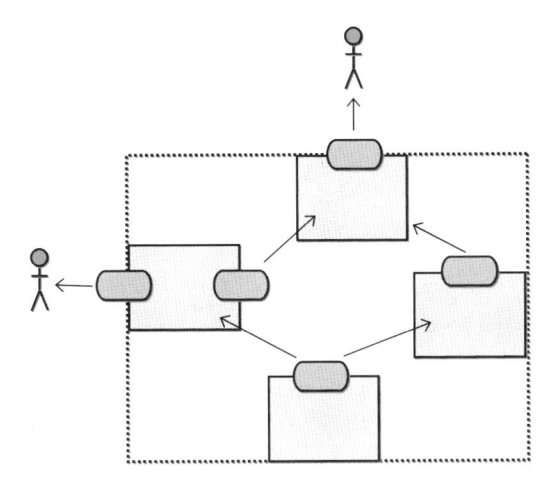

Fig. 2.2 Service network

2.4.1 Describing Agility Drivers

The drivers mentioned in the previous section touch upon many aspects of the enterprise, its context, and partners. In order to get a better understanding of the drivers and their contact points, we will use visualizations or models, as commonly used in many techniques. The concepts needed to do so can be found in modelling techniques such as ArchiMate (The Open Group 2012; Lankhorst et al. 2009), STOF (Bouwman et al. 2008), service science thinking (Spohrer et al. 2007; Salvendy and Karwowski 2010), and the Business Model Canvas (Osterwalder and Pigneur 2009). We give an informal description of these techniques here, a full formalization is beyond the goals of this section, but can be found in the literature mentioned above.

As can already be derived from the brief characterization of the seven drivers mentioned above, many of the drivers touch upon more than a single enterprise. In most cases, customers play an important role. Also, partners or competitors are relevant actors in the discussion. We therefore take as a demarcation of the object of analysis the *networked enterprise,* or service system networks: networks of connected service systems that have one or more associated value propositions—specific packages of benefits and solutions that a service system intends to offer and deliver to others (Fig. 2.2). Banks together with other financial service providers and customers form a service network, as do retailers with their suppliers.

Service networks are similar to value systems as used by Porter (1996). The concept is closely related to that of business models, defined as a blueprint of the way a (network of) organization(s) creates and delivers value for itself and its users through services or products. The business model therefore also refers to the internal structure and behaviour of the service system or network.

Table 2.1 Service network concepts

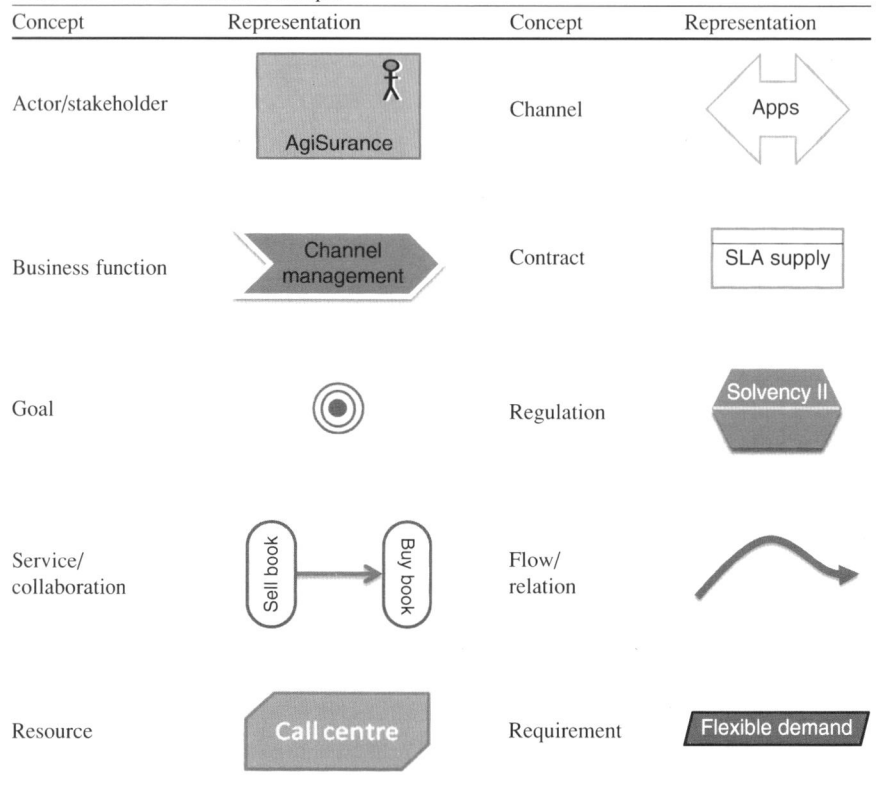

Concept	Representation	Concept	Representation
Actor/stakeholder	AgiSurance (person icon)	Channel	Apps
Business function	Channel management	Contract	SLA supply
Goal	(target icon)	Regulation	Solvency II
Service/collaboration	Sell book → Buy book	Flow/relation	(arrow)
Resource	Call centre	Requirement	Flexible demand

As described in Chap. 1, a *service system* is a dynamic configuration of resources that can create and deliver *services* while balancing risk taking and value co-creation. A service system is associated with an actor, such as a bank or an insurance company. So an actor delivers value through services. Services are delivered to other actors in the system though *channels*, such as intermediaries, Internet, mail, phones, call centres, etc. An actor has a certain intention or *goal* related to the service. Think of goals such as maximized customer satisfaction or yearly price reduction. A service can be formalized under a *contract*. The service system can be subject to regulation, such as Basel II and III, Solvency II, etc.

In order to describe the internal ways of working of the service system, we typically talk in terms of resources (people, stock, knowledge, systems), business functions (sales, customer relationship management, channel management, data warehousing, etc.), and their relations. All elements in the system can have requirements associated with them.

A legend with the concepts we use to describe the agility drivers can be found in Table 2.1.

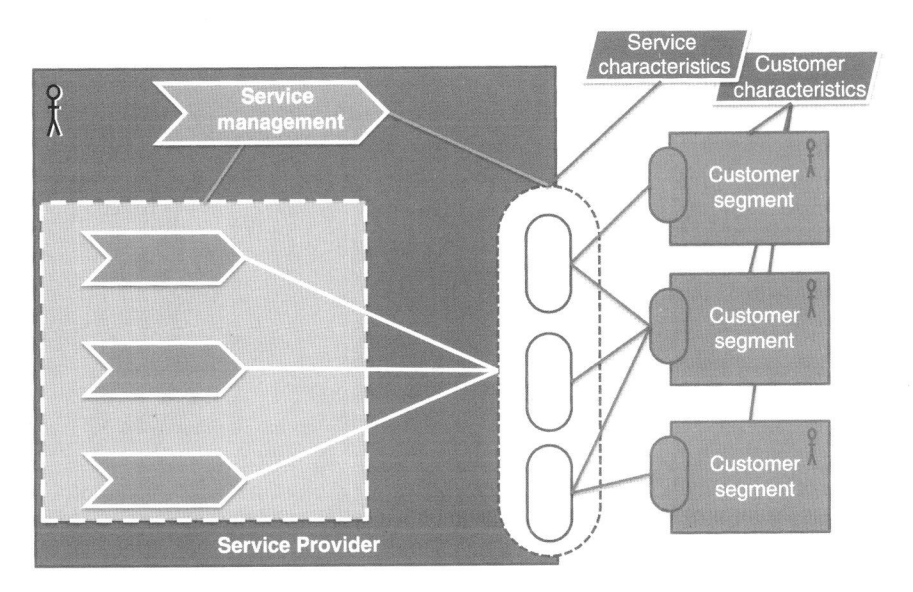

Fig. 2.3 Service dynamics

2.4.2 Product and Service Dynamics

The first possible driver for agility is product/service dynamics, that is, dynamics in the portfolio of products or services delivered to the customers. Agility is driven by factors occurring during the introduction of new services, phasing out services, and consumer-driven changes to services. We defined a business service as a coherent piece of functionality which is offered to the environment. The enterprise must therefore allow for flexible changes regarding its business services. Since business services are delivered by means of business functions and processes, which in turn are supported by application services, structural agility also needs to be realized within these applications. However, products and services vary from organization to organization.

Consequently, the characteristics that require agility also differ per organization. Therefore, before improving the agility of the enterprise's various structures, one has to determine which characteristics or aspects need to be agile. For example, suppose an insurance company offers insurance policies to its customers and wants to be able to introduce new policies in a fast and flexible way, in immediate response to events in the world (such as the financial crisis leading to a demand for conservative mortgages). The rights and obligations associated with such a policy deliver value to its customers. When adjusting the policy, nine out of ten times the associated business rules are altered, but the business processes, for example, for handling new applicants and or for claims processing, remain stable. Therefore, the business service, business functions, and application functions must allow for flexible rule elicitation, design, deployment, and change, but the business processes may largely be fixed and do not require significant agility.

This is illustrated in Fig. 2.3. The service provider can deliver a set of services to different customer segments. Services should be loosely coupled to the business

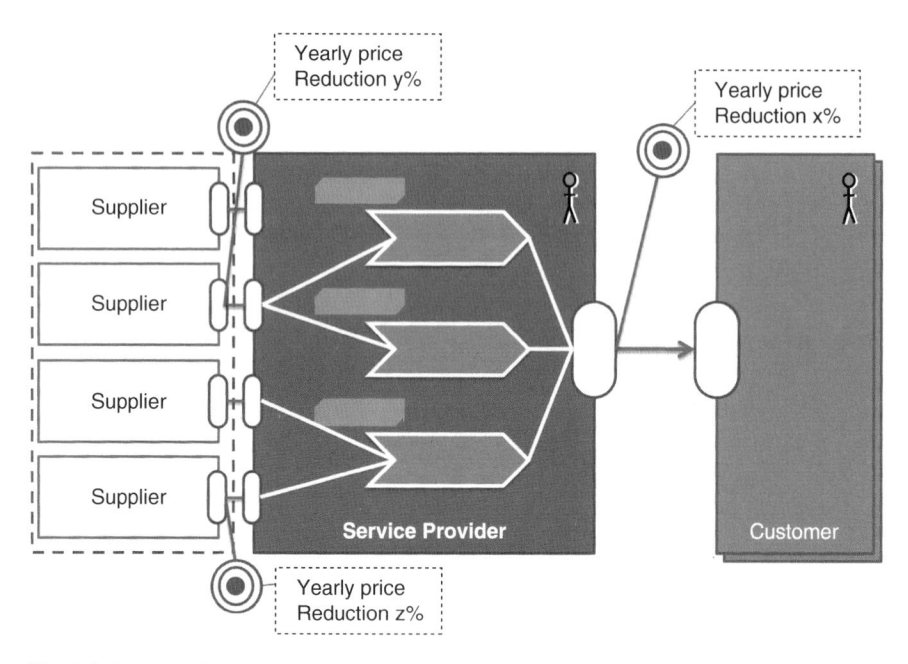

Fig. 2.4 Revenue dynamics

functions used to deliver them. Service management is needed to manage the flexibility and to monitor service characteristics and customer demand.

2.4.3 Revenue Dynamics

Revenue dynamics means that an organization has the ability to cope with changes in pricing strategies and other aspects that influence their revenue stream. Car navigation manufacturer TomTom and many similar high-tech firms are good examples. TomTom has to be able to reduce the price of a product and associated services every year or even every quarter (in addition to providing new added value). This has a strong impact on the way it produces and delivers the product. Cost reduction is pushed through every part of the service delivery system or service network. Since suppliers are an external part of the service delivery system, they will experience the same revenue dynamics.

The high-tech example is illustrated in Fig. 2.4. The goal of a yearly price reduction does not only affect the internal business functions and resources used but also disperse to the supply chain. Each and every actor in the network is faced with the customer characteristics in a certain way.

An example of revenue dynamics in two directions (upward as well as downward pricing) concerns television advertisements: the thirty-second spot. Prices depend on the date and time of the commercial, as well as the specific TV shows preceding and following the advertisement. In some advanced systems, it is even possible to dynamically negotiate broadcast times based on the actual number of viewers. The advertisements are fed in real time based on the bids of the companies advertising. This obviously has strong consequences for customer-service interaction, the underlying business functions, as well as the technologies supporting live feeds.

2.4.4 Volume Dynamics

For many services, demand can change over time, sometimes even drastically. Take, for example, the tax administration. Services supporting people to hand in their tax declaration have to be dimensioned for the peak times of delivery, the last few days before the deadline. The consequences thereof are severe. Not only are systems over-dimensioned on average but also supporting services such as the help desk or tax advisory services are completely geared towards those last few weeks before the deadline. A combination of temporary personnel and private cloud services might be of help here, but perhaps a complete rethink of the tax declaration system is in order, such as the concept of the 'shared information position' that the Dutch tax administration is contemplating, in which there is no longer a need for a separate tax declaration at one point in time.

Insurance companies also face this problem. In case of natural catastrophes, such as storm and hail, the number of claims sharply rises. The nature of the claims (e.g. broken windows or leaking rooftops) does not allow the insurance company to postpone claim handling. Moreover, postponing claims might lead to customers switching to another insurance company. This type of dynamics touches upon the key resources and processes of an organization. It might provide a good reason to outsource certain functions to dedicated, scalable, service providers, as is also the case with call centres, as illustrated in Fig. 2.5. Resource management becomes a key aspect in the performance of the service provider.

An alternative way of dealing with volume dynamics is through service diversification. Think, for example, of Amazon.com. Web shops have a highly irregular pattern of service use, both over the day and over the year (holiday season). If Amazon.com would have to dimension its infrastructure to the peaks in demand only, this would be very costly. In order to mitigate this, Amazon.com introduced other services based on its computing and storage competences, which have a very different pattern of use. Managing the portfolio of services and its combined characteristics becomes a key competence in this case, as shown in Fig. 2.6.

2.4.5 Channel Flexibility

If a company is dependent on a single channel, this can be a serious vulnerability in the business model. Customers might change the channel if they perceive it to be independent of the service. Take, for example, insurance companies. Some of them

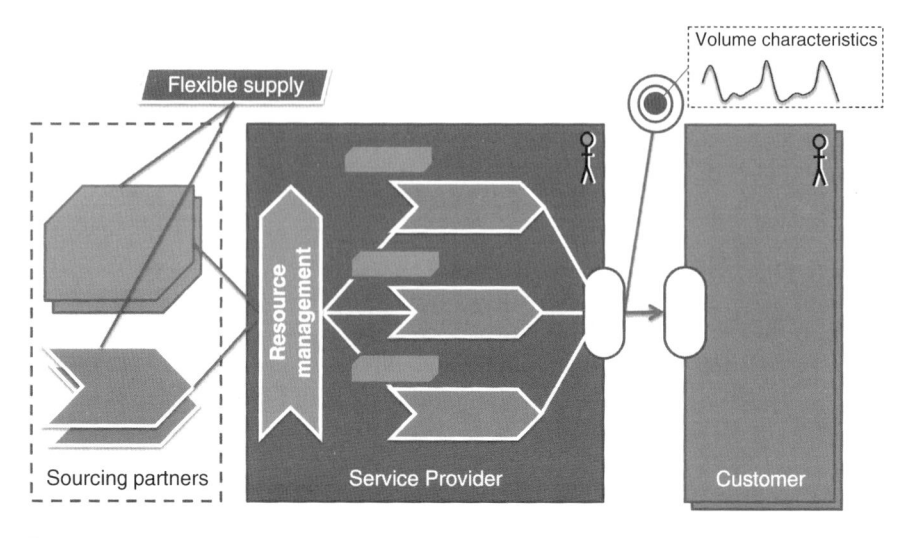

Fig. 2.5 Volume dynamics handled through resource flexibility

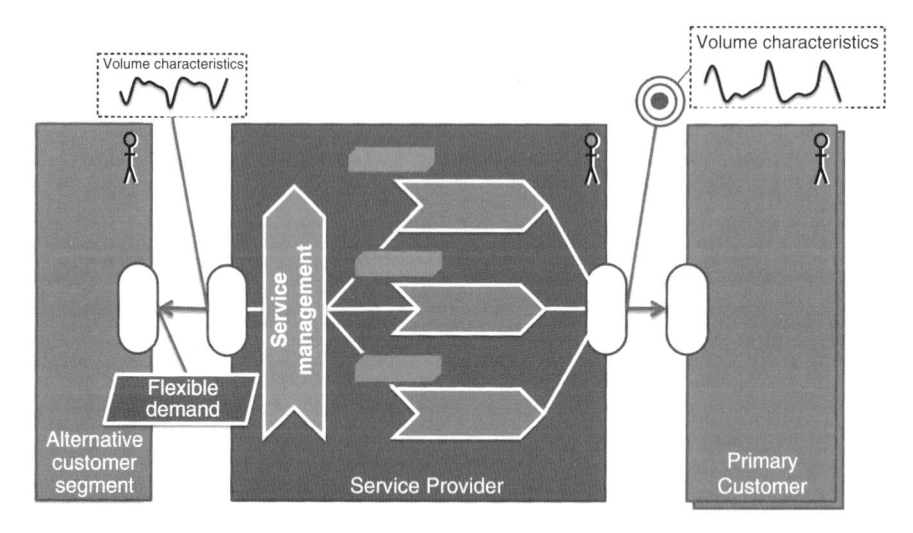

Fig. 2.6 Mitigating volume dynamics through diversification

rely on direct marketing as the main strategy; others rely on intermediaries to sell their products. And in the case of direct marketing, the change from mail to Internet is a profound one as well. A company that can strategically switch, include, or phase out channels definitely has a competitive advantage.

Adding or removing channels can have unanticipated consequences. An interesting example thereof is the introduction of mobile apps for banking in the Netherlands by Rabobank. The apps are highly successful and are valued by the customers, a cost-effective channel for the bank. A more detailed analysis,

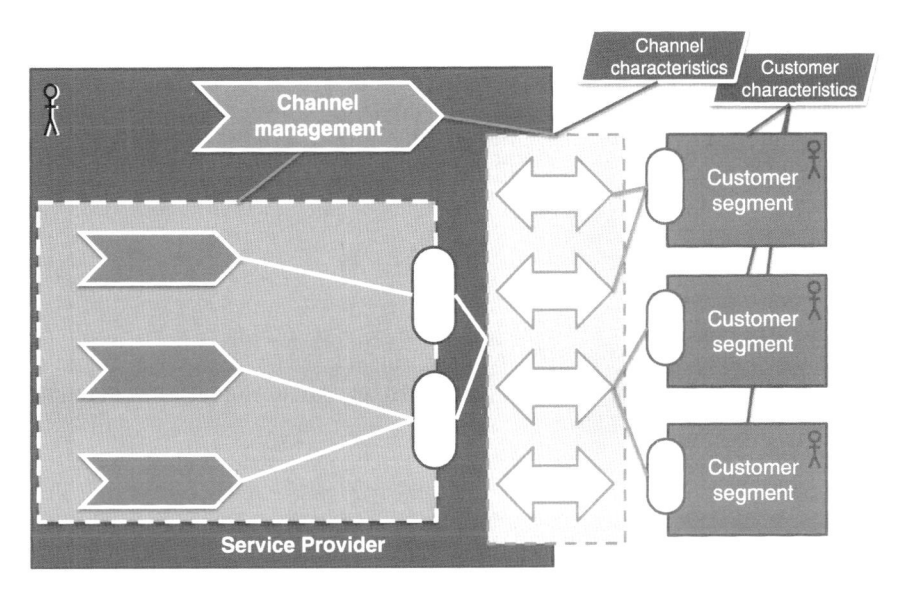

Fig. 2.7 Channel flexibility pattern

however, shows that Internet banking is an important channel for cross-selling, whereas cross-selling via an app is difficult or impossible. From a revenue perspective, therefore, adding the apps channel poses serious challenges.

So for channel flexibility, the channel and the business services should be loosely coupled. This implies that the characteristics of the channels have to be clear and should not constrain the services too much. Business services should be easy to combine to match these potential challenges. A person handling your needs at an insurance intermediary can handle a large variety of services bundled in that point of interaction, whereas digital channels are often much more discriminating (Fig. 2.7).

2.4.6 Supply Chain Flexibility

Most of the agility drivers mentioned until now are customer-facing. However, being able to adapt the supply chain to different demands, ideas, and conditions also is an important driver for agility. What would have happened if your supplier of high-tech components was based in Japan only after the tsunami? For that reason, many production companies use second sourcing strategies, also to constrain the power that suppliers have over their organization. Companies like Cisco and Nike are renowned for their supply chain flexibility, but it is a capability that many more companies have. Take, for example, Healthy People, a company making healthy fruit juices based on 'super fruits'. They are very keen on managing their suppliers, both from the quality perspective and to be able to quickly respond to the taste of consumers.

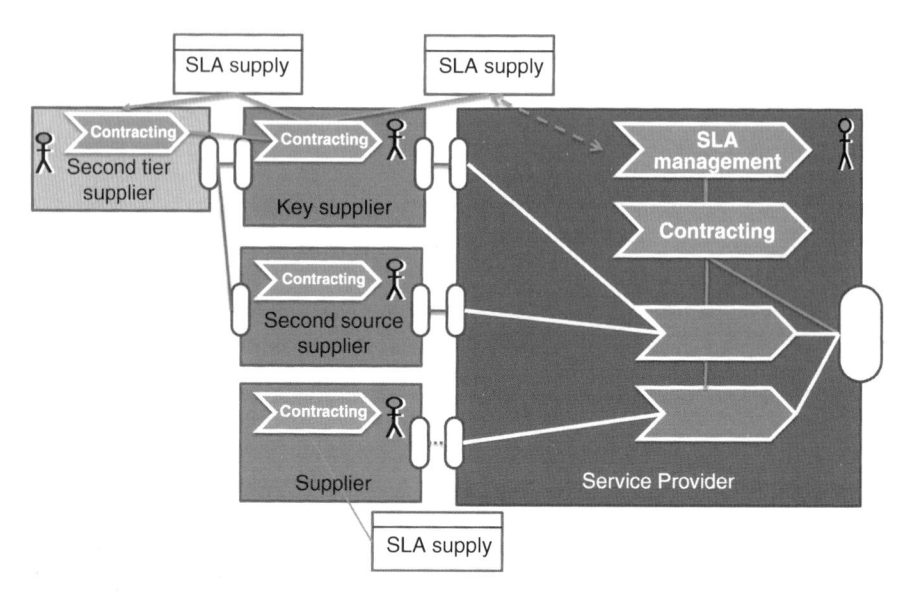

Fig. 2.8 Supply chain flexibility

Another example of supply chain flexibility is Voogd & Voogd, a fully authorized Dutch insurance intermediary. On top of their role as an intermediary, they introduced Voogd & Voogd-labelled insurance products, implemented through the insurances they can sell as an intermediary. This allows them to match the demand they see in the market of insurances to the supply of the different insurance companies in terms of price, coverage, and conditions.

Realizing supply chain flexibility is not as easy as defining it. It requires a high degree of standardization of business functions that supply chain partners realize, and requires additional supply chain management services. The pattern in Fig. 2.8 illustrates this.

Supply chain flexibility is often associated with standardization of IT to support supply chain integration. More importantly, however, the capabilities for contracting and SLA management of the service provider are a prerequisite to handle this type of dynamics.

2.4.7 Continuous Compliance

Continuous compliance means being able to stay conformant to changing laws and regulations. Compliance demands can affect multiple aspects, for example, the organization structure, the coordination of tasks, timing, accuracy, completeness and authorization of data, and the presentation of services. Furthermore, when laws and regulations change over time, the emphasis on specific aspects may change. Hence, an organization needs fundamental agility in every aspect of the business to

2.4 Business Drivers for Agility

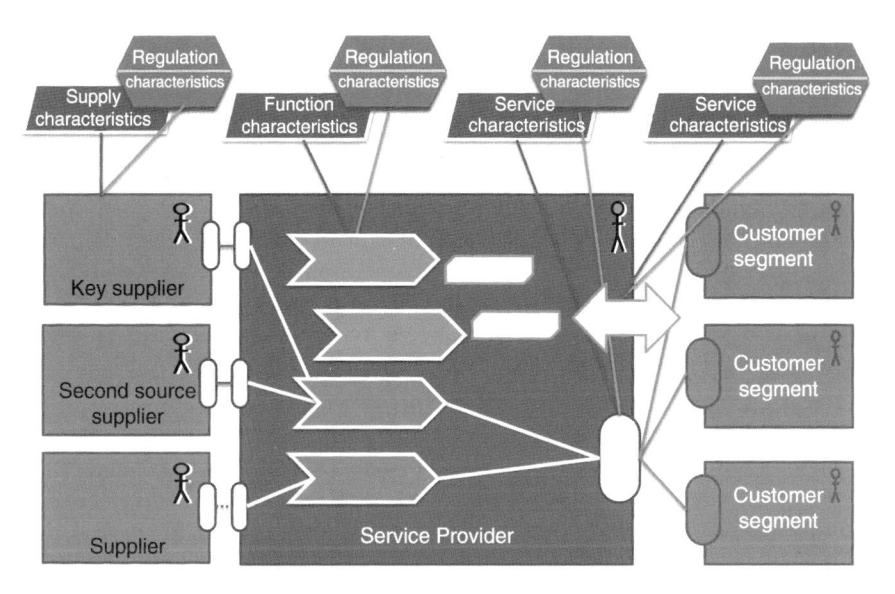

Fig. 2.9 Compliance dynamics

be able to absorb the changes demanded by compliance. Since this is impossible, organizations have to make choices (Fig. 2.9).

These choices must be based on the effects regulation had over the past years and on the types of changes expected in the coming years. For example, Basel's customer due diligence and anti-money laundering guidance focuses on the coordination of tasks and the timing, accuracy, and completeness of data. The Dutch 'Wet op het financieel toezicht' (Dutch law governing financial institutions) also affects the presentation of information to consumers. The fundamental agility therefore must be aligned with the specific demands of the regulations with which the organization must comply.

2.4.8 Technology Adoption

Adoption of technology is another driver for business agility. This adoption can be approached from two different fundamental situations: an (external) customer perspective and a supplier/internal customer perspective. From an (external) customer perspective, an organization can be forced to adopt new technology because its client base has adopted it. Take, for example, banks that support multiple operating systems for mobile phones to deliver the business function of banking. Adopting new technologies in the context of existing systems, services, channels, and resources of course requires these to be flexible enough to accommodate new developments. In particular, this concerns the various client-facing aspects and elements of the enterprise.

The second viewpoint is the supplier/internal customer perspective. Here, the organization allows for new technology when it improves its (internal) service delivery system. To provide this kind of agility, infrastructural services need to be highly decoupled from the application functions, so that the technology may be changed without unwanted effects on the supported application landscape.

Many well-known examples exist of technologies that inhibit this type of agility. The introduction of large-scale ERP systems like SAP, or CRM services such as Siebel, usually leads to a long-term dependence on these technologies. They provide a strong case for operational excellence, but this excellence comes at the price of strongly reduced internal flexibility. This rigidness, however, does not need to conflict with drivers such as channel flexibility or volume dynamics.

Chapter 3
Agile Architecture

M.M. Lankhorst and H.A. Proper

In this chapter, we will elaborate on the use of architecture in relation to agility. We start by clarifying what we mean by 'architecture' and 'enterprise architecture', since these notions are used in various ways within our field. Next, we explain what the roles of architecture can be: on the one hand, it can be used explicitly to design agile systems; on the other hand, it helps an organization to control agility and to keep a balance between stability and change. Finally, we outline how architecture processes fit within an agile context.

3.1 Introduction

The general opinion is that to manage the complexity of any large organization or system, you need architecture. But what exactly does 'architecture' mean? Even in building and construction, the term is ambiguous. It can denote the art and science of designing the built environment, a certain design style, as in 'gothic architecture', or it can refer to the design itself. The earliest use of the term 'architecture' in an IT context dates back to Amdahl et al. (1964), who define architecture (of the IBM S/360 mainframe system) as 'the conceptual structure and functional behavior as distinct from the organization of the data flow and controls, the logical design, and the physical implementation'.

Some say that, in the context of information systems, the term 'architecture' should be reserved solely to refer to a set of principles and constraints that should be applied to the design space. For instance, Dietz (2006) defines architecture as a 'normative restriction of design freedom', expressed in the form of principles governing the function and construction of systems. Most other definitions of architecture, however, refer to these structures themselves and not merely to the principles and constraints.

Many more definitions of enterprise, information, and IT architecture have been proposed; for an overview, see, for example, Op't Land et al. (2009) and Greefhorst and Proper (2011). The definition provided by TOGAF actually provides a dualistic view. The first one focused on the description of a system, and the second one on the structure and principles (The Open Group 2011):

1. A formal description of a system, or a detailed plan of the system at component level, to guide its implementation
2. The structure of components, their inter-relationships, and the principles and guidelines governing their design and evolution over time

Greefhorst and Proper (2011) also suggest to use a dualistic perspective on architecture by distinguishing *design principles* and *design instructions*. The design principles provide a declarative means to provide normative restrictions of design freedom, while design instructions (by way of, e.g. ArchiMate models) provide a more imperative way to provide restrictions of design freedom.

Fehskens (2008) fields valid criticism at many of these definitions, for example, that they are very IT centric. He suggests to define architecture as 'Those properties of an enterprise, its mission, and their environment, that are necessary and sufficient for the enterprise to be fit for purpose for its mission in that environment, so as to ensure continuous alignment of the enterprise's assets and capabilities with its mission and strategy'. Although this definition includes the goal or use of architectures—something missing from many other definitions—it runs the risk of encompassing 'everything' that is important in an enterprise. In our view, it is essential to focus on properties of the structure of an enterprise, as they can be *designed*, making it sensible to talk about their architecture in the first place.

In this book, we do not provide our own definition of architecture. Rather, we will simply use the most commonly used definition from the ISO/IEC/IEEE FDIS 42010 standard (ISO/IEC/IEEE 2011):

> *Architecture*: fundamental concepts or properties of a system in its environment embodied in its elements, relationships, and in the principles of its design and evolution

Although this definition also has its flaws, it is the most accepted in the architecture community. It is a refinement of the IEEE 1471 definition (IEEE Computer Society 2000), which itself was the result of an intense debate in the community but has now been used for over a decade. For example, the second definition of TOGAF has also been derived from this definition, and it is also used in the ArchiMate community (Lankhorst et al. 2009; The Open Group 2012).

Importantly, this definition also takes the perspective that an architecture is primarily a *conception* of a system, i.e. a mental construct. The standard, therefore, also distinguishes between architectures and architecture *descriptions*. Furthermore, the definition addresses a system *in its environment*; an architecture cannot be understood without looking at the system's context. Finally, it comprises *fundamental* concepts or properties; an architecture is not just the structure of physical components that make up a system, but remains invariant for different implementations. The focus on

3.1 Introduction

fundamental concepts or properties is made more specific by Fehskens' definition when he refers to 'The properties... necessary and sufficient for the enterprise to be fit for purpose for its mission in that environment'. The ISO/IEC/IEEE definition also accommodates both the notion of a system's structure and the general underlying principles.

An architecture helps you to get an integrated view of a system that you are designing or studying. We can apply this notion of architecture at different abstraction or aggregation levels. We may talk about the architecture of a piece of software, an information system, an organization, an enterprise, and even a network of enterprises. The ISO/IEC/IEEE standard takes no position on the question, 'What is a system?' Users of the standard are free to employ any system theory they choose. For example, 'system' could mean a software application, a subsystem, a service, a product line, a system of systems, or an enterprise. Systems can be man-made or natural.

It should be clear that these notions of architecture and system do not prescribe any particular order or procedure in their design or development. *Any* system has an architecture, even if it was not consciously designed. In the creation of a system or service, sometimes the architecture will come first, but in many cases, the architecture, design, implementation, and usage will co-evolve. This is particularly important when we want to combine architectural thinking and agile methods: architecture does not equate to 'Big Design Up-Front', the agile movement's bugbear. This is where the overused comparison with architecture in building and construction fails: there, fully detailed plans and designs are needed before construction starts, because change during construction of a building is too difficult and costly. But in business and IT, changes to the artefacts are often easier.

Moreover, in this context, the notion of architecture is used at different levels of granularity or scope and with different timescales: from the strategic, large-scale, and longer-term 'zoning plan' level, which is (or should be) more principle-based, to the blueprint level of design for individual systems and services, which is more dominated by models. The 'Big Design Up-Front' problems that the agile movement aims to avoid mainly arise when detailed models and blueprints are used at a wrong level of scale and scope. Regretfully, in practice it happens all too often that architects lose themselves in too detailed and specific 'designs', rather than focusing on those properties that are necessary and sufficient for the enterprise to be fit for purpose.

In this book, we focus on software-intensive socio-technical systems, which are a combination of business, organization, and people aspects and the information systems and technology supporting these. Important in this respect is the notion of *enterprise architecture* (EA), where an enterprise is defined as 'the highest level (typically) of description of an organization and typically covers all missions and functions. An enterprise will often span multiple organizations' (The Open Group 2011).

Fehskens (2008) observes how the interpretation of enterprise architecture has changed from enterprise-wide IT architecture to the architecture of the enterprise, and sees four kinds of use of the term:

- As a discipline or practice: 'I took a course on enterprise architecture'.
- As a process: 'Enterprise architecture enables business transformation'.
- As applied to a class of things: 'Every business should have an enterprise architecture'.
- As applied to a specific instance of a thing: 'We used TOGAF as the basis for our enterprise architecture'.

Given the previous definition of 'architecture' as being concerned with *fundamental* properties of a system, enterprise architecture is first and foremost concerned with the backbone of the enterprise: those fundamental design decisions that influence the essence of its operations, facilitate agility, and control risk, and are determined by its business strategy and needs (see also Chap. 2). Thus, enterprise architecture serves several important purposes in IT management:

- It offers a holistic view on the enterprise, creating insight into the various dependencies between and within business and IT, facilitating management decisions by clarifying their effects.
- Based on this holistic view, it provides a backbone for coherent operation and alignment between business and IT.
- It provides a backbone for compliance with rules and regulations, both internally defined and externally required.
- It provides a backbone for the integration of an enterprise with its environment.
- It gives explicit variation points where change may be expected and accommodated.

Later in this chapter, we will describe in more detail how (enterprise) architecture activities can be embedded within agile organizations and projects.

In Chap. 1, we already introduced the prominent role of services in our approach and elsewhere. Modern enterprise architecture methods use services as a pivotal concept in bringing together various business, information, and infrastructure aspects and domains. A prime example is the ArchiMate modelling standard for EA (The Open Group 2012; Lankhorst et al. 2009), also used elsewhere in this book. Service-oriented architecture (SOA) has become a prominent architectural style, not just in a technical sense (e.g. with Web services) but also as a way of structuring the business models, processes, and organization of an enterprise.

3.2 Architecture to Manage Agility

To some it may seem that architecture is something static, confining everything within its rules and boundaries, and hampering agility and innovation. Many proponents of agile methods are opposed to the use of architecture, categorically classifying it as 'Big Design Up-Front' (BDUF). They argue that stakeholders cannot know what they really need and the problem will change anyway before the project is completed, so you cannot provide any useful designs up-front. Indeed,

3.2 Architecture to Manage Agility

in many cases, stakeholders cannot formulate their requirements up-front and suffer from the IKIWISI syndrome ('I'll know it when I see it'). Moreover, the changing business environment makes stable requirements an illusion to begin with.

However, this is a misconception about the role of architecture. A well-defined architecture helps you in positioning new developments within the context of the existing processes, IT systems, and other assets of an organization, and in identifying necessary changes. Thus, good architectural practice helps an organization innovate and change by providing both stability and flexibility. The insights provided by an enterprise architecture are needed on the one hand in determining the needs and priorities for change from a business perspective, and on the other hand in assessing how the organization may benefit from technological and business innovations.

This also goes back to the distinction between process and system agility, as described in Chap. 2. To achieve a truly agile organization, we should not only use responsive, iterative, and interactive processes but also create organizational and technical systems that can easily be adapted to changing circumstances and requirements. In a competitive environment, an organization should focus its energy on being agile in those change options that differentiate it from its competitors or help it keep up with the market. Change in other aspects is simply a waste of time and energy, since it will not make the organization compete more effectively. Architecture provides the backbone for making such decisions; it forms the stable core of the enterprise and provides the variation points for agility.

Moreover, agility is not the only concern of an enterprise. Many trade-offs have to be made, of cost-efficiency vs. flexibility, vs. reliability, vs. other '-ilities'. A well-designed architecture helps in making such trade-offs, analysing different change scenarios with respect to these different properties, and in assessing their impact across the enterprise.

Thus, architecture serves several important roles in fostering agility: First, it gives designers and developers the insight into a system and its environment they need for making changes. Second, it provides a way of designing organization-level agility, for example, by employing specific architecture principles, defining standardized interfaces, creating reusable building blocks, and using infrastructures that speed up development. Third, it helps in focusing design effort on those points of variability or uncertainty that are important from a business perspective: where do we expect future changes to occur, and how can we facilitate these?

The latter points are illustrated by Fig. 3.1. Simply put, a well-designed architecture and infrastructure is an up-front investment ('A' in the figure) that makes later changes easier, faster, and cheaper (the coefficient 'b' in the graph is smaller than 'c'). Classical agile development states that you should avoid big design up-front, because you cannot know all. But when you do know which parts of your organizational and technical landscape can provide a stable infrastructure on which enterprise agility is founded, designing those parts up-front is certainly smart.

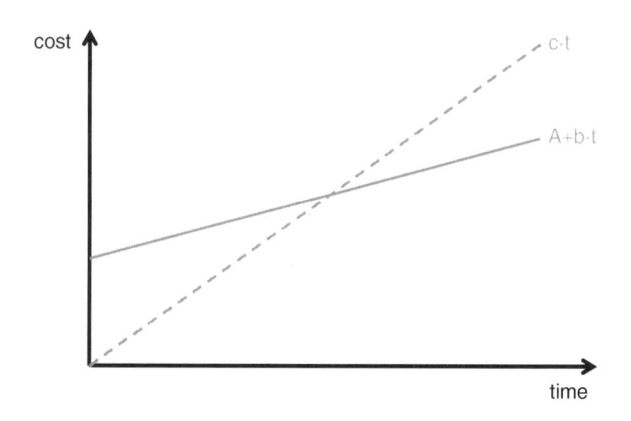

Fig. 3.1 Up-front investment vs. fully agile development

3.2.1 Agility Aspects

When considering an enterprise, there are two important capabilities that we might architect, directly related to the different kinds of agility we identified in Chap. 2:

1. The *execution* system, i.e. the 'things' needed for 'business as usual'. Most architecture approaches implicitly focus on this capability, and this is where the notion of system agility is focused.
2. The *innovation* system, i.e. the capability to innovate or change. This ranges from social processes, to the system development process supported by methods and tools. This is targeted by the notion of process agility.

In an agile context (or agile part of the enterprise), we see that these two systems blend together: the critical design focus should shift from having an efficient execution capability to developing an effective combination of the execution and innovation systems. Designing the execution system in such a way that it lends itself to quick changes within giving boundaries and ambitions is a prerequisite for the innovation capability to be effective. We will address the innovation system in Chap. 6; here, we focus on the requirements on the execution system in an agile context.

In Chap. 2, we have outlined the five aspects making up a system's agility: making changes, deploying these changes, dealing with their effects, integrating a system with its environment, and decoupling it from this environment (to be reused elsewhere). Many well-established architecture principles have been identified that positively influence the quality attributes comprising these agility aspects; for a broad overview of such principles, see (Greefhorst and Proper 2011, App. A).

Making Changes

The first aspect of system agility is the ease of making changes. This can be decomposed in customizability by the system's users, adaptability by system management, analyzability by designers, and changeability by developers. These are properties that have to be built in explicitly. In particular analyzability and changeability critically depend on a clear structure, i.e. the architecture of the system. Important and long-established architecture principles apply here, each related to the modularity of the system under concern:

- *Separation of concerns*: using layering and modularization to concentrate functionality in specific places and ensure that changes remain as local as possible.
- *Low coupling and high cohesion*: a low number of relations between subsystems and a high internal cohesion of each subsystem facilitate analysis and understanding, avoid changes propagating throughout the system, and hence greatly enhance the agility of a system.
- *Encapsulation*: if a system has clear interfaces and prevents the environment to depend on its internal implementation, this implementation can be changed without affecting that environment.

An important aspect related to the modularity of the system is the structure of the team. As Conway's law states, 'organizations which design systems [...] are constrained to produce designs which are copies of the communication structures of these organizations' (Conway 1968). In order for two system elements to be connected correctly, the designers and implementers of each element must communicate with each other. If a larger system or service development project requires multiple sub-teams, the team structure should therefore follow the high-level architecture of the system (and certainly not the other way around).

Deploying Changes

To deploy a system easily and quickly, qualities such as learnability, installability, testability, and manageability need to be addressed. This is particularly important in iterative development processes, where a system and its parts have to be tested, installed, and used many times over.

In agile development, testing occurs early and often, and not just at the end of development. Test-driven design is an important agile practice, and easily testable systems are therefore important in facilitating such an agile process.

Management (including maintenance) which takes a large effort compared to the actual usage time is non-productive. If changes to a system require a large management effort, this has a negative impact on agility.

Dealing with the Effects of Changes

In agile development, systems are changed often, and these changes may not always work out well. If something goes wrong during a change, the effects should be minimal and easily corrected, to minimize disruption of and risk to the day-to-day operations. The more often a system changes, the more important this becomes.

To this end, the architecture of the system should include facilities for, for example, redundancy and recovery.

Systems that are fault tolerant and can recover quickly and independently after a failure occurs can be tested and used more easily in uncertain or changing conditions and in circumstances that have not been predicted at its time of design. Furthermore, systems that have been designed with mechanisms to cope with possible bugs and errors can be deployed more easily in a 'half-finished' state, allowing for rapid testing in practice and short development cycles, thus promoting agility.

Integrating

For a system, whether technical or organizational, to be put in place rapidly, it must be easy to connect it to its environment. This requires attention to interoperability and conformance to applicable standards. A system that is highly interoperable is easily connected to other systems. This makes it easier to use it in new or changing environments, hence enhancing the agility of the system and of the organization of which this system is a part.

To some, use of standards may seem limiting to agility, since you cannot freely choose your own solution to a design problem. However, the use of standardized elements greatly facilitates the rapid development of new solutions from existing building blocks. Lego is a good example: you can build almost anything from these fixed blocks. Hence, agile architectures consist of interoperable elements that are easily configured and combined. A useful architectural principle in this regard is *design by contract* (Meyer 1991), where precise and verifiable specifications of a service are used, for example, with preconditions, post-conditions, and invariants.

Decoupling

If you want to change a part of some system, ideally this change does not influence or depend upon any other parts. The more dependencies you have to deal with, the more difficult, risky, and time-consuming a change will be. Therefore, a low level of coupling between system elements is an important property of agile systems.

Moreover, an important way of achieving development speed and simplicity is reuse. Reusing system elements requires that they have been designed in such a way that they can easily be decoupled from their environment and, conversely, that the environment does not depend unduly on specific implementation aspects of these elements. If a system or system element is easily replaceable, the organization using it is more agile, since it can respond more quickly when the need for replacement arises because of changing circumstances.

Building new systems from reusable components is an important way of improving agility. The Lego example above serves to illustrate this: because standardized, reusable building blocks are available, new systems can be built quickly and with a relatively low effort. Choosing the right elements that need to be reusable (but are themselves stable) is therefore highly important.

Designing a component for independence and reuse requires information on the potential contexts in which that component may be used in the future. A solid architecture backbone is indispensable to provide such a context. This does not mean that the architecture prescribes the design of each system element; merely that it clearly specifies the boundaries of these elements, i.e. the context, principles, standards, and interfaces in which they must fit.

3.2.2 Operating Models

As we have stated before, flexibility does not come for free, and there are other concerns to be addressed as well. It should be an explicit choice where you want to be agile as an enterprise, and which aspects can be standardized or otherwise fixed. A clear set of business goals and drivers (see also Chap. 2) is essential in making such a choice.

Explicit strategic guidance is given by the *operating models* of Ross et al. (2006). As they show with numerous case studies, successful enterprises employ an operating model with clear choices on the levels of integration and standardization of business processes across the enterprise:

- *Diversification*: different business units are allowed to have their own business processes. Data are not integrated across the enterprise. For example, diversified conglomerates that operate in different markets, with different products.
- *Replication*: business processes are standardized and replicated across the organization, but data are local and not integrated. For example, business units in separate countries, serving different customers but using the same centrally defined business processes. For example, a fast-food chain replicating its way of working through all its local branches.
- *Coordination*: data are shared and business processes are integrated across the enterprise, but not standardized. Example: a bank serving its clients by sharing customer and product data across the enterprise, but with local branches and advisers having autonomy in tailoring processes to their clients.
- *Unification*: global integration and standardization across the enterprise. For example, the integrated operations and supply chain of a chemical manufacturing company.

In those operating models that prescribe standardized processes or data integration, project-level agility is bounded by these organization-level choices: a project may not be allowed to define its own business processes or data models, but must comply with company-wide standards. At the organization level, however, this may actually enhance agility: because the organization is explicit about its operational choices, timely decision making is facilitated, and the type of response to changes in the environment may be known beforehand. Moreover, use of standardized processes or systems may help in quickly developing solutions to new requirements, as we have argued above.

In addition to the operating model, they provide a stage model of the architectural development of organizations:

1. *Business silos*: every individual business unit has its own IT and does local optimization.
2. *Standardized technology*: a common set of infrastructure services is provided centrally and efficiently.
3. *Optimized core*: data and process standardization, as appropriate for the chosen operating model, are provided through shared business applications (e.g. ERP or CRM systems).
4. *Business modularity*: loosely coupled IT-enabled business process components are managed and reused, preserving global standards and enabling local differences at the same time.
5. *Dynamic venturing*: rapidly reconfigurable, self-contained modules are merged seamlessly and dynamically with those of business partners.

The level at which you can achieve agility is related to these stages. Organizations that are at the first stage can only do local optimization, which precludes a coherent agile response at the organization level if, for example, changing market demands or regulatory pressure requires this. At stages 2 and 3, the standardization and optimization at the technology level facilitate a global response, but within the bounds of the current business- and organization-level structures. At stages 4 and 5, the business itself becomes adaptable, reconfigurable, and fluidly integrated with a dynamic environment.

3.2.3 Standardization and Variation

You might think that standardization is bad for agility. Standardizing in the wrong way can indeed be very detrimental, but you can also use standardized functions to enhance the agility of an enterprise's execution system.

Importantly, you have to differentiate between 'lengthwise' and 'crosswise' standardization and variation (Govers and Südmeier 2011), as depicted in Fig. 3.2. Lengthwise standardization means standardizing the steps that are taken over the length of a certain type of process, across different products, services, or customer segments. Lengthwise standardization can be good for agility. If all processes have the same series of steps, you can possibly reuse some steps in implementing a new stream. For example, if AgiSurance starts selling an extreme sports insurance, it may perhaps reuse parts of the registration steps from its property insurance products, parts of the valuation from health insurance, etc. Thus, lengthwise standardization provides you with a stable architectural backbone for variation across the standardized parts.

3.2 Architecture to Manage Agility

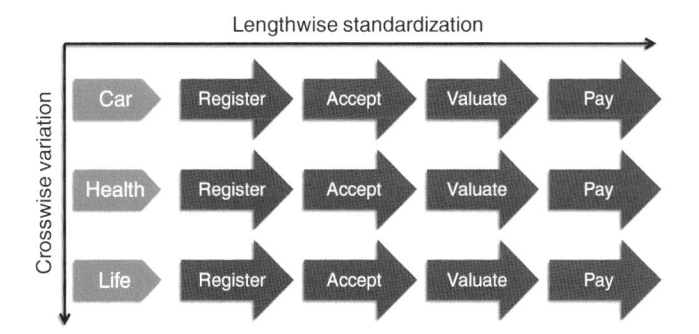

Fig. 3.2 Standardization vs. variation

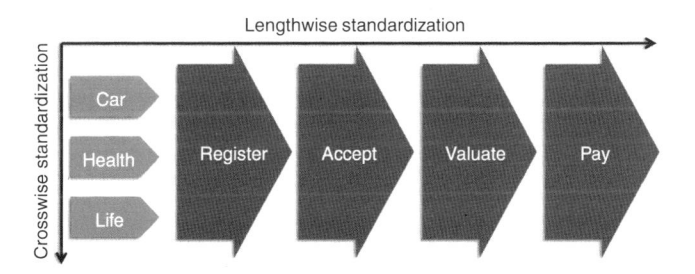

Fig. 3.3 Crosswise standardization

Crosswise standardization means using the same implementation of a process step across these different streams (Fig. 3.3). This may harm your agility, however. By conflating all specific cases into a single process step—let alone a single IT service—such a step will often become unmanageable spaghetti. The result is much too big and complicated, and because it is based on knowledge from many different domains (in the example of AgiSurance, different types of insurance products), nobody has the combined expertise to really understand it. Moreover, everything becomes dependent on everything else; in the example, if a specific type of insurance requires a different kind of valuation, the decision tree for all types of insurance may be impacted.

Finally, change dynamics are often different for various types of products or customer segments. Take the example of travel insurance vs. health insurance: in the Netherlands, the changes in health insurance are largely dictated by government regulation and have a yearly rhythm, where changes to processes and systems must be implemented within a limited time frame before January 1; for travel insurance, insurers may largely decide on their own when and what to change.

You should therefore factor out these types of decisions and not standardize them across different product types. This is one way of promoting the 'decoupling' aspect of system agility described in Sect. 2.3.3. You might do this by defining separate processes or services for each product or, perhaps even better, by treating decisions separately. In Chap. 4, we will show how decision models can be combined with process models to achieve this separation of concerns.

This view on standardization goes against the common wisdom on ERP implementations, where you often see crosswise standardization as well. This is one of the important causes for the lack of agility of many ERP implementations (Govers 2003).

In applying the operating models described in the previous section, you should also keep this in mind. In particular the business modularity and dynamic venturing stages highly depend on this type of structure and variability. The danger of over-standardizing at the optimized core stage should be avoided.

Example: AgiSurance Claim Handling Process

Our example company AgiSurance has decided that each insurance claim has to go through four steps: registration of the claim, acceptance (e.g. check for completeness), valuation (to assess the amount to be paid), and payment.

If AgiSurance would use crosswise standardization, it would use a single valuate step, for example, which has to incorporate knowledge of all the different insurance products that the company sells, and uses large and complicated decision trees (or other means) to compute the valuation results in individual cases. This would not be a good idea.

3.2.4 Model-Based Development

Another important architectural approach that can provide more system agility is the use of *models* and model-driven tools to facilitate the development and change process. This improves both the innovation and the execution capabilities of the enterprise, because it shortens the path from 'business idea' to 'business execution' and it improves the business insight in the operational reality as well.

Importantly, we do not want to force IT-oriented models onto business stakeholders, but rather advocate the use of domain-specific concepts and languages to capture and communicate relevant business knowledge. These models can then be targeted to suitable IT infrastructure, either by transforming them to technology-oriented models or software code, or even by directly interpreting and executing these models. Such a model-based architecture facilitates the rapid development and deployment of new business services.

In Chap. 4, we will describe this model-based development approach in much more detail. If we compare such an approach to writing software code in languages like Java, PHP, C, or Cobol, we see that much of this code is only intended as scaffolding to deliver the required functionality, but does not add business value itself. Writing code is also more error prone simply because there are more opportunities and places for mistakes. Moreover, a lot of the same code is written over and over again, compounding these problems even further.

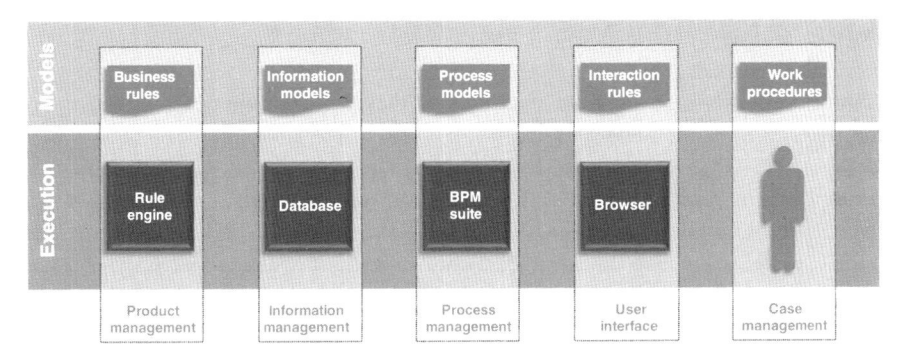

Fig. 3.4 AgiSurance's model-based architecture vision

Thus, model-based approaches can be both faster and more efficient in developing services. They are not without their own challenges, however. The up-front investment needed may be considerable, and a clear business case is needed to show when this will pay off, as we have already argued in Sect. 3.2 (see also Fig. 3.1). These approaches may also require extensive retraining of employees, both at the business and the IT side of you organization. In Chaps. 4 and 8, we will go deeper into these challenges and ways to overcome them.

> **Example: AgiSurance's Future Model-Based Architecture**
>
> In insurances, the parameters of individual policies change quite often. In its IT infrastructure, AgiSurance has therefore chosen to move towards a business rule engine solution, which should support the latter type of changes and provide a high level of flexibility. In Fig. 3.4, we see an abstracted view of AgiSurance's vision on its future IT landscape, in which several engines for the interpretation of models play a central role.

3.3 Architecture Processes in an Agile Context

To create a truly agile enterprise, you should design both your systems and your development processes with change in mind. This also holds for architecture products and processes. Thus, architecture should focus on the backbone of the enterprise and on guarding its essence. Moreover, architecture is invaluable in helping to take risky or high-impact design decisions.

An architecture will itself evolve over time. Architectural artefacts will therefore only have a temporary status. Architectures change because the environment changes and new technological opportunities arise, and because of new insights as to what is essential to the business. A good architecture process ensures that the various artefacts remain relevant and up to date, and avoids unnecessary waste.

3.3.1 A Risk-Driven Approach

Next to the organization's own strategy and maturity level, there are other important reasons for managing and controlling agility. In particular risk management and compliance with external laws and regulations may limit the freedom of organizations. Risk management policies may imply that the costs and effects of changes are thoroughly investigated before a solution or change may be developed and deployed. In an agile process, the available resources and the delivery schedule are usually fixed, but the functionality is flexible and delivered in order of the priorities given by business stakeholders. Laws and regulations are not so flexible; they must be fully implemented at the date set by lawmakers or regulatory bodies, so the schedule and requirements are fixed.

Next to the operational and financial risks addressed by laws, regulations, and company policies, there is also the risk in the development process: taking wrong design decisions may be very costly. A common adage for architecture in an agile context is that it should be 'just in time, just enough' (e.g. Wagter et al. 2005). You should defer committing to a design choice until you absolutely need to, thereby increasing flexibility and raising your chances of success. The question then becomes when do you need to take which architectural decisions? In particular, this concerns high-risk decisions, i.e. those that are both difficult and have a potentially high impact.

Taking a decision too early is dangerous, because you may need to do a lot of rework if that decision turns out to be wrong. Although some agile proponents say that it is easy to refactor your software (see the next section), it may not always be possible to easily turn back on an earlier decision. The aforementioned database structure may be an example of such a decision. Other examples are the use of existing infrastructure, performance or quality criteria, or the extensibility of your data model. Sometimes it may therefore be smart to have an analysis phase before starting an agile, iterative project. In that phase, you investigate the important risks, technical and otherwise, and you define the essence of the architecture. You can then use this as a project start architecture for the agile project, giving it sufficient guidance to avoid these risks.

There is also a lurking danger that the team starts with the simple stuff and postpones more difficult requirements and design decisions. For example, a Dutch social security institution saw its development of a new information system for a complicated new law fail, because (among other causes) it started with implementing the 'happy flow', tacked on some more difficult cases as exceptions to this flow, added the even more difficult cases, and so on, until the business process designs they used as the foundation for system development became completely unmanageable. This is a common hazard of incremental development processes. In prioritizing requirements, the common '80–20' rule ('let's focus on the 80% most common cases') is dangerous: perhaps these first 80% are easy to cover, but the 20% difficult cases may require a costly redesign of your solution.

A good heuristic in this respect is to take a *risk-driven approach*, where you address the most critical risks early in the project life cycle. If the necessary input for making a risky decision is not available yet, further analysis and investigation are needed. Perhaps you can build a so-called spike solution, a common technique in XP, to try out aspects of a design in more detail. If this is not possible and a decision is too risky to take right now, you should postpone it until the necessary input is available and the risk of making a wrong choice is low.

3.3.2 Refactoring and Technical Debt

A very important technique to cope with changing architectures and designs in incremental development is *refactoring*. In software development, this is defined as a 'disciplined technique for restructuring an existing body of code, altering its internal structure without changing its external behavior' (Fowler 1999). By applying specific semantics-preserving transformations, you can change software code (or other designs, e.g. business processes, data models, business rules, or even hardware designs) to accommodate new requirements, without altering its behaviour for existing cases. Before something is refactored, a solid suite of tests is created to ensure that the refactored result performs the same as the original.

Refactoring serves two main purposes: it improves maintainability and it increases extensibility. You should continuously improve the architecture, designs, models, and code. If they start to 'smell', for example, if new requirements seem progressively hard to implement, if the models are difficult to understand or explain, or if implementations nearly duplicate other code, it may already be too late.

In the previous example, if the social security institution had realized that their processes were gradually turning into a mess, it would have refactored them. For example, they could have separated the decision-making rules on client benefits from the generic workflow processes, keeping the latter stable and managing the complexity of the social security laws separately and explicitly.

Unfortunately, not every piece of design or implementation is amenable to refactoring. For example, if the architecture incorporates a legacy system or employs a commercial-off-the-shelf component, these may be fixed and unchangeable. Decisions on the use of such fixed elements are hence high risk and should be investigated early and thoroughly, as explained in the previous section.

Closely related is the role of architecture in avoiding what is sometimes called 'design debt' or 'technical debt'. Often, you need to take a temporary shortcut in your design, leading to an increase in complexity or a decrease in quality that you should resolve at some time in the future. Cunningham first drew the comparison between complexity and debt in a 1992 experience report (Cunningham 1992):

> Shipping first time code is like going into debt. A little debt speeds development so long as it is paid back promptly with a rewrite.... The danger occurs when the debt is not repaid. Every minute spent on not-quite-right code counts as interest on that debt. Entire engineering organizations can be brought to a standstill under the debt load of an unconsolidated implementation, object-oriented or otherwise.

Architecture is an important instrument to avoid that this debt gets out of hand. By explicitly providing the boundaries of the design space, it helps in providing a 'debt ceiling'. Temporarily, projects may be absolved from adhering to the architecture, but eventually their results must be brought back into the fold.

This is an important practice of the Dynamic Architecture (DyA) method (Wagter et al. 2005), for example, which has an explicitly controlled process for development without architecture. This process includes a management letter that stipulates how this deviation from the architecture is going to be resolved, for example, by limiting the lifetime of the project result and/or starting development of a long-term solution in parallel.

3.3.3 An Agile Architecture Process

The process of enterprise architecting as described by Op't Land et al. (2009) consists of three main activities:

1. *Create*: shaping the design of the desired situation, to address the goals and purposes as formulated by the enterprise, in cooperation with relevant stakeholders and within applicable constraints of time and resources
2. *Apply*: using the architecture as a steering instrument to guide the development and evolution of the enterprise
3. *Maintain*: keeping the architecture up to date and relevant, by monitoring the enterprise and its environment and responding accordingly

This EA process may seem a bit linear and at odds with the interactive and iterative way of working in an agile environment. You may get the impression that the architects first do all the thinking, and then an agile team is only needed for implementing their ideas. However, this is not how things operate in an agile organization. These architecture activities are not strictly ordered, nor do they always precede the more detailed design and implementation activities. Rather, these three streams should run continuously and in parallel with development, keeping the architecture relevant and up to date at all times and interacting closely with the various development teams.

However, these are merely the architecture activities. How can we combine these with all the other work going on in an agile organization and its development processes for services? First of all, agile and other iterative projects do not assume the enterprise architecture as a given. In a changeable context, the architecture cannot be too detailed for the distant future and must be amenable to adaptation if the need arises. This makes the aforementioned maintenance activities crucial in an agile context, and a constant awareness of the drivers for change is essential. The cycle between creation, use, and maintenance of the architecture is also relatively short; enterprise architectures should not be detailed 5-year plans, but provide the general direction in which an organization wants to move.

Second, each individual project will have its own activities for creating, applying, and maintaining (parts of) the enterprise architecture, and of course for their own project-level architectures. It is a good agile practice that architecture largely emerges from projects, and is not just invented from the top down. Only those aspects that really need to be decided at an enterprise-wide level (see also Sect. 3.2) should be given to the project at the start, for example, in the form of a project start architecture (Wagter et al. 2005). Conversely, the project-level architectures are an important source of information for the enterprise architecture.

This also holds for organizing the architecture work. An agile team is largely self-sufficient in its choice of methods and tools. However, for architecture products to be reusable in other contexts, a certain standardization of their contents will be needed, for example, in the use of models and description languages. Moreover, if parts of the system's infrastructure rely on a specific model-based approach (see also Chap. 4), then this constrains the architecture as well. Individual projects will also uncover their own best practices for architectural (and other) work, and sharing these with other teams requires some level of organization beyond the project scale. In Chap. 6, we will go deeper into the various scales and cycles at which an agile way of working operates.

Chapter 4
Service Modelling

M.W.A. Steen, M.E. Iacob, M.M. Lankhorst, H. Jonkers, M. Zoet, W. Engelsman, J. Versendaal, H.A. Proper, L. Debije, and K. Gaaloul

The development of enterprise services involves making design decisions at different levels, ranging from strategic to infrastructural choices, and concerning many different aspects, ranging from customer interaction to information registration concerns. In order to support an agile development process with short iterations through each of these levels and aspect, we need to manage the inherent complexity and support rapid feedback on the impact of design decisions across the various aspects of service development. The use of models can help to manage the coherence among the different aspects in service design and in facilitating and accelerating changes. Therefore, we propose a comprehensive framework and method for service modelling and model integration as an important ingredient of an agile service development methodology. This method is aimed at providing a shorter path between requirements and execution through the use of models to feed run-time execution engines, fast validation at the model level, support for communication with stakeholders, integration of different aspects, domains and fields of expertise, and consistency across the enterprise.

4.1 Introduction

Enterprise services are provided by a complex socio-technical system—the service system—comprising both human and technological resources. These resources need to be instructed on what to do, when, and how in order to deliver the required service. Service development is the entire process of designing, implementing, maintaining, and adapting services. The development of enterprise services involves making design decisions at different levels, ranging from strategic to infrastructural choices, and concerning many different aspects, ranging from customer interaction to information registration concerns. Think of information to be managed, partners to involve, channels to be used, and processes to execute in order to deliver the overall service. In addition, the distinction between business and

IT services is blurring, with the ongoing shift from people-delivered, possibly IT-supported, services to IT-delivered, possibly people-supported, services.

Service providers need to address the question of how to align their business operations and information technology to market demands, legal and regulatory requirements, and business strategy. There are many stakeholders involved, each with their own interests and concerns. In addition, services have to fit with the needs of customers, the organizational context, and the technological infrastructure. Marketeers will be interested in targeted market segments, channels, and proposed customer value; business operations managers in the impact on business processes; IT managers in the impact on applications and technology infrastructure; line-of-business managers in the division of roles and responsibilities; partner managers in the involvement of key partners; and so on, and so forth.

Next to the many aspects that need to be addressed when developing services, the other main challenge of service organizations is to deal with change (also see Chap. 2). They are continuously confronted with changes, such as changing market conditions, changing legislation, technological changes, changing volumes, changing partnerships, and the introduction of new channels. Therefore, we advocate an agile way of working, which is detailed further in Chap. 6. However, in order to support such an agile development process with short iterations through each of the design levels and aspect, we need to manage the inherent complexity and support rapid feedback on the impact of design decisions across the various aspects of service development.

It is simply not possible to be agile in such a complex endeavour without the use of suitable and coherent abstractions. In this chapter, we therefore propose a comprehensive framework for service development that takes the various aspects of services into consideration. This framework can serve as a map for plotting and relating the various concerns of stakeholders. The approach for composing a way of working as outlined in Chap. 6 can then be used to plan a route through this service development landscape. In particular, we can, on the one hand, position the various development artefacts within this framework and, on the other hand, use these to select and combine relevant agile practices (see in particular Sect. 6.7.2).

The framework is complemented with a method for integrating the different aspects. In this way, we obtain an integrated, model-based, agile approach to service development. This method enables a shorter path between requirements and execution, through the use of models to feed run-time execution engines, fast validation at the model level, support for communication with stakeholders, integration of different aspects, and domains, expertises, and consistency across the enterprise.

4.2 The Role of Models in Agile Service Development

As we explained in Chap. 1, we strive for an agile engineering approach to service development. Most mature engineering disciplines are firmly rooted in the use of formal, mathematical models for predicting the various properties of their design

4.2 The Role of Models in Agile Service Development

artefacts in order to make the right decisions. In this context, we use the following definition of a model:

> A *model* is a purposely abstracted and unambiguous conception of a domain.

This definition is taken from (Lankhorst et al. 2009) and is originally based on (Falkenberg et al. 1998). In this definition, a 'domain' is any subset of a conception of the universe—that is, the service world we are talking about—that is viewed as being some 'part' or 'aspect' of the universe. For complex worlds, such as the world of enterprise services, many different domains or abstractions can be envisioned, ranging from the financial and economic structure of the service network, via the individual organizations involved and their business processes and functions, to the IT implementations and infrastructures.

Models in general serve many purposes. By means of their abstraction from details, they help us focus on the essence, a specific purpose. This way, they provide us with more insight into a situation. This insight might be needed towards an informing purpose, analysis, decision-making, etc. This is the *descriptive* use of models.

Models may also be used *prescriptively* to provide guidance towards the execution of work. This could, for example, concern design activities or operational work processes. Because of the unambiguous nature of models, the guidance they provide is often clearer and more explicit than when natural language or simple pictures are used. In particular, when formalized rules or processes must be followed, using models may help avoid miscommunication or differences in interpretation and thus are a great help in project communication.

In Chap. 2, we outlined the various attributes of agility, both of agile processes and of agile systems. The use of models contributes to the realization of many of these agility aspects. Models help us in clearly establishing and prioritizing requirements and in achieving traceability between business goals, requirements, and design models, which is important to ensure that our designs really fit the needs of the business. Models also help in estimating the effort needed for a specific requirement, for example, because they give insight into the size of the functionality needed or into the complexity of a system's interactions. This aids in prioritizing requirements and improves the competency of the service development team in delivering on its promises.

Assuming that models are easier to create and maintain than software code, the use of models may help to accelerate and shorten the path between requirements and execution. If we automatically convert models to implementations, or even better, if we have an infrastructure that can directly interpret and execute these models, we can build and change services with less software coding or even no coding at all. Various kinds of 'engines', for example for business process or business rule execution, are becoming increasingly popular because of this. Thus, making changes becomes much easier, and the development process is accelerated. Fig. 4.1 illustrates this.

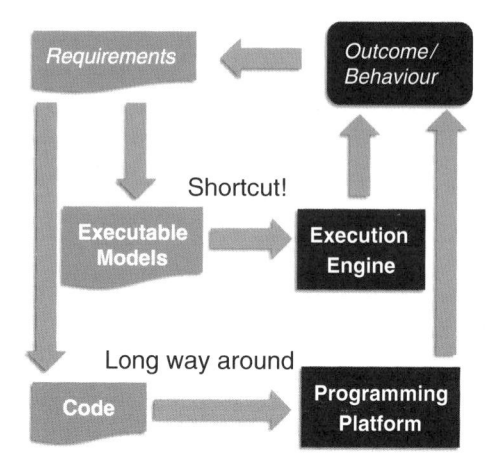

Fig. 4.1 Agility through model execution; when models are executable, one can take a shortcut and obtain faster feedback on design decisions

Furthermore, models may serve as an important means for communication with business stakeholders (also see Chap. 7). These stakeholders can be more closely involved in designing or changing a service, or in some cases they may even be able to make changes themselves. In particular, when the infrastructure is built using engines like those mentioned above, some types of changes may be made directly by end users, such as changing business rules or workflows. Thus, using models may improve stakeholder involvement, increase responsiveness to business needs, and speed up the development process.

Models also facilitate the deployment of a change, by shortening the development, testing, acceptance, and production process. Since less coding is involved, the development process takes less effort. But you can also use models to validate or verify a service design offline, for example, by means of simulation and model-based analysis techniques. You can detect errors at an earlier stage, when they are usually cheaper to fix, and you can predict behaviour, for example, resource consumption under heavy usage.

The usage of models that show the dependencies between different service aspects also helps you in assessing the effects of changes, for example, by seeing how they propagate through the models. This ensures consistency and avoids unexpected and unwanted side effects.

Finally, models may facilitate the integration and reuse of services. If you have model-based descriptions of service interfaces, finding and integrating these services is easier and can sometimes even be automated. Service composition and bundling, offering new combinations of existing services, is also facilitated if you can already check at the model level whether these services are compatible.

Importantly, and as discussed in Chap 6, we do not advocate 'big design upfront' of the entire service landscape. Rather, the modelling efforts themselves should be iterative and should follow good practices for agile modelling, as, for example, provided by Ambler (2002) and others. But as we already outlined in Chap. 3, an investment in a model-based architecture may well pay off in a much quicker and cheaper development afterwards. Some design up-front is therefore required.

4.3 Adoption Levels of Modelling

Although the use of models in service development clearly has advantages in terms of agility, coherence, consistency, and quality, there are also costs involved. Modelling requires effort, skills, and specialized tools. And scenarios in which models are directly executed require an infrastructure consisting of appropriate execution engines. Unfortunately, the benefits of modelling can usually only be obtained after these investments in infrastructure, tools, education, and human resources have been made. Therefore, a model-driven approach should only be adopted when the benefits outweigh the costs. Below, we describe a number of adoption levels for the use of models, each with their own set of benefits and costs. This can help organizations to choose the right level of adoption (Table 4.1).

Level 1—no models—speaks for itself. If no models are used in the development process, there are obviously also no benefits and no costs for making models. Be aware, however, that overall development costs may increase, because there are limited means to manage the inherent complexity of service design.

At level 2—informal models—service developers enjoy improved communication, while the modelling costs are still low. An 'informal' model has no formally defined syntax or semantics. Examples include Visio diagrams and PowerPoint drawings.

Table 4.1 Adoption of modelling

Level of model adoption	Benefits	Costs
1. No models	None	None
2. Informal models	Improved communication	Low
3. Isolated formal models	Unambiguous specification, analysis support	Know-how and tools for specific technique(s)
4a. Horizontally integrated formal models	Cross-aspect impact of change analysis, consistency across domains, reuse	Integrated tool-suite for modelling or model integration support, cross-domain modelling expertise
4b. Vertically integrated formal models	Traceability to requirements, impact of change analysis, forward and backward engineering support, for example, code generation	Dedicated tool-chain and target platform, model transformation expertise
5. Integrated formal models	Combined benefits of 3 and 4	Integration of tools and infrastructure components, combined expertise, and know-how from 3 and 4

At level 3—isolated formal models—proper modelling tools are employed to model some aspects of the service design. We use 'isolated' here as opposite of 'integrated', meaning that multiple models may be used, but without being formally related to one another. The minimum requirement for a model to be 'formal' is that its syntax conforms to a metamodel. Examples include BPMN process models and UML class diagrams. The advantage of formal models over informal models is that they are unambiguous and amenable to formal analysis, such that they can be used to predict properties of the service before it is implemented. Obviously, this level requires know-how and dedicated tools for the selected modelling techniques.

At the highest adoption level, 5—integrated formal models—it is assumed that models are used at most abstraction levels and across most of the aspects of the service design. Moreover, these models are all assumed to be views on one, usually left implicit, integrated underlying model of the service. This level demands a lot in terms of skills, tools, and infrastructure. Therefore, it may not be appropriate for every organization. There are two possible routes to achieve level 5: horizontal integration first (4a) and vertical integration first (4b). The desired benefits and the priorities of the organization determine which route is most appropriate and to what extent the other path is followed.

At level 4a—horizontally integrated formal models—service developers can reuse elements from one aspect model in another, check and enforce consistency across the aspects, and perform cross-aspect impact-of-change analyses. Models are 'horizontally' integrated when they are at the same level of abstraction, but possibly addressing different aspects, and consistently referring to each other's elements. This level of integration requires an integrated tool-suite for modelling or another form of model integration support and cross-domain modelling expertise. In Sect. 4.7, we detail further the specific requirements this scenario places on tools support.

At level 4b—vertically integrated formal models—service developers can trace design and implementation artefacts back to the requirements that motivate their existence, analyse the impact of changes in requirements or designs on the lower abstraction levels, and make use of automated support for forward and backward engineering, such as code generation. Models are 'vertically' integrated when they are at different levels of abstraction, addressing the same aspects, and have relationships defined between semantically conformant elements. This level of integration requires a dedicated tool-chain and target platform as well as model transformation expertise.

4.4 The ASD Framework

In this section, we present a model-based framework for agile service development. We focus in particular on identifying the kinds of abstractions that are required to support an integral and coherent service development process. In developing this framework, our aim was not to develop 'yet another' framework, but rather to combine the features of relevant existing frameworks that are relevant to (agile) system development.

Of course, we are not the first to propose a framework for enterprise service development. One of the best-known and oldest frameworks for the describing the design space of enterprises is the Zachman Framework for Enterprise Architecture (Sowa and Zachman 1992). It was first introduced in 1987 as the 'Framework for Information Systems Architecture' (Zachman 1987). The Zachman framework is a logical structure for classifying and organizing the elements and aspects of an enterprise (its ontology) that are significant to the management of the enterprise as well as to the development of the enterprise's systems. In its most simple form, the Zachman framework depicts the concepts on the intersections between the roles in the design process, in particular the *planner*, *owner*, *designer*, and *builder*, and the product abstractions: that is, *what* (data) it is made of, *how* (function) it works, and *where* (network) the components are located with respect to one another. Three additional columns of models depict *who* does what work, *when* do things happen, and *why* are various choices made.

A more recent framework with a strong impact on international standardization is the framework embedded in the ArchiMate language (The Open Group 2012; Lankhorst et al. 2009). The core of the ArchiMate language distinguishes between the structural or static aspect and the behavioural or dynamic aspect of enterprises. The structural aspect is further subdivided into active structural elements (the business actors, application components, and devices that display actual behaviour, i.e. the 'subjects' of activity) and passive structural elements, that is, the objects on which behaviour is performed.

In addition, ArchiMate makes a distinction between an external view and an internal view on systems. The service concept represents a unit of essential functionality that a system exposes to its environment. For the external users, only this external functionality, together with non-functional aspects such as the quality of service, costs, etc., is relevant. Services are accessible through interfaces, which constitute the external view on the structural aspect.

Finally, ArchiMate distinguishes three layers: the Business layer offers products and services to external customers, which are realized in the organization by business processes (performed by business actors or roles); the Application layer supports the business layer with application services which are realized by (software) application components; and the Technology layer offers infrastructural services (e.g. processing, storage, and communication services) needed to run applications, realized by computer and communication devices and system software.

There are many more framework and reference architectures with some relevance to service development. Standardization organizations, including OASIS, The Open Group, W3C, and OMG, have produced various standards and white papers containing guidance for developing service-oriented solutions; see (The Open Group 2009b) for an overview. However, these generally are of a technical nature and pay less attention to the business, organizational, decision, and interaction aspects of enterprise service development. Most methodologies and development tools also boast their own world views. TOGAF, for example, has its own Content

ArchiMate:	Active Structure	Behaviour		Passive Structure
Zachman:	Where	Who	How	When	What

| Interaction | Structure | Function | Coordination | Decision | Product |

3-tier pattern: Presentation   Business Logic   Data

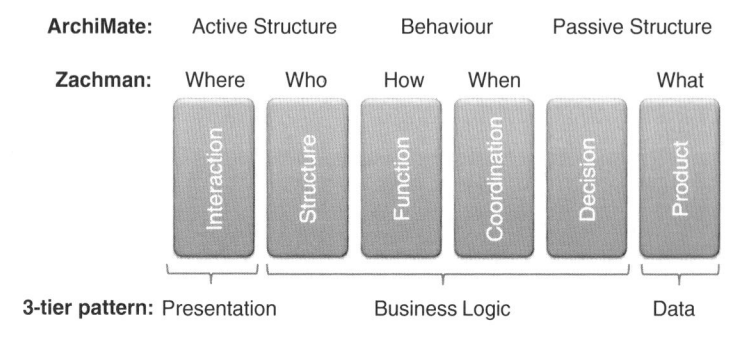

Fig. 4.2 The framework's aspects and their relationship to other frameworks

Framework, which categorizes architecture artefacts according to the TOGAF development phases (The Open Group 2011). The Design and Engineering Methodology for Organizations (DEMO) takes a language-action perspective and looks at organizations at an ontological, an infological, and a datalogical level and further distinguishes the construction, process, state, and action aspects (Dietz 2006).

While each of these frameworks has its merits, none of them covered all the aspects and perspectives that we encountered in agile service development. Nevertheless, they are complementary and contain many useful concepts that we can reuse in service development. We therefore saw the need to combine those features of the existing frameworks that are relevant to agile service development into a framework that is comprehensive and specific to agile service development.

4.4.1 Service Aspects

Our framework aims to support agility and flexibility in realizing service requirements, while managing the inherent complexity. A good practice for achieving such flexibility is 'separation of concerns'. Following Zachman, our framework is structured along two axes: service aspects and abstraction levels. By dealing with each aspect separately before dealing with the bigger picture, we can maintain a grip on the complexity and avoid that design concerns get mixed up. This supports agility by providing a single point of definition and change for each aspect. A well-known example of this principle from web application development is the use of the so-called three-tier architecture, separating presentation, business logic, and data. A similar subdivision applies to service development, where we need to address the interaction with customers, the provided functionality, and the information being managed.

However, the functionality or business logic of enterprise services is usually not so easily captured. Other principles help us to divide this aspect further. Service-oriented architecture (Erl 2009) and structured analysis and design techniques (Marca and McGowan 1987) suggest us to separate, decompose, and encapsulate groups of coherent functionalities into reusable building blocks, providing again services to their environment, resulting in a hierarchy of functional building blocks.

4.4 The ASD Framework

Workflow thinking has taught us to separate activities or tasks to be executed from the (human or system) actors executing them. Business process management (BPM) (von Brocke and Rosemann 2010) thinking suggests to separate the coordination of such functional building blocks. And a final good practice is to 'separate the know from the flow', that is, do not mix decision logic with coordination logic. Figure 4.2 shows the six resulting service aspects and loosely relates them to the ArchiMate and Zachman frameworks.

4.4.1.1 Interaction

The interaction aspect is concerned with the way in which the enterprise interacts with its environment. It includes the enterprise's collaboration with its various partners and how its clients interact with the business services it provides. These services may be delivered through an online channel, but traditional, human-centric services, delivered, for example, via the telephone or over the counter, are also part of this. Hence, the interaction between user and service may involve graphical user interfaces, online forms, etc., but also the classical person-to-person interaction and service.

4.4.1.2 Structure

The structure aspect concerns the way in which the enterprise organizes its human and technological resources. This includes the organizational structure, comprising the definition and allocation of roles, responsibilities, authorizations, reporting lines, etc., but also the information system structures, that is, the technical and application architectures.

4.4.1.3 Function

In the function aspect, we address the individual elements of business and application functionality that, orchestrated and coordinated together, deliver the actual substance of a service. This comprises both the (manual) tasks of employees and the (automated) service logic of applications. Individual functions (and the services they deliver) are coordinated via the coordination aspect; they use and produce information from the information aspect, and they employ rules and calculations from the decision aspect.

4.4.1.4 Coordination

The coordination aspect focuses on the various dependencies between the activities needed to deliver services. This includes, for example, the specification and (possibly automated) orchestration of business processes, workflow support, etc.

It comprises both the coordination within an individual organization and the coordination of activities with other organizations, which may be users of the service or partners in delivering it.

4.4.1.5 Decision

The decision aspect captures the logic of reasoning used in the service domain, to reach decisions, that is, how decisions are (to be) made. For example, in the domain of insurance policies or banking products, this pertains to decisions based on calculations and other (logical) derivations. Part of this logic may take the form of executable specifications, such as decision tables or executable business rules; other elements are typically used by people, both in delivering the service and in defining, checking, and enforcing an organization's 'rules of conduct'. However, the logic specified here should not include coordination, interaction, or organization logic, which belong to the other aspects.

4.4.1.6 Product

Finally, the product aspect is concerned with the things that the service produces and consumes and the way in which these products are registered and managed. Products can refer both to tangible business objects, such as cars and pizza's, but also to intangible information items, such as insurance claims and pizza orders.

4.4.2 Abstraction Levels

Each of the service aspects can be considered at different abstraction levels (Fig. 4.3). We distinguish between the specification space and the human and technical infrastructure on which specifications are realized and deployed. The specification space can be divided further into a requirements level, a design level, and an implementation level. These abstraction levels are detailed further below.

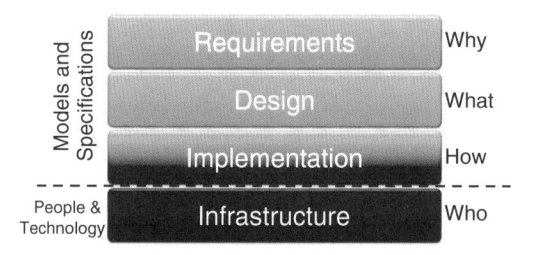

Fig. 4.3 The framework's abstraction levels

4.4.2.1 Requirements Level

The requirements level deals with the motivation and rationale behind the service, that is, its 'why', and comprises the service requirements from the business perspective. This level not only contains specifications of the requirements on the specific service under development but also includes specifications of the context in which the service is to operate. Therefore, at this abstraction level, we recognize the need for at least two types of models: a context model and a requirements model.

4.4.2.2 Design Level

The design level contains the 'what' of the service: the interactions, processes, functions, rules, and objects that are needed to realize the service. Designs are typically denoted in the form of some kind of model. Models, being formalized abstractions of reality that cover specific aspects of that reality and abstract from the rest, are a precise way of specifying services. The use of models as executable specifications is especially valuable from the perspective of agility. Because models can be checked in various ways before they are implemented, risks of changes can be managed and their effects can be predicted (within limits) before implementation. Furthermore, if implementing a change in the IT domain merely amounts to changing some models, an organization may react much more quickly to changing requirements than, for example, when large-scale software changes are needed.

4.4.2.3 Implementation Level

The implementation level describes the 'how', that is, how the service will be implemented, in terms of both the people and the technology involved. Ideally, this level can be skipped, that is, if the design models are directly executable on the infrastructure. However, more often than not, this is not realistic, which makes it necessary to also look into the implementation artefacts.

4.4.2.4 Infrastructure Level

Finally, we have the infrastructure level. This is where the rubber meets the road: the people and technology actually delivering the service. One the one hand, we find here people with suitable capabilities who deliver services through physical channels. To be able to deliver these services, they execute tasks, coordinate activities, manage other people, and enforce that rules are obeyed. On the other hand, there is the IT infrastructure which delivers services through online channels and comprises both generic hard- and software infrastructure and specific applications on top of that, such as DBMSs, BPMSs, rule engines, and web and application servers.

4.4.3 Overview and Use of the Framework

Putting all of the abstraction levels and aspects together results in the framework shown in Fig. 4.4.

The framework illustrates that enterprise services are realized through combinations of business functions, processes, IT, and more, all of which should be developed jointly. Of course, the framework is no more than that, a frame of reference. It does not specify a way of working, and there is no requirement to fill each cell of the model individually. Rather, it provides a way to position and relate the various design artefacts, where individual artefacts may cover more than one cell. For example, in the infrastructure layer, people (human resources) will often fill multiple positions at the same time, for example, being both 'manager' and 'coordinator'. Similarly, the more advanced IT systems, such as for case management, business process management, or business rule management, cover multiple levels and aspects. Conversely, some cells may remain empty for a specific service. For example, if no significant coordination with others is required, business process specifications may be superfluous.

Service organizations can use the framework to plot the models and abstractions they are already using in their service development process and highlight white spots that they currently do not cover. To give an idea on what to put where, we return to the AgiSurance case study introduced in Chap. 2.

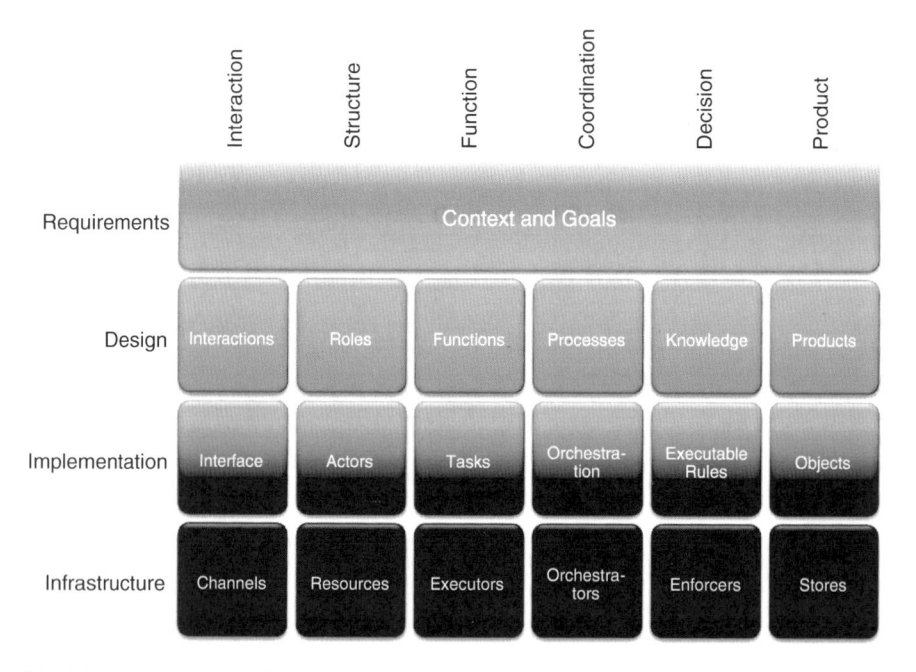

	Interaction	Structure	Function	Coordination	Decision	Product
Requirements	Context and Goals					
Design	Interactions	Roles	Functions	Processes	Knowledge	Products
Implementation	Interface	Actors	Tasks	Orchestration	Executable Rules	Objects
Infrastructure	Channels	Resources	Executors	Orchestrators	Enforcers	Stores

Fig. 4.4 Framework overview

4.4.4 Modelling AgiSurance

While AgiSurance offers many different insurance products, each with their own unique properties and rules, they also share some characteristics. For each product, there has to be an acceptance process and a claim handling function. In order to cope with the regularly changing product offering, AgiSurance wants to establish an agile service architecture, allowing easy configuration of new insurance products on a stable infrastructure. In the following, we focus on the redevelopment of the claim handling service. Currently, claims are received on paper and handled manually—a costly and error-prone process. Due to increased sales, AgiSurance expects a sharp rise in claims. Therefore, they want to optimize and partly automate the claim handling. The idea is to develop generic business and IT functions and processes for handling insurance claims that are fed with specific rules for decision-making and interaction for each product.

In Sect. 3.2.4, AgiSurance had already decided for a flexible, model-driven infrastructure, consisting of a database management system (DBMS), a business rule management system (BRMS), and a business process management system (BPMS). However, because of the relatively simple and stable processes for claim handling, they now decide not to use the BPMS, but to implement the processes directly onto a standard application server.

AgiSurance first constructs a *context model* and a *product model*, based on an analysis of contracts, policies, and insurance legislation. The context model is complemented with a *business requirements model* to define the stakeholders, their goals, and the requirements on the claim handling service. The organizational structure and the division of tasks and responsibilities do not really change, so these models can be copied from the corporate *business architecture*, defining organizational units, roles, functions, and high-level processes and the *handbook* with guidelines and procedures for employees. Next, the context and product models are detailed further into a *rule model* and an *information model*. The rule model will be executed directly on a rule engine; the information model is automatically transformed into a *database schema*. In parallel, a *user interface model* and a *service model* are devised. The service model lays the foundations for the application code and the process model. The user interface model is used to generate the *web pages* for the claim handling service.

Figure 4.5 plots the identified models and infrastructure elements on the ASD Framework. Here we can see that all the service aspects are covered to some extent and that detailed implementation level models can be traced back to higher level requirements models. Design artefacts can also be related horizontally, such as the service, rule, and information models, signifying that they refer to each other. Several models cover more than one aspect and/or level. The product model, for example, floats between the requirements and design layers and covers parts of the information, decision, and process aspects. By plotting the models on the framework, AgiSurance can identify where specifications are

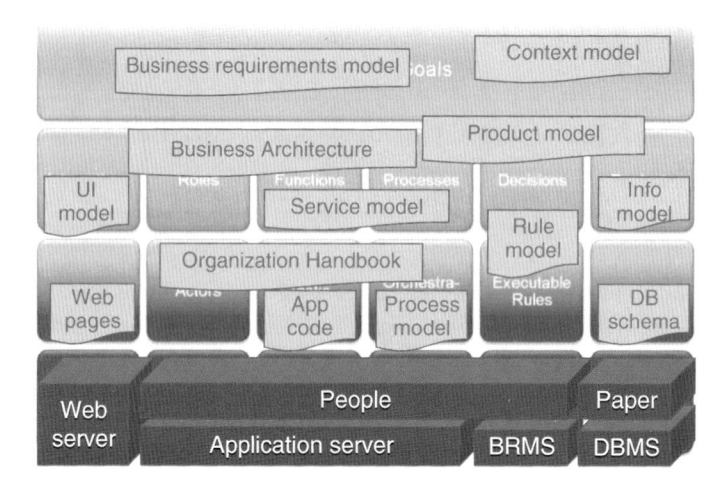

Fig. 4.5 Positioning AgiSurance models on the ASD framework

missing and where they should put their effort in verifying the consistency between models.

4.5 The ASD Conceptual Model

In this section, we describe the concepts underlying the various service aspects and their relationships. This gives body to the ASD Framework and is a first step towards integrating different models and specifications. The conceptual model is structured along the dimensions of the ASD Framework (see Sect. 4.4.3). First, we describe the concepts pertaining to the requirements level. At this level, models are increasingly used to formalize service requirements and to use them to relate design artefacts to organizational goals. Service requirements, in turn, depend on a conceptualization of the business domain, the context in which the service is to operate. Therefore, we introduce two modelling domains at this level: context and requirements. Second, we define concepts for each of the six design and implementation aspects. Each aspect constitutes a modelling domain. Finally, we define the relationships between the defined modelling domains.

The metamodels for each of the modelling domains were constructed by analysing a number of relevant and popular modelling techniques for the given domains. In a sense, we attempted to extract the best practices in conceptual modelling from a large number of existing techniques. Table 4.2 lists the modelling techniques that were analysed for each of the modelling domains. Each technique defines its own set of modelling concepts. Concepts that we encountered more than once (also those which could be considered synonymous) or which represent a key abstraction for the given domain, we selected as key concepts for that modelling domain.

4.5 The ASD Conceptual Model

Table 4.2 Relevant modelling techniques for each of the modelling domains

Modelling domain	Modelling techniques
Context	ERD, ORM, OWL, SBVR, UML class diagram
Requirements	ArchiMate motivation extension, i*, KAOS
Interaction	ConcurTaskTrees, Diamodl, UML use case diagram, UsiXML
Structure	ArchiMate, BPMN, DEMO, e^3value, UML
Function	ArchiMate, DEM, DFD, e^3value, IDEF0, SoaML
Coordination	ArchiMate, BPMN, DEMO, UML activity diagram
Decision	Decision tables, DMN, ECA rules, SBVR
Product	ERD, ORM, UML class diagram

4.5.1 The Context Domain

A *context model* is a conceptual model of the domain in which an enterprise conducts its business and in which the service(s) under development should operate. It describes the vocabulary and key concepts of the business domain, as well as their properties and relationships. Usually, the context or domain model is only associated with a structural view of the business domain, but it can equally well contain dynamic views describing the main business activities and their constraints and dependencies. A context model is often complemented with the constraints that govern the integrity of the model. Sometimes, the context model is referred to as *knowledge model* because it defines the basic facts and rules of the business domain. Thus, it is more than a list of dictionary-style definitions of terms.

The context model can be effectively used to verify and validate the understanding of the business domain among various stakeholders. It is especially helpful as a communication tool and a focusing point both among the different members of the business team and between the technical and business teams. In addition, the context model forms the basis for defining requirements on the service(s) to be developed. Therefore, it is important that a context model itself is independent from design or implementation considerations.

The importance of context or domain modelling has been highlighted by many before us. As a consequence, many methods and techniques exist for it. The structure of a domain is often modelled using object-oriented techniques, such as UML class diagrams, or the more basic Entity Relationship Diagrams (ERD) (Chen 1976). In case UML (OMG 2011a) is used, domain concepts are represented as classes, their relationships as associations, and their properties as attributes. Constraints can be specified using the Object Constraint Language (OCL) (OMG 2010). However, the UML has been criticized a lot for being incomprehensible by domain experts that are not software engineers.

There are several alternatives from the data and knowledge representation community, such as the Web Ontology Language (OWL) (W3C 2009), Object

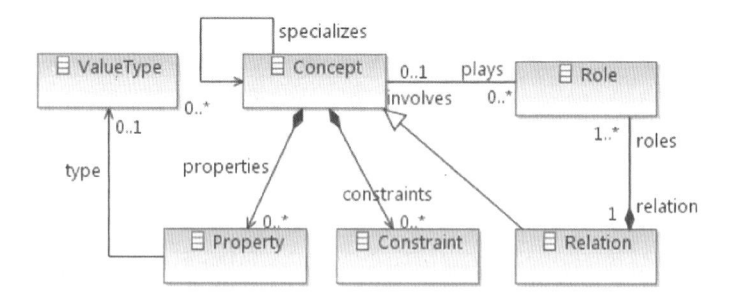

Fig. 4.6 The context metamodel

Role Modeling (ORM) (Halpin and Morgan 2008), and the Semantics of Business Vocabulary and Business Rules standard (SBVR) (OMG 2008), that take a more fact-oriented approach to modelling the domain. In these techniques, properties, relationships, and other rules or constraints are all seen as 'fact types'. Sometimes, these techniques enable automatic reasoning, for example, to derive new facts.

By analysing and comparing the modelling techniques mentioned above, we have derived the following set of key concepts for context modelling:

> *Concept*: an abstraction or generalization of a phenomenon that may occur in the domain.
> *Property*: an attribute, characteristic, or quality of a concept. Each property has a type specifying the range of values it can take.
> *Relation*: an association between two or more concepts, each having a particular role in the relation.
> *Value Type*: a range of values that properties can take.
> *Role*: the position of a concept or the part played by a concept in a relation.
> *Constraint*: a limitation, restriction, or rule controlling the possible instances of concepts and relations and values of properties.

Fig. 4.6 depicts the context modelling metamodel, relating the key concepts defined above.

4.5.1.1 An Example Context Model

In finance, context models are to a large extent defined by the legal 'space' in which the financial institution operates. They need to comply with legislation based on international directives and standards, such as Solvency II, Basel III, and IFRS. Within this legal space, or more precisely their interpretation of the legal space, financial institutions define a product model defining their products and services. Both legislation and financial products and services are generally defined in

4.5 The ASD Conceptual Model

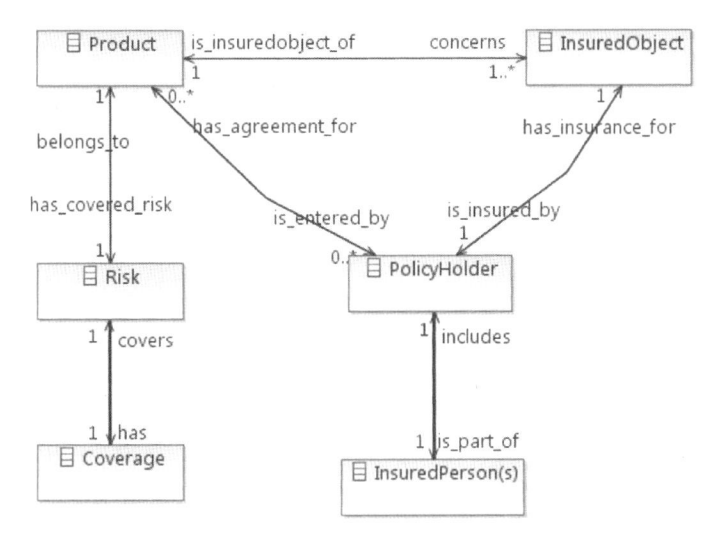

Fig. 4.7 Part of the AgiSurance context model in UML

legal documents (laws, contracts, policies). Drawing up a context model then consists of interpreting these documents, formalizing the definitions and rules contained within them.

In Fig. 4.7, we show some of the results of such a context modelling exercise for AgiSurance, our example insurance company. A UML class diagram is used to model the domain concepts and their relations.

4.5.2 Requirements Modelling

Whereas the context model defines the inherent structures and constraints of the environment in which the enterprise has to operate, the *requirements model* captures the strategic direction and desires of the enterprise itself. A requirements model describes the motivation for the service(s) under development. It identifies the stakeholders and their concerns and defines their goals or objectives.

In addition to clarifying and formally specifying the requirements for a service, requirements modelling is useful to achieve forward and backward traceability between objectives and design artefacts. Forward traceability is the ability to analyse the impact of a change in requirements. For example, when a business objective changes, it becomes possible to analyse which services, and the components realizing those services, are affected by this change. Backward traceability can be used to determine the value or *raison d'être* of a design artefact. Backward traceability answers questions like the following: 'Why was this service here? Who was responsible for this service? What is the added value of this service to the enterprise?'

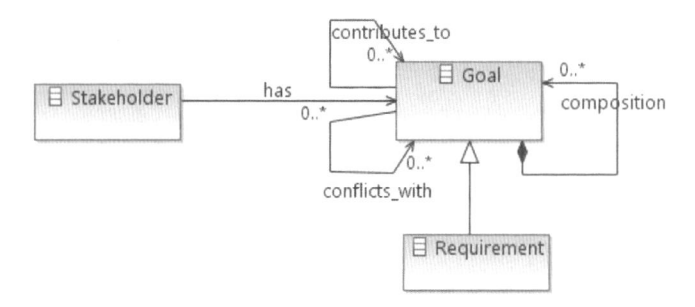

Fig. 4.8 The requirements metamodel

Within the goal-oriented requirements engineering literature, we can identify a number of relevant modelling techniques, such as KAOS (Van Lamsweerde 2003) and i* (Yu 1997). Several of these were analysed and compared in the design of the ArchiMate Motivation extension (Engelsman et al. 2011). KAOS is a language that refines system goals to concrete requirements. In i*, intentions of stakeholders (goals, beliefs) and their dependencies are modelled. Intentions are refined into tasks an actor has to perform to realize them.

Since the ArchiMate Motivation extension (The Open Group 2012) is based on these earlier techniques, we adopt the most essential concepts from ArchiMate as key to requirements modelling:

> *Stakeholder*: the role of an individual, team, or organization (or classes thereof) that represents their interests in, or concerns relative to, the outcome of the architecture.
> *Goal*: an end state that a stakeholder intends to achieve
> *Requirement*: a statement of need that must be realized by a system.

A number of different links are possible between these constructs. A goal can be associated with one or more stakeholder. There are two relations available for goal refinement. First, we have the goal decomposition relation. A decomposition of a goal is the conjunction of the set of subgoals that constitute the goal, in such a way that an immeasurable goal is decomposed into goals with measurable indicators, and a goal with measurable indicators is decomposed in subgoals with subindicators. The decomposition relation is used to operationalize goals. A goal influence relation is used to demonstrate that the satisfaction of one goal positively or negatively influences another goal.

A third link is the goal conflict relation. Two goals are conflicting if the satisfaction of one goal prevents the satisfaction of the other and vice versa. In this case, both goals are mutually exclusive.

Figure 4.8 illustrates the underlying metamodel for requirements modelling. The main idea behind this metamodel is that a stakeholder may have a number of desires or intentions. An *intention* can be anything, most likely a desired state of the world.

4.5 The ASD Conceptual Model

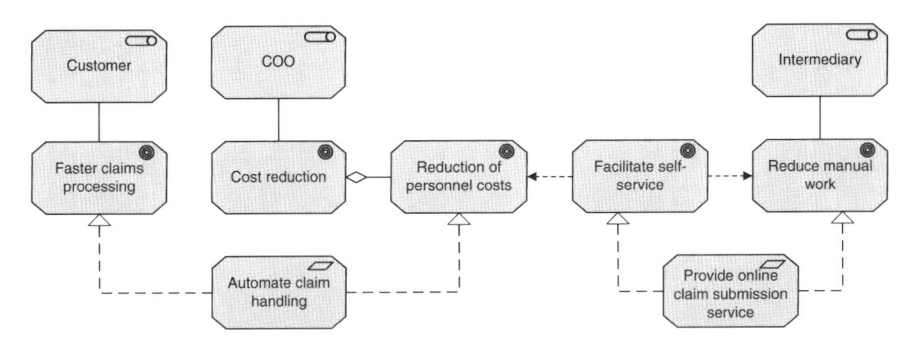

Fig. 4.9 A business requirements model for AgiSurance

An intention only becomes a goal when a stakeholder is willing to commit resources to reach that state of the world. The previously discussed relations are used to refine goals into requirements. A *requirement* is a concrete goal that can be assigned to a single actor. A *goal* is a desired state of the world which is not yet concrete enough to be assigned to a single actor.

4.5.2.1 An Example Requirements Model

Figure 4.9 shows part of the business requirements model for AgiSurance using the ArchiMate Motivation extension. It shows three stakeholder roles: the chief operating officer (COO) of AgiSurance, whose main goal is cost reduction; an intermediary, whose main goal is to reduce the manual work he has in filing claims on his customers' behalf; and a customer, who wants claims to be processed faster such that he will receive the insurance money in time to cover the incurred damage. The diagram further shows that the main goals and contributing goals will be realized by the two requirements 'Provide online claim submission service' and 'Automate claim handling'.

4.5.3 Interaction Modelling

In the interaction aspect, we design and model the way in which the various parts of the enterprise interact with customers, partners, and each other to deliver the service. Such interactions can be specified at various levels, ranging from an identification of collaborations and channels to the detailed design of user interfaces.

Although the scope of interaction design for enterprise services is much broader, involving, for example, also physical channel design, many insights can be gained from the more established discipline of user interface engineering for software applications. In fact, user interfaces are a kind of service interface. User interface engineering involves human factors engineering, user interface design, and graphics design (Nielsen 1993). For each of those subdisciplines, separate developers and designers with different competences are needed. Such perspectives and competences are clearly relevant to service interaction design as well (see also Dividino et al. (2009)).

In user interface engineering literature, authors have distinguished multiple levels of interaction modelling (Nielsen 1993; Aquino et al. 2008; Calvary et al. 2003; Vanderdonckt 2005; Versendaal 1991):

- Task level
- Concept level
- Interface level (abstract (user) interface)
- Navigation and presentation level (concrete (user) interface)
- The implemented (user) interface

In our framework, the task level is largely covered by the structure and function aspects, while the concept level is covered by what we call the context model. What remains are abstractions for modelling the actor–actor, actor–system, and system–system interactions. Most literature in this area focuses on actor–system interactions, that is, on how to model human–computer interfaces, for example, Vanderdonckt (2005) and Trætteberg (2009). Actor–actor interactions can be modelled in languages, such as ArchiMate and UML, that both support the Collaboration concept.

> *Collaboration*: a (possibly temporary) configuration of two or more roles (see structure aspect) that cooperate to jointly perform certain collective behaviour.
> *Interface*: a point through which a role offers access to its services.
> *Interaction Element*: part of a user interface, for example, a window, button, or checkbox. Also, non-visible parts of the interface, such as an input event and a command, are interaction elements.

Since our aim is to integrate multiple modelling techniques, we have chosen here for the most abstract definition of the interface concept. It can be used to represent business interfaces or channels, but also to represent user interfaces (screen dialogues) and application-to-application interfaces (e.g. WSDL). When we dive deeper into the implementation level, we may also need concepts to model page navigation and presentation, such as page, field, command, and page flow.

In Fig. 4.10, we present a metamodel for the key concepts of the interaction aspect and their most important relationships to concepts from other aspects, that is, the role concept from the structure aspect and the service concept from the function aspect.

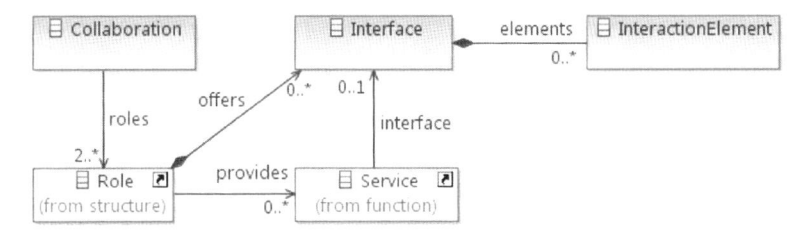

Fig. 4.10 The interaction metamodel

4.5.4 Structure Modelling

In the structure aspect, we design and model the way in which the enterprise is organized internally to deliver its services. This involves the definition of the human, organizational and system actors within the enterprise, as well as the relationships between them. A simple example of a structure model is the organizational chart, depicting the hierarchy of organizational units and positions within an enterprise.

Often, the structural aspects of an organization are covered by models that have a broader scope. Interaction, process, function, and value models usually include a partial specification of the structure of the service system. In the Business Process Modelling Notation (BPMN) (OMG 2011c), for example (also see Sect. 4.5.6), activities are assigned to pools and lanes representing organizational units, roles, and role hierarchies. In ArchiMate, the Open Group standard for enterprise architecture modelling (The Open Group 2012), the structure aspect is covered by the static structure aspect of ArchiMate. This includes business-level concepts, such as Business Actor and Business Role, but also application- and infrastructure-level concepts, such as application component, device, and node.

The structure of a service system can be captured using the following key concepts:

> *Actor*: an entity within the enterprise that can be assigned behaviour and responsibilities, such as a person, organizational unit, or application component.
> *Role*: an abstract kind of actor and a collection of responsibilities and potential behaviours. An actor can be assigned to a role, indicating that the actor will fulfil all responsibilities and behaviours specified by the role. An actor may be assigned to multiple roles, and a role may be assigned to multiple actors.
> *Location*: a logical or a physical location relevant to the enterprise (such as branch office, city, or country).

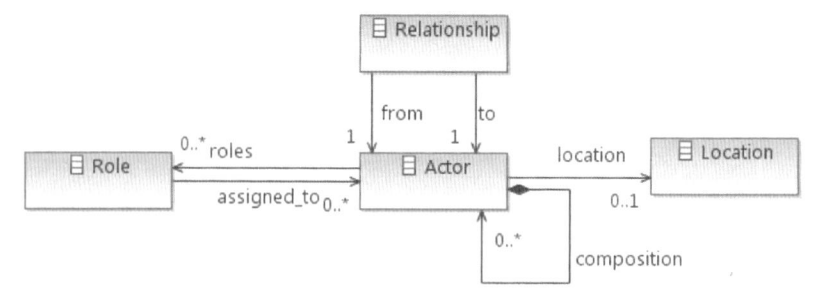

Fig. 4.11 The structure metamodel

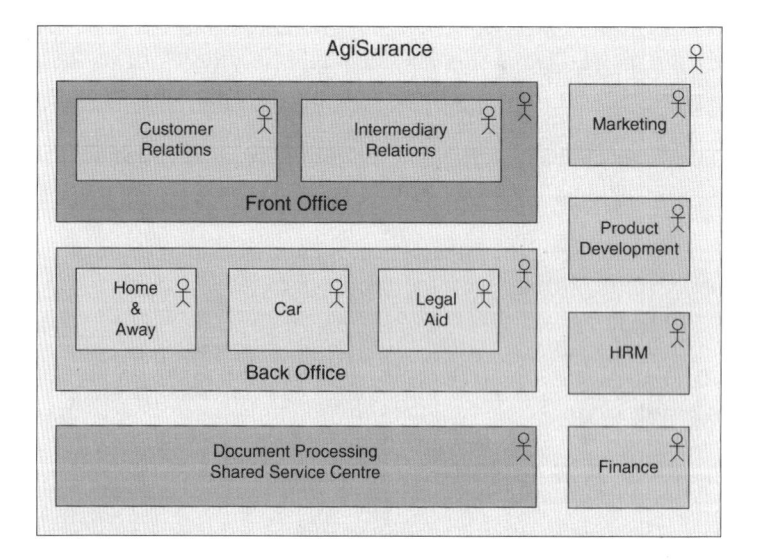

Fig. 4.12 An organizational structure model for AgiSurance in ArchiMate

Actors can be related to each other through composition: one actor can contain other actors. Other relationships can be imagined, such as reporting, ownership, or assignment (of a role). In addition, actors can be assigned a location. Figure 4.11 illustrate the key structure modelling concepts and their relationships.

4.5.4.1 An Example Structure Model

AgiSurance's corporate business architecture consists of three models: the organization model, the business function architecture model, and the high-level business process architecture model. The organization model specifies the organizational structure and the hierarchical relationships between departments (see Fig. 4.12). In this figure, hierarchy is modelled as containment (nesting).

4.5.5 Function Modelling

In the functional aspect, we design and model the activities or functional building blocks that are required to deliver the service under development. Together with the coordination aspect, it specifies the behaviour of the service. Where the coordination aspect focuses on the flow (the logical or temporal ordering of activities), the functional aspect focuses on the decomposition of complex behaviour into smaller, manageable, and reusable functions and their interconnection through input/output relationships. Functional decomposition makes it possible to structure the complexity of organizations and systems. The decomposition gives structure to the tasks and activities in an orderly manner, independent from the executing mechanism.

Functional decomposition, as a technique for describing systems as a hierarchy of functions, is a widely applicable principle. It was first introduced in the area of information systems engineering as the Structured Analysis and Design Technique (SADT) (Marca and McGowan 1987), later formalized by the IDEF0 (Integration Definition for Function Modelling) (IDEF 1981) standard. Data flow diagramming (DFD) (Stevens et al. 1974) is another technique often used in information system analysis, which focuses more on the flows of information between functions (called 'processes' in DFD).

The principle of functional decomposition is also present in service-oriented architectures and business function architectures. Therefore, techniques used to model these, such as SoaML (OMG 2009) and Dynamic Enterprise Modelling (DEM) (van Es and Post 1996), are also relevant to the functional aspect.

The e^3value methodology models a network of enterprises creating, distributing, and consuming things of economic value (Gordijn and Akkermans 2001). The e^3value technique can be used to model value exchanges between enterprises. This may result in a business value model, clearly showing the enterprises and final customers involved and the flow of valuable objects (goods, services, and money). Such models can be used to analyse the economic viability of each enterprise within a service network.

Central to the functional aspect are the concepts of 'function' and 'flow'.

> *Function*: a coherent unit of behaviour with the purpose of performing and/or fulfilling one or more missions or objectives and identified by a verb or verb phrase that describes what must be accomplished.
> *Flow*: a steady, continuous stream or supply of something. Different types of flow may be distinguished, such as information, physical, and value flows.

Functions consume and produce flows, respectively, their inputs and outputs. Each function can be decomposed into 'subfunctions', thus creating a hierarchy of functions. Functions are executed by 'mechanisms', which can be automated systems, individuals, a group of people, or a combination of systems and people. In the metamodel, we model this as an assignment to a role (from the structure aspect). The execution of a function and its subfunctions takes place under 'control'

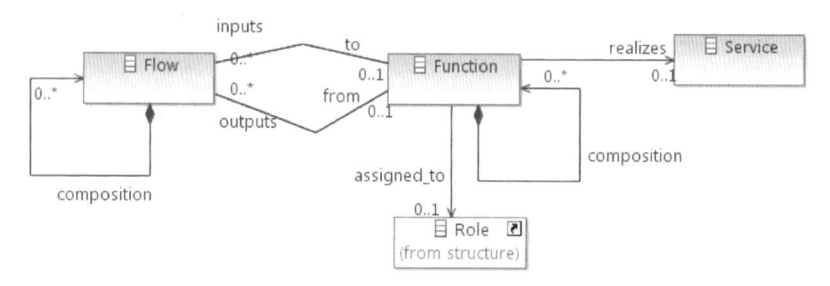

Fig. 4.13 The function metamodel

of something or someone. This can be a workflow, a set of rules or some other kind of control function that is associated with the function.

Once the functions have been named and defined, we can start to think about the services they realize. We repeat the definition from Chap 1:

> *Service*: a unit of functionality that a system exposes to its environment, while hiding internal operations, which provides a certain value (monetary or otherwise).

The key concepts for the function aspect and their relationships are illustrated in Fig. 4.13.

4.5.5.1 An Example Function Model

Figure 4.14 shows the business function architecture model for AgiSurance in ArchiMate. It is an example of a model that is mainly concerned with the functional aspect: it defines the functions, their decomposition, and the information flows relating them to each other and to external roles.

4.5.6 Coordination Modelling

In the coordination aspect, we design and model the way in which activities, both automated and human activities, are coordinated to deliver the service under development. It comprises both the coordination of activities within the enterprise and the coordination of the interaction with other organizations, which may be users of the service or partners in delivering it. The literature on service coordination generally distinguishes between a centralized form of coordination, called orchestration, and a decentralized, emergent form of coordination, called choreography (Papazoglou and van den Heuvel 2007).

4.5 The ASD Conceptual Model

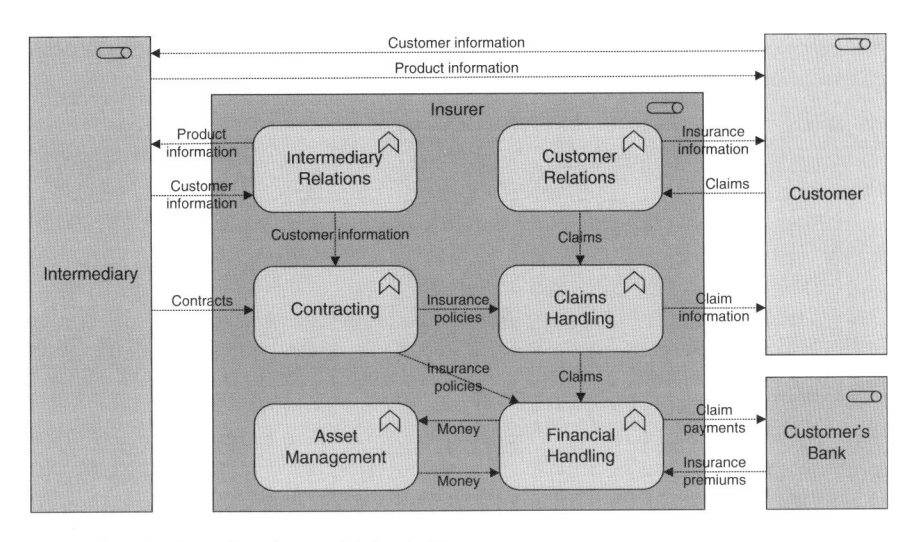

Fig. 4.14 A business function model for AgiSurance

Many modelling techniques, both tool-independent and proprietary, are available to model activities and their dependencies. The concepts that are used in these techniques show a lot of overlap, although there are some differences in focus. Some techniques are limited to modelling the processes of a single system or organization, while others explicitly address the interactions between parties.

The Business Process Modelling Notation (BPMN) is a standardized business process notation which is defined and specified by the Object Management Group (OMG 2011c) and has become the de facto standard for graphical process modelling. BPMN process models are composed of flow objects such as routing gateways, events, and activity nodes. Activities, commonly referred to as tasks, represent items of work performed by software systems or humans. Routing gateways and events capture the flow of control between activities. The Unified Modeling Language (UML) offers activity diagrams, to model the flow of activities within a process, and sequence diagrams, to model the detailed interactions between actors in a specific scenario.

Central in coordination modelling is a set of behaviour elements that express the way in which an actor (e.g. a system, person, or organization) acts in relation to its environment. Typically, behaviour elements can be defined at different levels of granularity. We distinguish two levels of behaviour elements:

Process: a grouping of behaviour based on an ordering of activities. It is intended to produce a defined set of (internal or external) products. A process may be decomposed into more fine-grained (sub)processes.

Activity (or *action*): an atomic behaviour element, performed by a single role within a certain time frame at a certain location. It can represent a function or task (from the function aspect) that is subject to coordination.

Some coordination modelling formalisms explicitly discern collective behaviour of two or more roles:

> *Interaction*: a common behaviour element, carried out by two or more roles in which each role is responsible for its part in the interaction. A *transaction* is an interaction that is treated as a unit to satisfy a specific request.

In general, a process does not consist of a single sequence of activities. It may contain, for example, branches (choices) or parallel activities. For this purpose, all process modelling languages provide several types of *gateways*:

> *Gateway*: a coordination element that controls the flow of a process, handling the forking, merging, and joining of paths within a process.

A process can be influenced by internal or external *events*, which may, for example, trigger a new process instance or interrupt a running process. A process may also raise events.

> *Event*: something that happens (internally or externally) and triggers a process or activity.

Finally, some process modelling formalisms explicitly model *states*. Behaviour elements then result in *transitions* between states.

Coordination elements can be related in different ways, depending on the particular modelling technique that is used. We distinguish two main types of relationship: triggering and dependency:

> *Triggering*: a relationship that defines the control flow, that is, an explicit ordering of activities within a process.
> *Dependency*: a relationship that defines how the execution of one activity depends on the completion of other activities or on the availability of certain product items.

The coordination aspect is closely related to other aspects. Processes or activities may be *assigned to* roles from the structure aspect. They may *access* (create/read/write/update) product items, and they may *refer to* decisions or rules (Fig. 4.15).

In the graphical notation of most process modelling languages, there are 'placeholders' for elements from the other aspects, for example, *items* or *data*

4.5 The ASD Conceptual Model

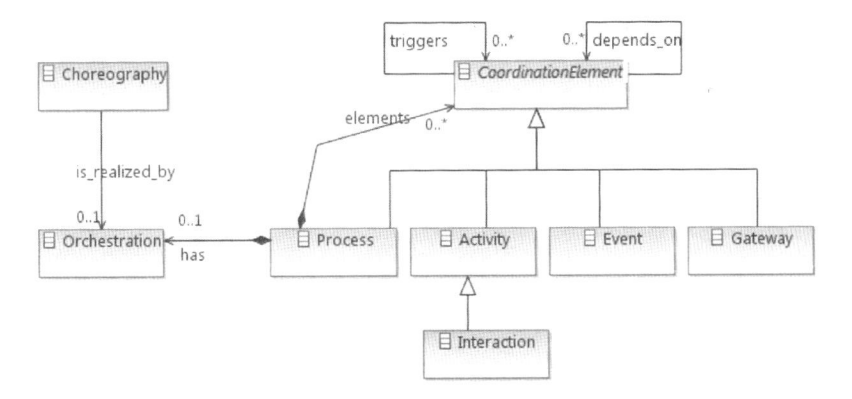

Fig. 4.15 The coordination metamodel

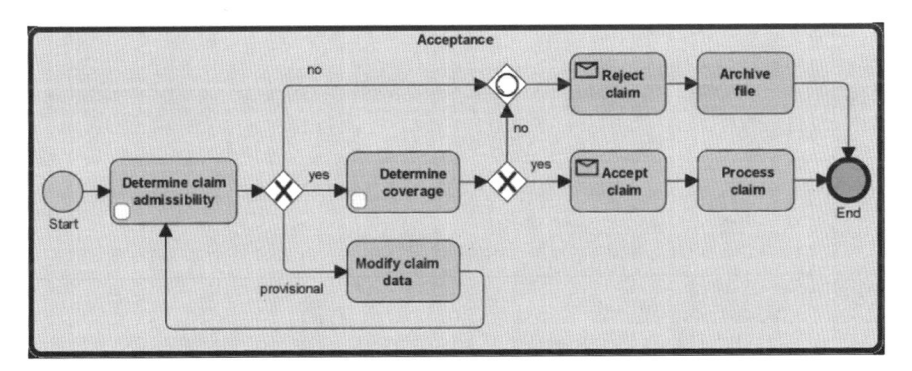

Fig. 4.16 A coordination model for AgiSurance's acceptance function in BPMN

objects that can be accessed by behaviour elements or *decision activities* that refer to decisions.

4.5.6.1 An Example Coordination Model

One of the processes within the claim handling function of AgiSurance is the acceptance process (see Fig. 4.16). AgiSurance first determines the admissibility of the claim and then the amount of coverage, upon which an acceptance or rejection letter is sent.

4.5.7 Decision Modelling

As mentioned before, the decision aspect captures the logic of reasoning used in the service domain to reach decisions, that is, how decisions are (to be) made. In this aspect, we therefore design and model the (business) logic to be used by the service under development. A decision is made to determine a conclusion regarding a specific case, based on domain-specific norms (Breuker and Van de Velde 1994). We illustrate the process of deriving a conclusion from domain-specific norms by an example based on the AgiSurance case. Consider, for example, the claim acceptance process at AgiSurance in which the activity 'determine claim admissibility' is executed. First, data is collected from and about the claim and the incidents that are reported. Second, this data is compared to predefined norms defined by AgiSurance. Once the data has been compared, a conclusion is derived.

The decision described is a straightforward operational decision. Other kinds of decision exist, such as strategic/chaotic or strategic/complex decisions. Examples of such decisions are crisis management and merger and acquisition decisions. These kinds of decision are outside the scope of this book; here we focus on operational patterns and fact-based decisions.

Elaborating on the previous paragraph, we further detail a decision by identifying the key concepts it consists of or to which it is closely related. A decision consists of a combination of conditions and conclusions. Both conditions and conclusions are represented by fact types. A fact type is a general classification of a real-world fact, for example, age, caring criteria, number of accidents, and credit rating. Depending on the modelling language used, a specific combination of conclusions and conditions is allowed.

Currently, there are multiple techniques within the professional as well as the scientific domain to describe decisions and underlying facts. Six of the most common languages to model decisions are (Zoet and Ravesteyn 2011):

1. If-then sentences
2. Decision tables
3. Decision trees
4. Score cards
5. Event-condition-action rules
6. Event-condition-action-and-alternative rules

Although the six languages display many similarities, differences exist regarding the underlying concepts as well as the relationships they allow. Nevertheless, Zoet and Ravesteyn show how the languages can be translated to each other.

In addition to the actual modelling languages, an important topic currently emerging is the manageability of decision models. The expert system community long wrestled with this problem, but according to Arnott and Pervan (2005), this research is focusing on the wrong application areas and has no connection with industry anymore. Vanthienen and Snoeck (1993) came to the same conclusion almost a decade earlier, proposing a first solution based on normalization theory. Currently, multiple decision management methods are being developed. A management method that is industry-based is The Decision Model (von Halle and Goldberg 2009). A method emerging from the scientific community is described in Zoet and Ravesteyn (2011). We discern the following key concepts for modelling the decision aspect:

4.5 The ASD Conceptual Model

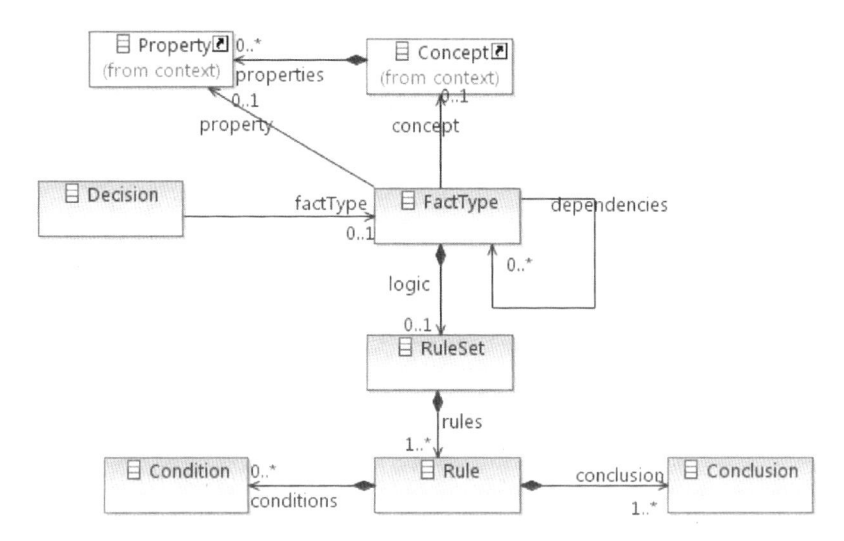

Fig. 4.17 The decision metamodel

Decision: a conclusion reached after consideration of a number of facts and the way in which that conclusion is drawn from those facts
Fact Type: a general classification of a fact
Rule Set: a group of statements that defines or constrains a specific aspect of the business
Rule: a logic statement connecting one or more conclusions to a set of conditions
Condition: an assertion used as antecedent in a rule
Conclusion: an assertion used as consequent in a rule

The key decision modelling concepts are closely related to the context modelling concepts, as we can see in Fig. 4.17.

4.5.7.1 An Example Decision Model

The acceptance process of AgiSurance contains two decision activities: 'determine claim admissibility' and 'determine coverage'. The first is modelled in Fig. 4.18 using the Decision Modelling Notation (DMN) from von Halle and Goldberg (2009). It shows that the claims admissibility depends on the customer's payment behaviour (has he paid his insurance premium) and the correctness of the data in the claim form. In reality, there will of course be many more conditions for the acceptability of a claim. The picture only shows the graphical representation of the decision model. Not visible are the decision tables for each of the fact types.

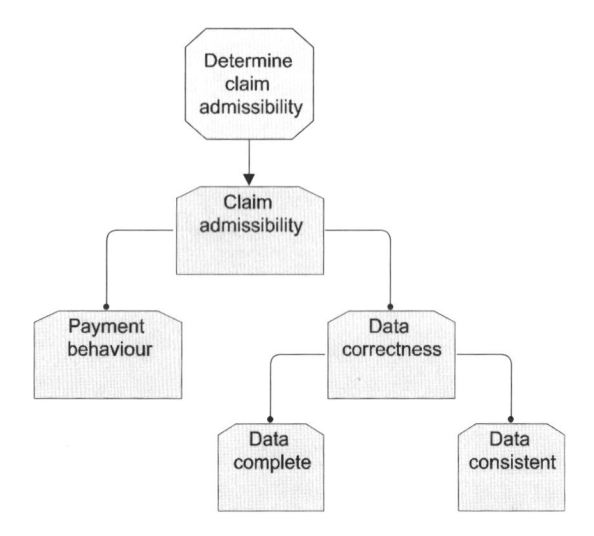

Fig. 4.18 Decision model for claim admissibility in the Decision Modelling Notation

4.5.8 Product Modelling

In the product aspect of a service, we design and model the products that are produced and consumed by the service under development. These can be physical products, but more often, these will be informational products. Every service uses and manages a certain amount of information. For insurance services, this can include information on customers, sold policies, and claims received. The product modelling concepts are highly interwoven with almost all other modelling concepts. The interaction modelling concepts display the information products, and when modelling decisions, the fact type refers to information types (Fig. 4.19).

Product modelling is very similar to context modelling, and many of the same techniques can be used, for example, ERD, ORM, and UML (also see Sect. 4.5.1). A product model is usually more detailed and more concrete than a context model, because it is the basis for implementation in database and message schemas. Therefore, we adopt a more restrictive set of concepts close to those of ER diagrams, with the addition of concepts for modelling physical products:

> *Product*: a thing that is produced or consumed by services. There are two kinds of product: physical *objects*, such as people or cars, and informational *items*, such as orders and claims. Often, items are used to represent real-world objects in an information system. Products can be composed of other products, their parts.
> *Entity*: a specification of a class of information items. One entity can specialize another, that is, inherit the more general entity's properties.

4.5 The ASD Conceptual Model

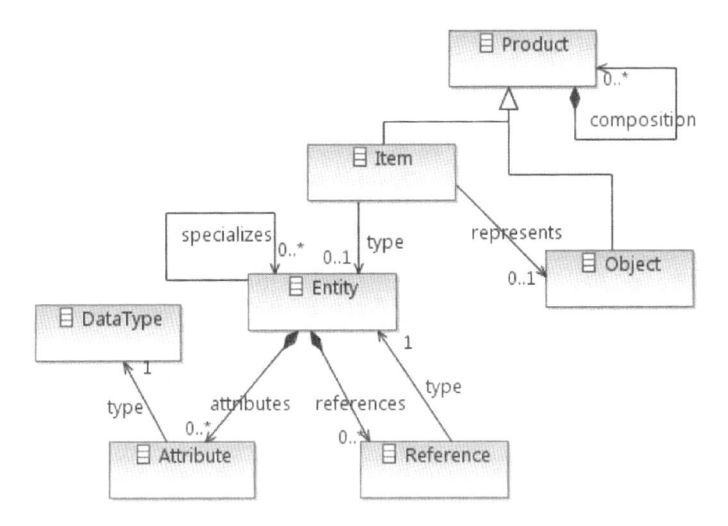

Fig. 4.19 The product metamodel

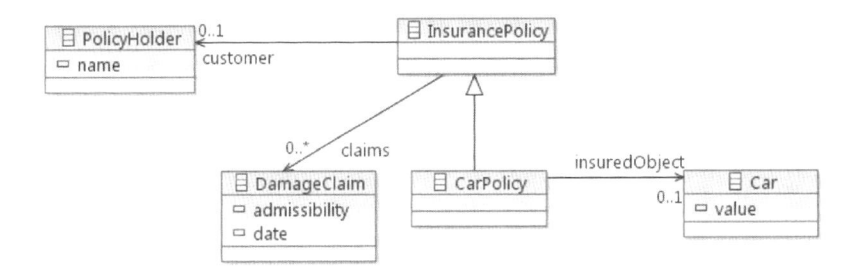

Fig. 4.20 Fragment of the product model for AgiSurance

> *Attribute*: a property belonging to an entity, for example, its name, age, length, or amount. Attributes have a type, which defines the values it can take.
> *Reference*: a relationship from one entity to another entity, for example, a car entity refers to its owner (a person entity).

4.5.8.1 An Example Product Model

Figure 4.20 shows a small part of the AgiSurance information model (the entities, their attributes, and references) pertaining to the handling of insurance claims. Here a UML class diagram is used to model these information products.

Table 4.3 Key concepts for each modelling domain

Modelling domain	Key concepts
Context	Concept, property, relationship, value type, constraint
Requirements	Stakeholder, goal, requirement
Interaction	Collaboration, interface
Organization	Actor, location, relationship
Function	Function, flow, service
Coordination	Process, activity, interaction, gateway, event
Decision	Decision, fact type, rule, rule set
Product	Product, object, item, entity, attribute, reference

4.5.9 Integrated Service Metamodel

The analysis of existing modelling techniques above has resulted in the identification of the key concepts for each of the modelling domains in the ASD framework. These concepts are summarized in Table 4.3.

Most existing modelling techniques cover more than one of the modelling domains. This helped us in identifying relationships between concepts across the domains. ArchiMate in particular covers many of the identified modelling domains. The ArchiMate core language defines and relates concepts for the interaction, organization, function, coordination, and information domains. In version 2.0 (The Open Group 2012), this core is extended with concepts for modelling also the requirements domain. Other languages, such as BPMN (OMG 2011c) and the Decision Model Notation, cover a smaller intersection of the ASD conceptual model, but still identify relationships between their concepts and other languages. In The Decision Model (von Halle and Goldberg 2009), the authors clearly specify how *decisions* are related to *activities* in BPMN and how *fact types* are related to *concepts* and *properties* in a context model or, similarly, to *entities* and *attributes* in a product model. Figure 4.21 provides an overview of the metamodel for the ASD conceptual model including these relationships. For readability, we have left out those concepts that do not have relations with concepts from other aspects.

4.6 Model Integration

The ASD framework is an instrument to divide a service design into smaller set of more manageable abstractions. However, '... having divided to conquer, we must reunite to rule' (Jackson, 1990). Therefore, the framework must be complemented with a method for integrating the different aspects and abstractions. To this end, we propose to use a metamodel-based approach akin to, for example, the approach suggested by De Lara and Vangheluwe 2004. The basic idea is to relate different models via a common, integrated metamodel or ontology, in our case the ASD conceptual model presented above. The conceptual model defines and relates the key concepts for each of the modelling domains. There is no need to create some

4.6 Model Integration

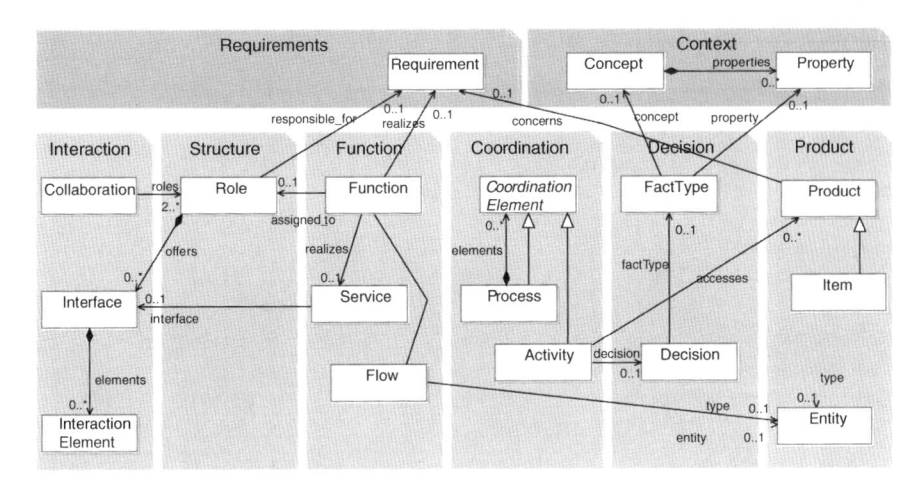

Fig. 4.21 Integrated metamodel

kind of super metamodel that incorporates all possible concepts for all possible aspects. It is sufficient to focus on the key concepts, because our objective is to support consistency checking and traceability, not to do fully semantics-preserving transformations. We presume the latter to be supported by specific tools, such as BPM suites and model-driven code generators.

The relations between the concepts from the various modelling domains enable us to relate actual models used in a service design. We use the following procedure to do so:

1. First, we define mappings from the used domain-specific modelling languages (DSMLs) to the ASD integrated metamodel.
2. Second, we use the defined mappings to translate each of the models to a corresponding ASD model, that is, a model that conforms to the ASD integrated metamodel.
3. Third, the resulting models are merged into one integrated model. Model elements that represent the same real-world object or phenomenon are matched and merged into one model element. For example, when a process model refers to a particular actor and the organizational model contains an actor with the same name, then these actors are candidates for being merged. Model merging can be done in a naïve name-matching manner, possibly augmented with the help of a thesaurus to match synonyms, but it can also be based on more elaborate semantic matching algorithms. In any case, it is sensible to make this an interactive, user-controlled process.
4. Finally, the integrated model can be used to query for the existence and consistency of relations between elements from different aspect models.

Let us illustrate this procedure using the AgiSurance case study. In Sect. 4.4.4, we already introduced the various models that AgiSurance made for redeveloping its claim handling service (see Fig. 4.5). Subsequently, we showed parts of these

Table 4.4 Language mappings

AgtSD concept	ArchiMate	BPMN	DMN	UML
Role	Business role	Pool/lane		
Function	Business function			
Flow	Flow relation			
Process	Business process	(Sub)Process		
Activity	Business activity	Activity		
Gateway	Junction	Gateway		
Decision			Decision	
Fact type			Fact type	
Rule set			Rule family	
Concept/entity	(Business) Object			Class
Property/attribute				Attribute

models in Sect. 4.5 when we introduced the conceptual model. Different modelling languages were used: ArchiMate and its motivation extension, BPMN, the Decision Modeling Notation (DMN), and UML. The first step now is to map the used modelling languages onto the ASD integrated metamodel. These mappings are summarized in Table 4.4 below. For the sake of simplicity, we present only those parts of the mappings that are relevant to the case study.

A Business Role in ArchiMate, and Pools and Lanes from BPMN are mapped to the Role concept. Processes, activities, and gateways also occur in both these languages and are mapped to their corresponding concept from the coordination aspect. The decision aspect concepts, however, only occur in the DMN in this case study. UML was used for context and product models.

Next, we translate the given ArchiMate, BPMN, Decision, and UML models using these mappings (step 2) and integrate the resulting models (step 3). The integrated model we obtained is illustrated in Fig. 4.22. We use the UML object diagram notation, with rectangular boxes representing the model elements. The boxes are labelled with the name of the element and followed by their type (the name of the corresponding metamodel concept). Due to space constraints, the figure only shows an excerpt of the model, highlighting the elements related to the determination of the admissibility of an insurance claim.

The model should be read as follows: three roles have been defined in the structure domain as part of the business function architecture (see Fig. 4.14): 'customer', 'insurer', and 'assessor'. The assessor role is contained within the insurer role (not depicted in Fig. 4.22). From the business function architecture, we can also derive the following elements in the function domain: a 'claims handling' function, which is the responsibility of the insurer role, and a 'claims' flow from the 'customer' role to the 'claims handling' function. Within the coordination domain, a process called 'acceptance' has been defined which belongs to the claims handling function. This 'acceptance' process contains an activity 'determine claim admissibility', which has been assigned to the 'assessor' role. The latter activity refers to a decision called 'determine claim admissibility' in the decision domain. The corresponding 'claim admissibility' fact type refers in turn to the

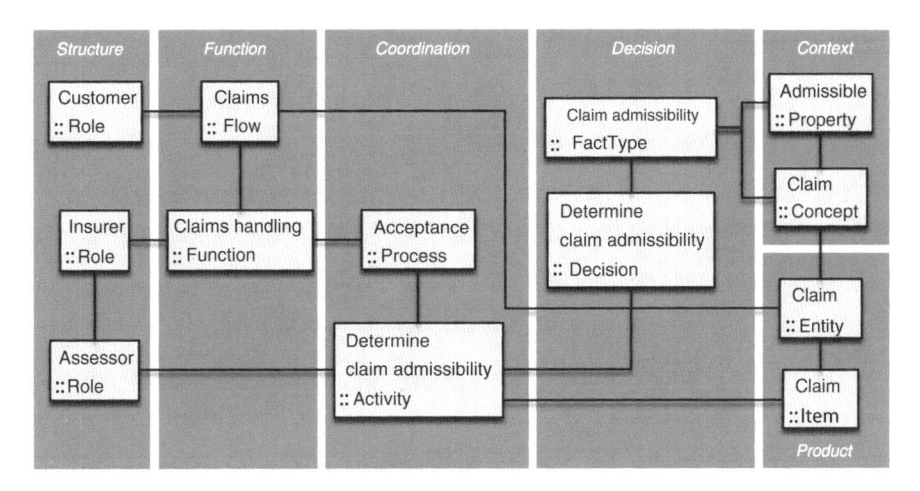

Fig. 4.22 Part of the integrated model for AgiSurance

'claim' concept and its 'admissible' property from the context domain. In the product domain, we also find a 'claim' entity and a 'claim' information item, which are associated with the corresponding context model concept.

4.7 Requirements for Tool Support

The model integration approach presented in the previous sections of course poses important requirements to service development tools and operational infrastructures. As we already described in Sect. 4.3, we can distinguish different levels of adoption of modelling. Up to level 3, 'isolated formal models', no additional functionality is needed beyond what individual modelling tools already offer. For the two highest levels, however, more is required.

At level 4b, 'vertically integrated formal models', it should be possible to relate models from different abstraction levels. This means that the relations from requirements via design and implementation down to the operational infrastructure, and vice versa, can be traced and that models are used to configure individual infrastructure elements. An example of this would be the use of a business process management engine that is configured with BPMN 2.0 (OMG 2011c) models, which in turn are related to more abstract architecture and requirements models.

This type of functionality is already offered by many integrated tool suites. However, if the upper-level models are designed in different tools than the lower-level models and the execution environment, a clear interface between these levels needs to be established. Existing standards such as XMI (ISO/IEC 2008) can be used to specify the necessary interchange formats and many modelling tools support this (although they are often better at importing than at exporting models, for obvious reasons). Usually, however, this is a unidirectional transformation, down towards the implementation and infrastructure; if we also want traceability back up the chain, a feedback mechanism needs to be implemented. Such traceability is currently offered only by single-vendor, integrated tool solutions.

At level 4a, 'horizontally integrated formal models', we want to be able to relate and integrate models from different aspects. This helps in ensuring consistency and coherence between these aspects and allows for various kinds of analyses of these models, as explained before. This integration implies that we must relate elements in different models with each other and hence that we need to 'address' such elements.

One approach to this is the use of a single-tool environment that 'owns' the various models covering different aspects. This is the approach taken by many business- and architecture-oriented modelling solutions, such as Be Informed Studio, Aquima, BiZZdesign Architect, and IBM Rational System Architect.

However, at the lower levels of abstraction, different types of models are often managed by different tools; for example, process models are tied to BPM suites, business rule models to BRM tools and engines, class and object models to software development environments, etc. This implies that these tools need to talk to each other, or at least to some common environment that links them together. In that case, each model element would ideally have a globally unique identifier that any tool can use as a reference, even if that particular element is in a model managed by a different tool. However, at the moment, the only realistic solution is to store these models in a single shared repository on which these different tools operate. This is the route taken by most vendors of larger modelling and requirements management tool suites.

Unfortunately, such repositories are often not open to third-party tools. Although many repositories are based on standards such as EMF (Steinberg et al. 2008) or MOF (OMG 2011b), this is not enough. We also need open, standardized interfaces and (semantic) standards for relating concepts, based on a clear metamodel such as the one presented in the previous sections.

To demonstrate the feasibility of this integration approach, we have already connected different tools in both the horizontal and vertical direction. BPMN models created with the business process tool BiZZdesigner (from BiZZdesign) were related with the context and product models from the knowledge modelling solution of RuleManagement Group, via decision models in the DMN. In the previous section, we already showed part of the integrated AgiSurance model that was developed in this case study (Fig. 4.22).

The hardest part, however, may turn out to be the integration between the different elements and platforms at the infrastructure level. The complexity of integrating various components, for example, via an enterprise service bus, should not be underestimated. Not only does this integration require clarity about the functionality and semantics of each of these elements, but it must also conform to various non-functional requirements. If high or bursty volumes must be processed, for example, the performance may become a bottleneck. The complexity of such a landscape may require extensive proofs-of-concept. Models may also be of help here, for example, to perform quantitative analyses or simulations. For more on such analyses, see, for example, Lankhorst et al. (2009), Chap. 8.

Chapter 5
Patterns for Agility

M.E. Iacob, M.M. Lankhorst, and A. Schrier

The use of patterns is an important practice in the agile software development community. There are many sources for patterns. In this chapter, we will examine several pattern collections and explore their potential contribution to system agility. We illustrate our pattern approach by a detailed examination of our collection of architecture patterns for multichannel management. The chapter is organized as follows: after a first part in which we define design patterns and discuss their most important characteristics, we describe our classification of several collections of patterns with respect to their contribution to agility. We conclude this chapter with an example of pattern usage in practice.

5.1 Introduction

Design patterns originate from Christopher Alexander's architecture work in building and construction (Alexander 1979) and were adopted by the software engineering community and many other disciplines. To quote Alexander (Alexander et al. 1977):

> As an element in the world, each pattern is a relationship between a certain context, a certain system of forces which occurs repeatedly in that context, and a certain spatial configuration which allows these forces to resolve themselves. As an element of language, a pattern is an instruction, which shows how this spatial configuration can be used, over and over again, to resolve the given system of forces, wherever the context makes it relevant.

Since the publication of 'Design Patterns' by Gamma et al. (1994), patterns are well known in software architecture as well.

> A *design pattern* is a generally applicable solution to a common design problem, codified in a standardized form providing a configuration of elements that together solve the problem.

Similar to architecture patterns in civil engineering, software design patterns can be used at different levels of granularity, from large-scale enterprise-level reference architectures (analogous to city planning) to small, code-level solutions (comparable to the fitting of a window in a wall). Patterns for a particular domain can be organized in the form of a *pattern language*, which is defined as a network of patterns at different abstraction levels that refer to each other.

The use of design patterns to support design agility is a critical skill of service developers. For example, studies indicate that significant effort and money is spent on the modification of information systems after their initial release. Refactoring a system (Chap. 2) is not always the answer to new requirements; sound design is needed to prevent such costs, and it is useful to invest in simple, clear, and extensible designs. Such a strategy is facilitated by the consistent usage of design patters across the enterprise. This has the following positive effects:

- Since patterns encapsulate best practices with respect to a whole class of problems, they facilitate the reuse of design knowledge in different contexts.
- Patterns provide service designers with a higher-level language for talking about their designs, without them having to go into the technical details of the implementation.
- Patterns facilitate the use of proven design principles and styles, such that the resulting service design will have a sound foundation.
- Patterns may help to increase business and technology alignment by mapping business aspects of services onto the software realization of those services.
- Patterns may help exploit the existing information systems infrastructure by combining software components into new business and application services, thereby increasing reuse and ultimately enterprise agility.

A pattern names, abstracts, and identifies the key aspects of a common design structure, such that it can be reused and applied over and over again in creating new designs. In this chapter, we use the following general pattern structure, mainly based on the structure introduced by Coplien (1996) and consisting of the following elements:

- **Name**: A short descriptive name of the pattern.
- **Problem**: Which problem does this pattern solve?
- **Context**: In which circumstances is this pattern useful?
- **Forces**: Which forces have to be balanced? Which goals and constraints apply?
- **Solution**: What solution does this pattern offer? What is the structure of the pattern?
- **Rationale**: What is the motivation for the chosen solution?
- **Consequences**: How does the pattern resolve the forces? What are the positive and negative effects of using the pattern?
- **Known uses**: How is this pattern used in practice?
- **Related patterns**: How is this pattern related to other patterns?

5.2 Conceptual Model

To review a large and diverse collection of patterns and to establish their possible contribution to both service design and agility, we needed a conceptualization of design patterns to help us identify their most important characteristics and structure them in a uniform way. For this reason, we have developed a pattern conceptual model (shown in Fig. 5.1) that has also served as data model for the pattern catalogue tool we developed. Next, we briefly describe this conceptual model.

The central concept is that of *service pattern*, which is specified in terms of the template introduced in the previous section. As said before, a service pattern may also be related to other patterns. Such relations are captured by the *concept inter-pattern relation*. A relation links two patterns (a source and a target), and it has a description.

Since our focus is on agile systems and design, we include the *agility contribution* concept in order to be able to specify the effects of each pattern on the different aspects of system agility; these aspects have been defined and discussed in Chap. 3.

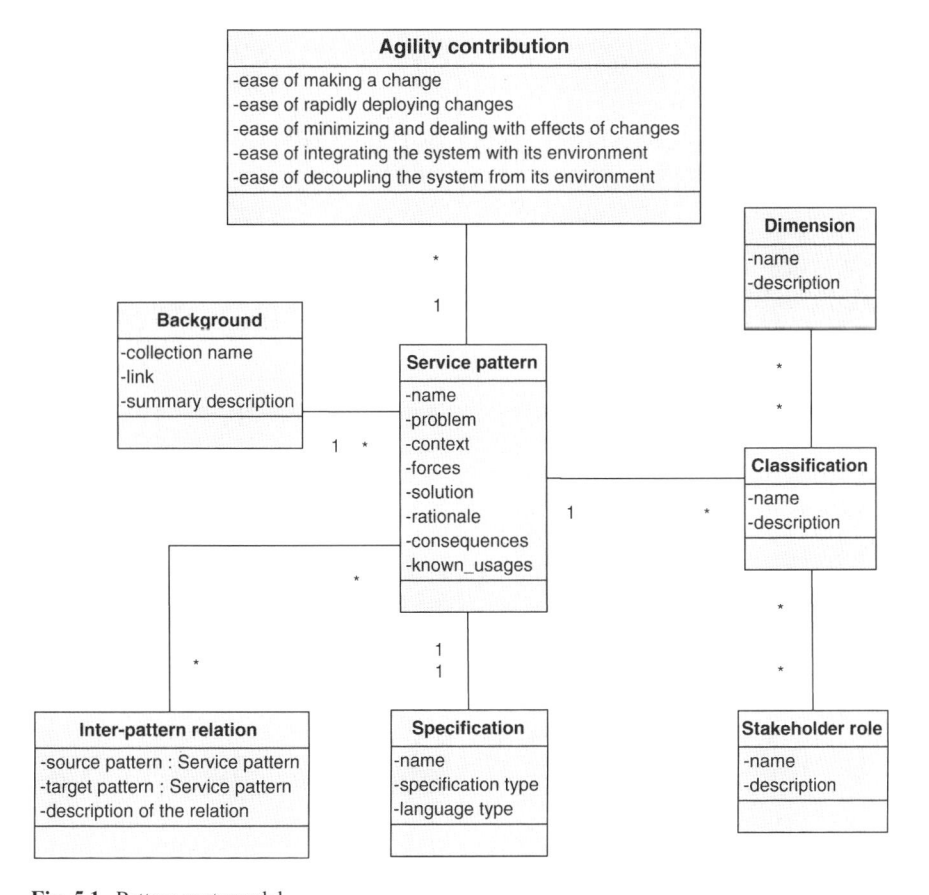

Fig. 5.1 Pattern metamodel

Also, some of the patterns may have a solution element described in terms of a model. The *specification* concept has been introduced to accommodate such models. Finally, we want to provide pattern *classifications* following several criteria, which we call *dimensions*, and according to the *stakeholder roles* the pattern addresses.

5.3 Pattern Classification

We have defined a set of classification criteria and used these to assess service design patterns. The selection of these criteria and the evaluation/classification exercise was organized as follows:

1. We set up a workshop with six experts and agreed upon a set of classification criteria and the possible values associated with each criterion.
2. We first evaluated the discriminatory power and accuracy of our classification/evaluation instrument in a pilot test. Thus, we asked four experts independently to assess one pattern collection, the Enterprise Architecture Patterns for Multi-channel Management. Comparing their results, we discovered that there was a significant overlap between two dimensions (domain and problem type), and another one was difficult to assess (abstraction level) since it often produced inconsistent results (this dimension was particularly sensitive to the subjective interpretation of the rater). We decided to drop the latter and to merge the former into one criterion.
3. We then assigned each collection to two raters and asked them to assess it independently using the consolidated classification instrument. They also had to compare the results and resolve conflicting classifications.

We considered the following classification criteria (i.e. 'dimensions') to evaluate patterns: activities, problem type, role, and contribution to agility. Although the last one is an evaluation criterion rather than a classification criterion, we consider it very important as it shows the perceived usefulness of a particular pattern for system agility. Thus, these criteria reveal essential characteristics for the usage of the patterns in the context of agile service development and facilitate a fast discovery of suitable patterns in a particular design situation.

5.3.1 Activities

Within the iterations of an agile project, there are many recurring activities, such as:

- *Communicating*, for example, stand-up meetings, stakeholder interaction, requirements elicitation.
- *Strategizing*, defining the general, long-term direction of the organization.

- *Envisioning*, identify scope and business goals for the effort and develop a common, high-level vision on the service.
- *Defining requirements*, to find out what the stakeholder requirements and other constraints on the envisaged service are, prioritization.
- *Eliciting knowledge*, for example, interviewing experts, analysing applicable documents, etc.
- *Analysing*, to get clarity in the problem at hand, the implications of requirements from different stakeholder groups, coherence between requirements, the context in which the envisaged service must operate, including external connections, legacy systems, COTS software to be used, etc.
- *Organizing*, i.e. defining roles and responsibilities, reporting lines, etc. within the service development project.
- *Planning*, for example, timeboxing, sprints, migration planning, resource allocation.
- *Architecting*, to obtain high-level decisions on the solutions structure and its fit within the context.
- *Designing*, to flesh out the solution in more detail. Different disciplines will have their own design steps.
- *Realizing*, to realize a solution in business processes, business rules, human tasks, software code, etc.
- *Integrating*, to combine partial solutions (e.g. from different disciplines like software development, business process engineering, business rules design).
- *Deploying*, to address software and hardware deployment, deployment of business processes on BPM engines, etc.
- *Implementing*, to address implementing the deployed solution in the organization, including change management etc.
- *Measuring*, for example, monitoring project progress with burn-down charts, etc.
- *Evaluating*, for example, quality assurance, user experience testing, other forms of testing and validation, to make sure the service performs as required.
- *Documenting*, writing down relevant aspects of the service, its design, use, etc.
- *Managing*, to address the operational management, governance, and maintenance aspects of the deployed service and all its related artefacts.
- *Decommissioning*, to phase out or replace the service.
- *Learning*, explicitly reflecting on and improving your way of working.

Note that these activities are *not* sequential phases (like in a waterfall process). In an agile or iterative development process, these are recurring activities that gradually refine and extend the solution to the problem at hand, while going through the aforementioned cycles/iterations.

5.3.2 Problem Type

The problem type of a pattern characterizes the typical issues that the pattern addresses. We focus on the service being designed and not on the agile processes being performed; this is treated elsewhere. Some examples of problem types we encountered are as follows:

- *Organization* (as part of the business system), for example, ownership, governance, compliance, roles and responsibilities, reporting
- *Usability*, user interaction, for example, GUI design, navigation paths, customization
- *Communication*, for example, conversation, interaction, message passing
- *Coordination*, for example, workflow, orchestration, event-based
- *Interoperability*, for example, transformation, translation patterns
- *Knowledge representation*
- *Data structure*
- *Data access*, for example, directly, through gateways
- *Compliance* (of systems) with rules and regulations
- *Security*
- *Scalability and performance*
- *Reliability and availability*
- *Transaction*

5.3.3 Role

The role dimension of our pattern framework describes the typical role users of the patterns may play. Lankhorst et al. (2009) (Chap. 7) identify three different types of roles (called 'purposes' there).

1. *Designing*: Supporting architects and designers in the design process from initial sketch to detailed design. Typical roles include product and service developers, enterprise, knowledge and software architects, business process designers, software engineers, and interaction designers.
2. *Deciding*: Assisting managers in the process of decision making by offering insight into cross-domain architecture relations, typically through projections and intersections of underlying models, but also by means of analytical techniques. Typical roles involved are CxOs, business line managers, product/service managers, and project managers of service development projects.
3. *Informing*: Helping to inform any stakeholder, in order to achieve understanding, obtain commitment, and convince adversaries. Associated roles include end users, clients, and employees. This is also related to the stakeholders involved.

5.3.4 Contribution to Agility

With this dimension, we assess the impact each design pattern may have on the agility of the designed service or system. For this purpose, we use the agility aspects from the definition of agile systems as presented in Chap. 2:

1. The ease of *making a change* to a system
2. The ease of rapidly *deploying* changes
3. The ease of minimizing and dealing with *effects* of changes
4. The ease of *integrating* the system with its environment
5. The ease of *decoupling* the system from its environment

5.4 Pattern Catalogue

We have built a catalogue of patterns, classifying many different patterns with respect to the aspects from the previous section. The sources of these patterns can be found in several books and online pattern libraries, listed below. Their selection was guided by three criteria: comprehensiveness, relevance for service design, and agility. We also used the agile service development framework (Chap. 4) to direct our search and to check whether these collections together ensure a satisfactory coverage of the relevant aspects and layers.

Design Patterns: These patterns are the classical 'Gang of Four' pattern descriptions of Gamma et al. (1994) for good object-oriented software design. Good object-oriented software design strives for ease of extension, adaption, and reuse of the designed software. All classical properties of object-oriented design (e.g. abstraction, encapsulation, polymorphism, etc.) are there, because of their importance in designing 'agile software'.

Enterprise Application Architecture Patterns: This is a rich collection of enterprise software application design patterns by Fowler (2002).

Enterprise Integration Patterns: Hohpe and Woolf's book (Hohpe and Woolf 2003) provides a vocabulary and visual notation to describe large-scale integration solutions across many implementation technologies by means of patterns. The book concentrates on using asynchronous messaging architectures for loose coupling of independent applications. It explores in detail the advantages and limitations of asynchronous messaging architectures.

Organizational Patterns: These patterns by Coplien and Harrison (2004) focus on software development management. The patterns can be broadly divided into two categories: process patterns, which govern developmental processes, and organizational patterns, which deal with organizational structure. Many of the popular agile development methodologies like Scrum and Extreme Programming borrow from Organizational Patterns, but, these patterns are not restricted to agile software development only.

EAM Patterns: The Enterprise Architecture Management (EAM) pattern catalogue from TU Munich (Ernst 2008) contains three main categories of patterns for EAM: methodology patterns (M-Patterns), which focus on methods for architecture (and IT) management; viewpoint patterns (V-Patterns), which address various ways of depicting architectural information; and information model patterns (I-Patterns), which concern the storage of architectural information.

Workflow Patterns: This collection (van der Aalst et al. 2003) is the result of a collaboration between Wil van der Aalst (TUE) and Arthur ter Hofstede (Queensland

University of Technology). Its aim is to provide a conceptual basis for process design. The patterns provide a thorough examination of the various modelling perspectives (control flow, data, resource, and exception handling) that need to be supported by a workflow or a business process modelling language.

Patterns for e-Business: The e-business patterns from IBM (2010) are categorized in sub-classes: Business, Integration, Composite, Application, and Runtime patterns. The business patterns are high-level patterns, while the application patterns refine these patterns so that they can be implemented in automated systems. There may be more that one application pattern to automate a business pattern. A runtime pattern describes the logical architecture required to implement the application pattern. The integration patterns help to implement a full solution, integrating individual business patterns. Composite patterns represent commonly occurring combinations of Business patterns and Integration patterns and typically solve major portions of functionality within a solution.

SOA Patterns: Thomas Erl's book SOA Design Patterns (Erl 2009) gathers 85 individually documented design patterns for service-orientated architectures, covering patterns for the design, implementation, and governance of service inventories; patterns for contract design, security, legacy encapsulation, reliability, scalability, and a variety of implementation and governance issues; service composition patterns that address the many aspects associated with combining services into aggregate distributed solutions; compound patterns (such as Enterprise Service Bus and Orchestration); and recommended pattern application sequences that establish foundational processes.

Ontology Design Patterns: The Ontology Design Patterns (ODP 2010) address the design of knowledge/domain models in the form of ontologies.

User Interface Design Patterns: These UI patterns originate from the Yahoo! Design Pattern Library (Yahoo 2010). It includes patterns for layout, navigation, selection, rich interaction, and social user interface aspects.

Rule Patterns: This collection is a true pattern language by Graham (2007), concerning business rule management, consisting of two parts. Part I is concerned with requirements, process, and architecture and Part II with knowledge elicitation, product selection, and application development.

Multichannel Management Patterns: This is a catalogue of patterns for multichannel management (Lankhorst and Oude Luttighuis 2009): functional structures for designing organizational and technical solutions that help organizations to manage and align the various information channels they use in communicating with their customers.

5.5 Example: Multichannel Management Patterns

Due to space constraints, we will present the results from this classification exercise for only one pattern collection. We chose the enterprise architecture patterns for multichannel management (Lankhorst and Oude Luttighuis 2009), mainly for the following reasons:

5.5 Example: Multichannel Management Patterns

- This collection is small and manageable for illustration purposes.
- The focus is on business services design rather than on software design.
- Most patterns in this collection have a clear impact on agility.
- Finally, this collection is a result of our previous research.

Since the early 1990s, organizations have been using a variety of customer service channels. Next to the traditional channels, such as mail, fax, reception desk, or telephone, customers have access to digital channels like websites and e-mail. These service channels have different characteristics and are used for communication, interaction, transaction, and distribution of products and/or services. Many organizations, especially in government, struggle with the integration and management of these service channels. In particular, channel synchronization needs to be addressed. Channel synchronization and coordination is required as customers expect information and services to be consistent across channels.

Relevant architecture patterns for multichannel management were collected from applicable literature and real-life architectures, especially in different governmental organizations in the Netherlands, and various existing technological solutions in which useful patterns are apparent. This resulted in the identification of some thirty patterns, which are explained briefly in Table 5.1.

Many of these patterns are concerned with the synchronization of content, channels, and/or providers to ensure a seamless experience for the client. As we can observe, these patterns have different granularities. Some patterns address localized, small problems, and others, higher-level architectural decisions. Like the pattern language suggested by Alexander et al. (1977), this catalogue of interrelated patterns helps architects to solve design problems at different levels of abstraction. An example is the *Mid-Office* pattern, which encompasses linkage between front-office and back-office systems and processes. This pattern uses other, more fine-grained patterns such as *Document Management* and *Business Process Management* that address specific aspects within the general problem field of front-office and back-office integration.

For illustration purposes, we give a description of one pattern—the *Mid-Office* pattern—that follows the pattern structure outlined in Sect. 5.1.

Name: *Mid-Office*

Problem: In many organizations, the back office is organized along the lines of the applicable expertise, both in an organizational sense and in terms of the application landscape. These back-office systems are often not available around the clock, are not meant to be accessed directly by clients for security or performance reasons, and do not provide an integrated image of the client situation. This hampers, for example, the creation of a modern Web front end for e-services or an overview of a client's situation in the call centre. The *Mid-Office* pattern provides a set of solutions for bridging this gap.

Context: A mid-office architecture is often used as a temporary phase in the migration from monolithic legacy systems to a service-oriented architecture, which distinguishes between:

Table 5.1 Multichannel management patterns

Name	Description
Service selection	The client is presented with service options in order to find the right service from the right provider through a fitting channel
Personalization	A personal client profile is kept to adapt the selection, delivery, and realization of services to his/her situation, needs, and desires
Channel combination	Synchronous usage of two or more channels, for example, calling up a company while browsing through its website
Channel stack	Usage of one channel through another, for example, a call centre agent who uses the company's website to explain things to the client
Co-browsing	Synchronous usage of (especially) the Internet channel (website) by company employees and the client to assist the latter
Service combination	Combining services from different providers and offering these in an integrated way through the same channel
Intermediary	An intermediary matches supply and demand of services and integrates these to provide a good match with the client's needs
Service team	A service team is responsible for integrated client service, across channels and combining front- and back-office activities
Funnel	Depending on the complexity of the client's question, this is funnelled via the website, call centre, to back-office specialists
Redirection	A client is redirected by one channel (and service provider) to another channel (and possibly another provider)
Case transfer	A service provider transfers a client case to another provider
Access	The client identifies himself and is authenticated, authorized, and provided with access to a particular service
Delegation	The client delegates the authorization to use a service on his behalf to someone else, for example, to an intermediary
Portal	Online services are offered in an integrated way via a web portal
Electronic form	Infrastructure for structured electronic forms
Wizard	Automated assistant that helps with finding the right service, filling in forms, etc.
Knowledge base	Storing the business logic and other knowledge behind different products and services in a specialized system to facilitate reuse in different channels and applications, easy adaptation, etc.
Rule engine	Encoding business logic as formalized rules that can be executed automatically by a rule engine
Mid-office	Facilities to link (legacy) back-office applications to multichannel front-office solutions (e.g. call centre, website, e-mail)
Business process management	Controlling the execution of business processes through a specialized component, separated from the application logic
Content management	Centralized management of content that is used in different channels and applications (e.g. in print, on the website, etc.)
Document management	Central, digitized storage and access of all incoming and outgoing documents
Case management	Centralized storage of all information pertaining to a specific customer case (i.e. service usage), accessible by all employees handling this case
Virtual dossier	Bringing client data together from different sources, via indices and synchronization (instead of centralized storage)

(continued)

5.5 Example: Multichannel Management Patterns

Table 5.1 (continued)

Name	Description
Central administration	Concentrating client data in a single place, for usage across different channels, applications, departments, and organizations
Operational data store	A solution that caches or copies back-office data for use by front-office applications and/or employees, usually for performance and availability reasons
Business intelligence	Measuring and analysing current and past client data (in particular regarding channel and service usage) to provide information to support management decisions
Publish-subscribe	Automatically distributing changes in data to systems that have registered their interest, in particular to keep client and service data in sync across channels

- Core, centralized databases with, for example, client, case, service, and product data
- Specialized services requiring specific expertise and systems
- Generic functionality such as document management, external communication, financial services, etc.

Forces: The goal of the *Mid-Office* pattern is to link front-office facilities, providing services to clients (e.g. website, call centre) to back-office applications and departments that realize these services.

Solution: Figure 5.2 shows the main structure of this pattern. In the figure, we have used the ArchiMate modelling language (The Open Group 2012). The services for data access, process management, and business logic are typically linked with an enterprise service bus. This bus is not depicted in the figure and is not considered part of this pattern (but it could be viewed as a supporting pattern). The pattern addresses the following aspects of the ASD framework:

- Interaction: Multiple front-office applications can serve different channels, for example, the website, the call centre, or the front desk.
- Function and coordination: The back-office applications are concerned with business logic, as is the business process engine. Furthermore, the pattern identifies a number of required services.
- Information: The operational data store and case warehouse are part of the data layer.

Rationale: The architectural solution chosen for the mid-office pattern is based on a fundamental principle of software architecture, namely, the separation of concerns, through different architecture tiers: a presentation tier, an application logic tier, and a data tier. This principle was adopted and extended in the mid-office pattern to enterprise architecture, in which the data tier consists of back-office applications responsible for the processing of persistent data transactions, the mid-office consists of applications incorporating the organization's business logic (and the temporary data processed by them), and, finally, the front-office which mostly

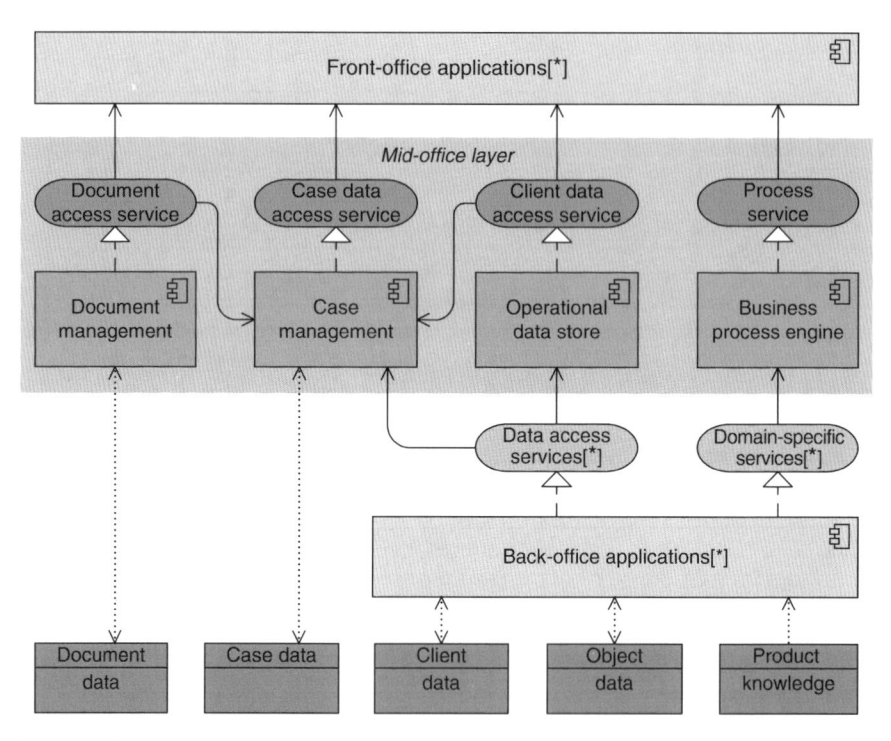

Fig. 5.2 Mid-Office pattern

consists of channel management applications (e.g. portals, websites, call centre, or front desk) and which represents the organization's presentation tier.

Consequences: The main advantage of the *Mid-Office* pattern is that it helps organizations to provide a unified, integrated face to the customer, while making the transition from a stovepiped back-office application landscape to a service-oriented architecture. The main disadvantage of this pattern is that it could serve as an excuse to prolong the life of an outdated back-office application landscape, preventing an organization to reap the benefits of a cleaner, more manageable service architecture that removes duplications of functionality and data. Another disadvantage is that some vendors offer integrated suites of applications as their 'mid-office solutions', whereas the various elements of the pattern could be implemented rather independently and phased out step by step while moving to a SOA.

Known uses: This pattern and its variants are widely used by large financial institutions such as banks and insurers, who have often grown through mergers and acquisitions, resulting in a scattered and fragmented back-office landscape (not to be confused with the 'middle office' organizational unit of investment banks). It can also be observed within Dutch municipalities [Eg06, BL08], in a multitude of variants.

Relationship with other patterns: The *Mid-Office* pattern combines a number of other patterns to arrive at an integrated solution:

- *Business Process Management*: to control business processes (workflows) across the borders of applications and departments
- *Case Management*: to register the progress of a client case (service usage) across applications and departments
- *Document Management*: to provide a centralized database of all in- and outgoing client communication
- *Operational Data Store*: to provide a safe, reliable, and 24×7 accessible data warehouse for back-office data

We conclude this section with our evaluation of a selection of the multichannel pattern collection with respect to the aforementioned criteria, which also includes the Mid-Office pattern. All these patterns are used by architects and designers in creating multichannel solutions, so their role classification is always 'designing'. This is therefore left out in Table 5.2.

5.6 Patterns at Work

In the previous sections, we have explained how we classified several pattern collections along different dimensions. In our way of working, which will be explained in more detail in Chap. 6, the use of patterns is one of the inputs for several 'agile practices'. Given the generic nature of the idea of patterns, they can of course be applied in all practices where general design knowledge can be reused. But more specifically, since we have classified these patterns with respect to, among others, the problem types they address, the role of the pattern user, and the activities in which they are used, we have three avenues for pattern selection.

First, the role of the pattern user is important. Via the three types of stakeholder or user roles—designing, deciding, and informing—you can make a first rough selection. Most patterns in our catalogue have been classified as patterns for designing; this is not surprising, since this is the most common use of patterns.

Next is an investigation of the activity in which you want to use these patterns. The agile practices that constitute our way of working (Chap. 6) have been mapped to the same series of activities described in the previous section. Given a specific activity, this gives you a pre-selection of potentially relevant patterns from those that are relevant to the specific user role you first selected.

The final step is to investigate the design or communication problem at hand. Of course, this cannot be standardized or simplified into a step-by-step procedure. The expertise of business specialists, architects, designers, or other pattern users is an essential factor. Nevertheless, the high-level classification of problem types given in the previous section helps these experts in the selection of potentially relevant patterns along this third dimension. Furthermore, the type of agility required in solving this design problem must also be factored in.

Table 5.2 Multichannel management pattern classification

Name	Activity	Problem type	Contribution to agility
Personalization	Communicating	Usability	Ease of changing, by offering personalization options to users, ease of integrating
Service combination	Communicating, defining requirements, organizing service development	Coordination, interoperability	Ease of integrating, by defining a process that combines different services into one 'super service'
Intermediary	Communicating, defining requirements, organizing service development	Coordination, interoperability	Ease of decoupling, ease of integrating, by having a third-party perform service selection and integration in lieu of the client
Service team	Defining requirements	Coordination, interoperability	Ease of integrating, by having a team of employees handle all service requests and provide an integrated response
Portal	Communicating, architecting, modelling, designing	Usability	Ease of integrating, by offering a single, integrated front end for multiple services; ease of changing, by offering a customizable Web front end for services
Electronic form	Communicating	Usability	Agility-neutral
Rule engine	Architecting, designing, realizing, integrating, deploying	Knowledge, coordination	Ease of changing, by separating business knowledge from software implementation and process flow and making it configurable in the form of (human-readable) business rule models
Mid-office	Architecting, designing, realizing, integrating	Coordination, interoperability	Ease of integrating and decoupling, by creating an infrastructure between back-office and front-office systems that allows (1) the use of multiple back-office systems in delivering services and (2) changing or replacing these back-office systems without affecting front-end services
Business process management	Analysing, modelling	Coordination	Ease of changing, by separating process flow from business knowledge and making the flow configurable through human-readable models. Ease of integrating, by concentrating process logic in a single place, where changes can be made when, for example, a new service becomes available
Virtual dossier	Communicating, realizing, integrating	Coordination, knowledge, security	Ease of integrating, by creating an infrastructure to combine information from different sources and presenting this a unified way

Example: AgiSurance Application Architecture

In AgiSurance's transformation towards becoming a product leader in insurance products for niche markets, many different design problems occur. But a specific and important one is the need for rapidly combining standardized but configurable insurance policy components to create custom insurance products that fit specific markets. The lead architect (a 'designing' role in terms of the pattern classification) is working on the design of the architectural backbone of AgiSurance that has to provide this flexibility (an 'architecting' activity).

In terms of the type of agility required, the need for combining different insurance elements points towards the 'ease of integrating' (in terms of the types of agility contribution) of the different services that provide the implementation of these elements. Furthermore, these services should themselves be highly configurable, to accommodate the specific needs of these niche markets, i.e. they should provide 'ease of change'. Finally, it should be easy to provide these products via many different channels, online, through various partners, etc. Triggered by the latter requirement, we now look for relevant patterns in our example catalogue of multichannel patterns. The following patterns appear particularly relevant:

- *Service Combination*: This will help with integrating different services to create these new, modular insurance products.
- *Mid-Office*: Given the still separate back-office applications of AgiSurance, integrating the software services they offer might be facilitated with such a mid-office solution. Also, a future migration of these back-office applications may be facilitated because a mid-office decouples the back and front end.
- *Business Process Management*: This helps in creating a model-based process flow that links together the relevant services.
- *Rule Engine*: To make these insurance products highly configurable, the internal business logic can be defined via executable business rules.
- *Portal*: Given the importance of the Internet channel to AgiSurance, a portal solution, with an integrated front end for insurance services, seems useful.

In Fig. 5.3, we see a small section of the first plateau of AgiSurance's application architecture. This is the medium-term target situation, in which the back-office applications of AgiSurance's departments are wrapped in a service layer and linked via a mid-office solution. The model clearly shows the application of the Mid-Office pattern. We also see that the back-office applications of AgiSurance no longer 'own' the client data; this is now stored in the CRM system. Moreover, these applications are now wrapped in a service layer and the 'Insurance policy services' are now partially provided by a business process engine. In the near future, AgiSurance intends to replace these back-office applications by a fully rule-based solution, making it much easier to change specific insurance parameters and decisions.

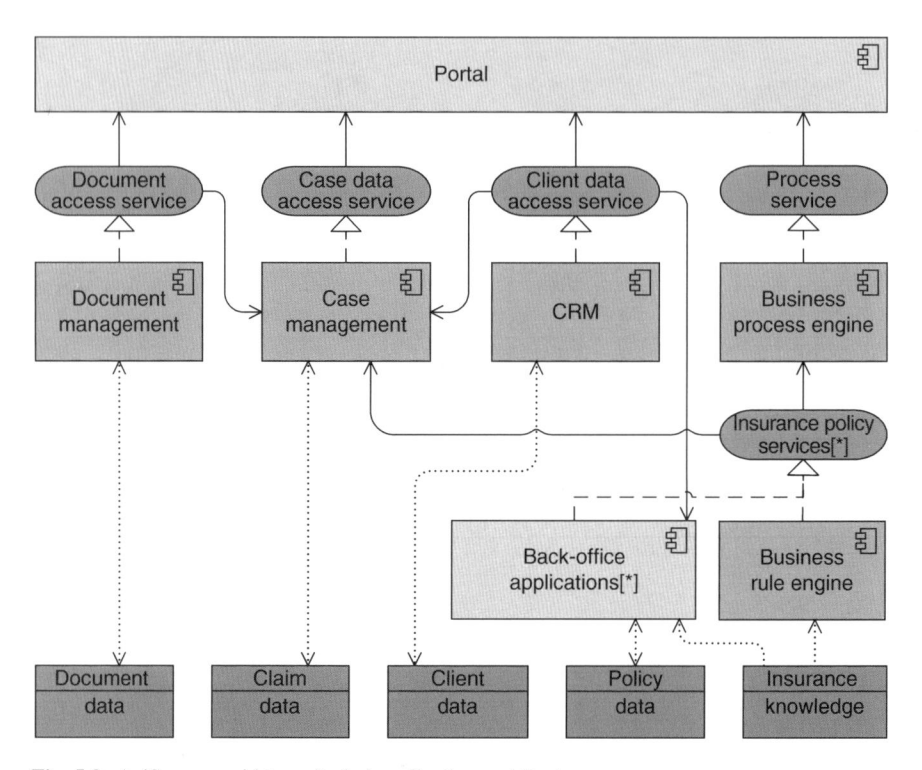

Fig. 5.3 AgiSurance mid-term 'to be' application architecture

Chapter 6
An Agile Way of Working

M.M. Zoet, A.W. Heerink, M.M. Lankhorst, S.J.B.A. Hoppenbrouwers, and W. van Stokkum

6.1 Introduction

As we have outlined in the first two chapters, the ability to react flexibly and timely to changing circumstances is a key characteristic of agile enterprises. Every organization is subject to expected or unexpected changes that affect the services that they offer. These changes can be self-imposed or come from the environment in which the organization operates. To remain competitive, organizations may have to respond to these changes, for example, by introducing new services, modifying existing ones, or phasing out obsolete services.

The contribution of architecture, models, and patterns to enterprise agility was addressed in Chaps. 3–5. In those chapters, we looked at the design of flexible organizations and information systems. In this chapter, we will dive deeper into the notion of *agile processes*: ways of working that are focused on rapidly delivering business value, in close relation with all relevant stakeholders, and open to changing requirements and circumstances.

When you think about organizing a development process, it is sometimes helpful to view service development (or any other type of development) as resulting from the 'innovation system' of your organization (see also Sect. 3.2.1): the system that produces or changes the execution system that actually provides services. The innovation system typically includes many different things, in very different configurations: the people performing the development but also the software involved (from compilers to modelling tools); the documentation used (including models); the methods, practices, techniques, and patterns involved; and so on. In a participative form of development (so typical of agile service development), the innovation capability also includes the people engaged on a regular basis in using or managing the service system being developed.

It is important to address service development from a systems thinking perspective. This helps you to think rationally and, literally, systematically about the whole set of factors, actors, processes, and components that are relevant for the service. Concerning the whole service system at once, instead of developing it in a piecemeal fashion, also helps you avoid sub-optimization, for example, having excellent business processes and IT systems, but a bad fit between them. Of course, we might distinguish many different aspects and subsystems and consider countless different ways of 'modelling the innovation system'. In a way, this whole chapter applies such a systematic view on service development. Also, fields like 'method engineering' and 'project management' arguably deal with innovation systems all the time—even if they do not mention them explicitly or do not use systems thinking in their approach. We certainly do not claim that systems thinking is always the best approach in process management (social factors and situated uncertainty play too large a role in projects for that), but if we work towards the creation and improvement of methods and tools, which are typically rational generalizations used for specific situations, and if we simply want to better understand complex projects and processes, then systems thinking can help a lot indeed.

The way in which an organization organizes its innovation system for business service should match its desired agility. For example, if the organization needs to define new services on a daily basis, then a heavy, waterfall-like development process is unlikely to deliver the required rate of results. On the other hand, in situations where service quality, legal requirements, or safety are key, a structured development process with extensive testing and audit procedures may be a better choice than a poorly documented ad hoc process. Consequently, there is a close relation between the agility required by an organization and the way in which it develops and changes its services. Ideally, the organization's way of working must be determined by the required agility, not vice versa.

In Chap. 2, we described how to operationalize this notion of process agility, by decomposing it into five aspects:

1. The *responsiveness* to business needs
2. The *speed* of delivering business value through working results, i.e. the response time for dealing with new requirements
3. The *competency* of the organization, i.e. delivering optimal results, in terms of both quantity and quality, with limited resources
4. The *flexibility* of the process, i.e. its adaptability to changing circumstances, learning experiences of team members, etc.
5. The *sustainability* of the way of working, for example, whether it can be applied in the long run without resulting in demotivated employees or strained customer relationships

In this chapter, we show how you can accommodate these five aspects while developing services. In particular, our focus will be on the construction and adaptation of an agile way of working that fits the particular needs and circumstances of an organization, programme, or project.

6.2 A Situational Approach to an Agile Way of Working

With many aspects and sources of agility discussed in the previous chapters, we have still neglected one source: agile ways of working, from which the use of 'agility' in a software and service context arose in the first place. As mentioned in Sect. 2.1, the Agile Manifesto (Beck et al. 2001) states that 'we have come to value responding to change over following a plan'. This implies that a fundamental requirement of an agile organization is to have a service or software development method being able to sense changes and react accordingly is. This in turn translates responsiveness to be a fundamental requirement for agile methods:

> 'An *agile method* is a method that uses light-but-sufficient rules of project behaviour and human- and communication oriented rules'. (Cockburn 2002)

Responsiveness is realized by having 'light-but-sufficient rules' and 'human- and communication-oriented rules' (Qumer and Henderson-Sellers 2008). Current agile development methods such as XP, Scrum, and DSDM (see also Sect. 2.2) adhere to these principles. However, they all have their own predefined set of 'light-but-sufficient rules' or practices.

> A *practice* is a common way to do something.

Different methods provide different practices, which may well be useful outside the context of the original method. Its practices allow XP to be effective in small to medium size software development projects, while Scrum and DSDM are also usable for large and non-software-related projects (Qumer and Henderson-Sellers 2008), but they lack the specific software engineering guidance XP provides. Examples of other characteristics that determine when an agile practice can be used are project size, team size, development style, and physical environment (Qumer and Henderson-Sellers 2008).

These characteristics have different instantiations per organization or project. For example, project X might work on a small service with a team size of seven people, while project Y builds a large enterprise system and has several teams totalling 100 people. Project size and team size are situational factors that influence the situation at hand and thereby the practices best applied.

Because situational factors are different at different organizations, different development methods are required. However, pre-packaged methods like Scrum and DSDM do not always fit entirely, and they may lack practices that you need in your specific situation. Therefore, a more general approach to service development is required. In this chapter, we describe our approach to the construction and use of such an adaptive way of working. This approach is based on the one hand on best practices and experiences from the agile community and on the other hand on the scientific foundations of the method engineering field (Brinkkemper 1996; Ralyté et al. 2007).

6.3 Practices, Goals, and Stakeholders

As outlined in the previous section, we want to define a process for constructing agile ways of working that fit particular situations. In order to do this, we first need to have a closer look at the underlying concepts and their relationships: goals, situational factors, and practices.

6.3.1 Practices as Method Fragments

As defined in Sect. 6.2, a practice is a common way to do something. Practices are embedded in methods as *method fragments*. For example, the Scrum method, outlined in Sect. 2.2, consists of multiple practices such as Daily Stand-up Meeting, Sprint, and Product Owner. The actual process and product part of a daily stand-up meeting are described in a method fragment. Organizations adopt specific methods as their way of working to formalize the processes they execute and provide guidelines they want to adhere to. For example, an organization may have business processes in place to define services or products for particular customers, use CMMI for process improvement, and communication guidelines to market new services. However, organizations also extract practices from specific methods and adopt them to their own situation. For example, an organization may combine Scrum's meeting practices with XP's software engineering guidance and the Project Start Architecture from DyA (Wagter et al. 2005). Besides these formal and well-defined processes, organizations also have many informal, undocumented ways of working. These also are practices executed by the organization.

Different practices are used in different phases of the service life cycle, from inception to decommissioning. Examples of such phases include planning, delivering, operating, and managing the service. In various research projects and through practical experiences, many practices have been identified and collected that can be used in the life cycle of a service. In this book, we focus (1) on practices that are potentially relevant for agile service development and (2) on practices that promote agility. Of course, many more practices may be identified, but these are out of scope.

> An *agile practice* (for service development) is a practice that promotes one or more aspects of agility when developing services.

6.3 Practices, Goals, and Stakeholders

Table 6.1 Description of agile practices

Element	Meaning
Name	A short, descriptive name of the practice
Problem	A description in a few sentences of the problem that this practice tackles. Specifically, which aspects of process agility (speed, responsiveness, competency, flexibility, and sustainability of the process) does this practice address?
Solution	What way of working does this practice offer for the stated problem?
	Who are the people involved in applying this practice, what are their roles, how do they cooperate, interact, or communicate?
	What is the motivation for the solution? Why is this solution suitable? What are the underlying principles/heuristics/theories justifying the solution?
	Which trade-offs have to be made in applying this practice and which forces must be balanced? For example, a system's properties may be less predictable beforehand because design choices are made at a late stage when a given practice is applied. If possible, state these trade-offs in terms of the situational factors they concern
Situation	In which circumstances is this practice useful, i.e. in which context can the proposed solution be applied (and when not)? For example, having daily face-to-face meetings requires a co-located team and is not possible in a geographically distributed situation (so perhaps a different practice must be applied to achieve the same effect). Described in terms of the situational factors outlined in Sect. 6.3.3
Artefacts	What kinds of (tangible and intangible) artefacts, and if applicable what kinds of models in particular, does the practice use and produce?
Known uses	What are examples of using this practice?
Related practices	How is this practice related to other practices? Is it often applied before, after, or together with other practices? Are there alternative practices that solve the same problem in a different way?

The agility aspects that we consider include process agility aspects (responsiveness, speed, competency, flexibility, and sustainability) and system agility aspects (the ease of making a change, of rapidly deploying changes, of dealing with effects of changes, of integrating the system with its environment, and of decoupling the system from its environment), as defined in Sect. 2.3. Note that an agile practice is not necessarily agile in itself; it can be a rigid practice that contributes to an agility problem. For example, Scrum is widely recognized as an agile software development method, although the Scrum methodology itself is standardized (in terms of roles and meetings) and well described, and Scrum certification programmes are in place (see, e.g. Schwaber and Beedle 2002).

Some of these practices have become 'standard solutions' for 'specific problems', and are often described in the form of patterns (see Chap. 5). Within the field of information systems and service development, almost all existing practices emphasize the development process of the actual realization and operation of the service. Fewer practices are related to business aspects of the service such as its business model, revenue streams, or market segments. All these practices have been described in a template, merging similar practices from different sources. This template was inspired by the way design patterns are described (Chap. 5). For each of the practices, the elements given by Table 6.1 have been provided.

6.3.2 Identifying Practices

Having discussed practices and the manner in which we describe them, we now take a closer look at already existing practices and the manner in which practices evolve. Let us start with an example of a filled-in practice template (Table 6.2).

This example is taken from the practices described by Ambler (2003). Many such collections and catalogues exist. For example, in (Agile Advice 2006), seven core practices to support an agile way of working have been identified. Coplien and Harrison (2004) present organizational practices that strongly correlate to success in software development processes. Popular agile development methods such as Scrum (Schwaber and Beedle 2002), DSDM (DSDM Consortium 2008), and Extreme Programming (Wells 2009) provide various concrete practices to deal with, for example, project roles, iteration planning, and engineering. Ambler has identified several practices to support agility through modelling (Ambler 2002), architecture (McGovern et al. 2003), and information structures (Ambler 2003).

Another source of relevant practices are the principles from Lean. Its main idea is to maximize customer value while minimizing waste. Lean originates from the car manufacturing industry (Ruffa 2008). This idea of minimizing waste has also been applied to the software development domain, resulting in Lean software development methods (Poppendieck and Poppendieck 2003).

Often, practices from various sources are very similar. For example, the practice 'Engage Customers' from (Coplien and Harrison 2004) is similar to the practices 'Active Stakeholder Participation' from (Ambler 2002), 'Involve All Stakeholders' from Ian Graham's Rule Patterns (Graham 2007), and 'All Hands On Deck Early On' from Xebia's Lean Architecture principles (Xebia 2010). We have classified similar practices, documented them in a standardized template, modelled their dependencies and relations, and developed an instrument to select relevant practices based on the situational factors of an organization. The process we followed is depicted in Fig. 6.1.

Of course, our library of practices is not a closed set, and new ways of working will continually arise. However, agile practices should not be designed from scratch or invented sitting behind a desk. Like patterns, agile practices evolve from real-life situations and practical experience. When a certain way of working has a proven track record, it can be added to our library.

6.3.3 Situational Factors

Now that you know what practices are, where to find them, and how to describe them, how do you select the *right* practices, which fit your circumstances? To this end, we need a concept to describe these circumstances: situational factors.

Of course, every organization is different; nevertheless, some common characteristics or factors can be recognized that are important in choosing your way of working.

6.3 Practices, Goals, and Stakeholders 117

Table 6.2 Description of active stakeholder participation (Ambler 2003)

Element	Meaning
Name	Active stakeholder participation
Problem	Systems and services often do not match the expectations of their prospective users and other stakeholders. How can you ensure that the system or service being built conforms to these (often implicit) assumptions and expectations of stakeholders?
Solution	A high level of participation is required to make software development efforts effective, and often, it is not sufficient in many organizations, particularly in those where politics and not reason are the order of the day. Project success often requires a greater level of involvement by project stakeholders—domain and technical experts should be actively involved with modelling (yes, creating the actual models, not just giving information to a modeller), senior management needs to publicly and private support your project, operations and support staff must actively work with your project team towards making your production environment ready to accept your system, other system teams must work with yours to support integration efforts, and maintenance developers must work to become adept at the technologies and techniques used by your system
	Often, these stakeholders are busy people with full schedules. Devoting enough time is difficult but necessary. If continuous on-site availability is not possible, options such as regular, periodic stakeholder meetings, or asynchronous communication methods (e.g. email) can be explored
Solution	A high level of participation is required to make software development efforts effective, and often, it is not sufficient in many organizations, particularly in those where politics and not reason are the order of the day. Project success often requires a greater level of involvement by project stakeholders—domain and technical experts should be actively involved with modelling (yes, creating the actual models, not just giving information to a modeller), senior management needs to publicly and private support your project, operations and support staff must actively work with your project team towards making your production environment ready to accept your system, other system teams must work with yours to support integration efforts, and maintenance developers must work to become adept at the technologies and techniques used by your system
	Often, these stakeholders are busy people with full schedules. Devoting enough time is difficult, but necessary. If continuous on-site availability is not possible, options such as regular, periodic stakeholder meetings or asynchronous communication methods (e.g. email) can be explored
Situation	People: This practice requires having on-site access to people, typically users or their representatives, who have the authority and ability to provide information pertaining to the system being built and to make pertinent and timely decisions regarding the requirements and prioritization thereof
	Product: This practice is applicable for many different kinds of products and services. However, it is particularly useful for those products that are new to their prospective users, i.e. they cannot easily state their requirements because they have no comparable experience; have an interactive character, i.e. a lot of user interaction; lend themselves to iterative development and refinement (and hence, less applicable for products with very strict compliance or quality requirements)
	Process: This practice is particularly useful in case of an iterative development process that allows for feedback loops in which stakeholder considerations can be taken into account and a development process during which the requirements and/or the environment of the product or service may change

(continued)

Table 6.2 (continued)

Element	Meaning
Artefacts	None
Known uses	Actively practised in all agile methods
Related practices	Communicate powerfully
	Domain expertise in roles
	Product owner
	Sprint review
	Planning game
	Ask the business and other knowledge elicitation patterns

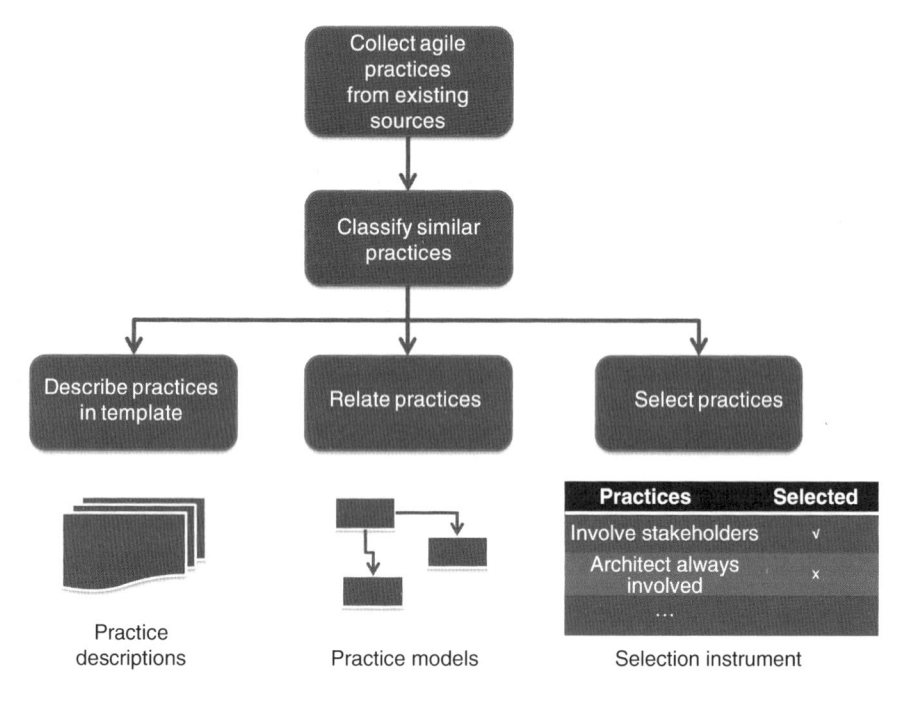

Fig. 6.1 Identification of agile practices

Examples of such factors are the organization size, number of business units, number of customers, company policy, and customer involvement. These common characteristics are called situational factors.

> A *situational factor* is a property of the environment in which a service is developed and/or used, which affects development processes and/or the services offered by the organization.

These situational factors can either be self-imposed (internal) or arise from the environment in which the enterprise operates (external). An example of an external situational factor is legislation. For example, the Basel Accords on banking supervision require banks to mitigate risks. This affects both their financial buffers, i.e. their financial risks, and their organization, systems, and (physical and IT) infrastructure, i.e. the operational risks. As a consequence, banks are, for example, tightening their rules on lending money to clients. The accords also comprise requirements on operational risk management, including aspects ranging from the risks of system failure and data loss to fraud and workplace safety.

In Chap. 2, we already outlined the common business drivers for agility, which provide an important source of such external situational factors. Internal situational factors affecting the way of working include, for example, the business strategy of an enterprise, the capabilities of its workforce, organizational culture, or project budget.

Based on the definition and explanation above, you might argue that a situational factor can be virtually anything. In a sense, this is true, but not every situational factor is applicable to every design problem (Winter 2011). Of course, generally applicable factors do exist, such as organization size or industry. However, design domains such as enterprise architecture, business process management, software product management, and agile service development all have specific situational factors affecting their management and implementation (Winter and Bucher 2006; Winter 2011). Here, we specifically focus on situational factors affecting agile service development. These factors have been clustered into the following categories:

- Business strategy
- Business drivers
- Barriers to change
- Service requirements
- Process requirements

Section 2.4 has introduced seven types of business drivers. Investigating the business drivers of the enterprise shows us the aspects in which its services need to be agile. In the next section, we will explain the analysis of these business drivers and the tool we developed for this purpose.

Although these business drivers indicate the need for agility from different perspectives, realizing this agility can be quite hard. Barriers within the enterprise may delay or prevent changes. Therefore, we also have to identify and deal with such barriers.

In addition to the situational factors concerning the entire organization, we also have to look at situational factors that are unique to the specific service at hand. For example, certain markets or user groups may pose specific requirements or constraints. Based on these service requirements, a first specification for the project has to be formulated (although in an agile project, this will often be only a high-level description of the needs and ideas and certainly not a detailed design). During this step, the environment of the service has to be investigated. This step provides you with the prerequisites (boundaries) with which the service needs to comply. Examples of such restrictions are existing (technical) infrastructures, compliance with laws and regulations, organization structures, and possibly even (management) culture.

After the relevant situational factors for the service have been determined, the final element of this step is to determine the situational factors for the development process. Examples of situational factors that can significantly affect the process are the availability of people (both development team members and stakeholders such as users and managers) and the synchronization needed with other projects and processes in the organization.

6.3.4 Stakeholder and Goals

Moving from practices to situational factors brings us closer to the stakeholders of the agile service. Stakeholders influence situational factors by settings goals. Moreover, stakeholders also affect or can be affected by the organization's actions. Let us repeat the applicable definitions from Chap. 4:

> *Stakeholder*: the role of an individual, team, or organization (or classes thereof) that represents their interests in, or concerns relative to, the outcome of the architecture
>
> *Goal*: an end state that a stakeholder intends to achieve

Examples of stakeholders (or rather stakeholder roles) are the board of directors, shareholders, customers, employees, architects, project managers, legislative authorities, etc. Stakeholders each have their own goals. For example, shareholders may expect a high return on investment, customers may require value for money, and IT managers would like to have a robust and reliable IT infrastructure to support the organization's business. Goals are not always aligned; different stakeholders will often have conflicting goals. For example, building a highly reliable and robust infrastructure desired by the IT manager may be too expensive from the CFO's point of view.

For any organization, it is important to know its stakeholders and their goals, because they affect the actions that the organization takes or should take. Does the organization optimize shareholder value and make the shareholders happy, or does it want to be best in class with respect to customer satisfaction and make the customers satisfied? Or both? It is the task of management to balance the interests of all stakeholders.

Moreover, stakeholders and stakeholder interests vary over time, and so do the goals that these stakeholders pursue. This challenges organizations to continuously monitor stakeholders and their goals and to adapt its service offerings to keep stakeholders satisfied.

A wide range of different stakeholder goals can be associated with the services an organization offers. These goals do not just relate to the functionality of the services but also address other areas. From a business agility point of view, three important areas stand out: the value offered to customers, the business model behind the service offering, and the various risks involved:

- **Service value.** This relates to the added value delivered to stakeholders. Which services should the organization offer to strengthen its portfolio? What investments should be made? What are the cash cows, stars, or dogs in the portfolio? Which stakeholders would benefit from these investments? And which types of changes do you expect in the future, either based on market demand or by creating your own offerings?
- **Business model.** A business model describes the rationale of how an organization creates, delivers, and captures value (Osterwalder and Pigneur 2009) (economic, social, or other forms of value). For example, do customers have to pay for the service? What price do they pay? Which partners are required to run the service? What infrastructure is required to operate the service? Many of these questions are addressed by Osterwalder's Business Model Canvas, which is a strategic instrument to develop and sketch business models. We will use this later on to show in which areas your enterprise may require agility.
- **Risk management.** Another important goal is to control the various risks involved in providing particular services. A proper risk analysis helps to identify these risks and set service goals. For example, if dropping service quality will cause customers to run to competitors, then quality assurance is probably high on the wish list of some stakeholders. Moreover, being agile is in itself a way of mitigating risks.

> **Example: AgiSurance High-Level Goals**
>
> AgiSurance knows that for its niche of event insurances, for example, the music festival insurance mentioned before, it has to respond rapidly when an event is announced; otherwise, its competitors will conquer this market. It has therefore defined a short-cycle development process that can deliver a fully operational, simple insurance product within a week's time. These products themselves are to be highly tailorable, to fit with the specific characteristics of events (e.g. indoor vs. outdoor accommodation, location, duration) in order to provide maximal customer value.

6.4 Constructing a Situational Way of Working

Using situational factors, stakeholders, and goals as inputs, we can use various practices to construct a custom way of working that fits that particular situation. Our situational method engineering approach, which fits the general iterative character of agile methods, is outlined in Fig. 6.2.

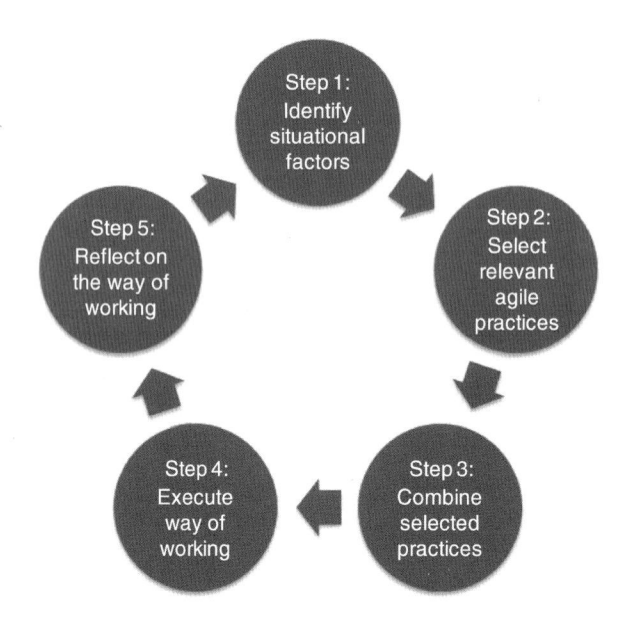

Fig. 6.2 Overview of the way of working

Step 1 First, we identify which factors determine the business need for agility of an organization. These are based on the organizational strategy, business drivers, available resources, and in particular the characteristics of the services that the organization provides. For example, does the organization need to offer new services on a regular basis or frequently change their parameters? Or is the service portfolio stable, but do the channels to access these services often change? Or perhaps the services and the channels are stable, but their realization is subject to changing rules and regulations. These agility aspects depend on the environment in which the organization operates; the culture, processes, and people in the organization itself; and the services that the organization intends to offer. As these can be different for each organization, this requires a situational approach. Existing approaches such as business requirements engineering (Engelsman et al. 2011) and goal-oriented method engineering (Quartel et al. 2009) can be used to facilitate the identification of relevant agile aspects. The process of defining goals based on the business drivers is elaborated in Sect. 6.4.

Step 2 Once we have identified the relevant situational factors and agility aspects, we select relevant practices that support agility in these aspects. We have collected a large number of agile practices from various sources in the agile community, which may contribute to achieving the desired agility in the way of working. Based on the agility contribution of each practice, we can decide whether a practice contributes to the required agility aspects and qualify as building blocks for our way of working. Furthermore, the set of practices needs to cover a sufficient part of the service development process, to provide designers and developers the necessary guidance. The selection of practices is further discussed in Sect. 6.6.

Step 3 Next, we must combine the method fragments underlying the practices into processes. Yet, this is not always easy: for example, practices may operate on different timescales, depend on each other's outputs, or pose conflicting demands on stakeholders or resources. How can one relate these fragments? This requires some form of causal ordering that helps us decide how practices depend on each other, which practices should be carried out first, and which come next. Is the practice iterative, and if so, what is the duration of the iteration cycle? Such a causal ordering of working practices outlines possible processes that an organization could follow to meet the required agility goals, but it does not prescribe one specific process. Combing practices into processes is further discussed in Sect. 6.7.

Step 4 Of course, executing the way of working is the core of any method. This is not blindly following a series of predefined steps but consciously applying relevant practices and monitoring their effect. Moreover, not every situation will be covered by an appropriate practice, and we should always exercise our professional judgement and make adequate decisions. In Sect. 6.8, we show how this is done in practice.

Step 5 Internal and external events not only affect the services that an organization offers; they also affect the way of working within the organization. Moreover, experiences from executing the way of working are important inputs for future iterations. Is the current way to develop services still the best approach? Should you intensify communication with stakeholders? Is the quality of results sufficient? We should regularly reflect on the way of working itself to achieve agility and ensure the competency and sustainability of our process. This adaptive, learning behaviour is an essential characteristic of agile methods. For example, the Sprint Retrospective of Scrum, a meeting held after each sprint to reflect and collect experiences, is explicitly intended to improve the way of working of the team.

This, then, is where we close the loop: these experiences are used as inputs to the next iteration and may influence the choice and application of agile practices. Thus, we continuously improve and adapt the agile service development process itself.

In the next sections, we will provide more detail on each of these steps and show how they can be combined to build and execute an agile way of working.

6.5 Step 1: Identify Situational Factors, Goals, and Practices

Having discussed the various concepts related to an agile way of working, we have now arrived at the question how (agile) practices can be selected based on goals and situational factors. To this end, first, we need to set appropriate goals, and next, we select those practices that help us to fulfil these goals.

6.5.1 Setting Goals

Goal planning is only concerned with goals, not with how to achieve them. Goals may apply to all aspects and elements of an enterprise, ranging from strategy, organization, and culture to architectures, business processes, and technology. Moreover, these goals may range from very high level to quite detailed and operational. Also, goals are often related, and there can be a hierarchy or network of super-goals and sub-goals.

If you set out to define or discuss goals, it is important that they are all real and urgent; vague and distant goals are not going to be very useful and certainly not in an agile project that aims to deliver value in the short term. To avoid 'over-specification' (i.e. people getting carried away by listing goals), every goal must be 'real' to at least some stakeholders and preferably already part of their planning or of their conversations about the work they do.

A systematic way of lining up goals and activities, enriching, checking, and changing them, and eventually declaring them fulfilled, requires no more than a well-structured document that can easily be changed during the project (keeping previous versions for later reference). This reflects both the progress in goal fulfilment (project progress) and the changes in project goals (product agility) as well as changes in process goals (agile way of working). To create such a document, we adopt the business requirement analysis language from Engelsman et al. (2011), which has also been used as the basis for the requirements concepts in Sect. 4.5.2.

6.5.2 Situational Factors: Strategy and Business Drivers

As outlined in Sect. 6.3.3, we have different types of situational factors. First, we need to investigate the strategy and business drivers of the enterprise, because this will help us find out in which aspects our services need to be agile. To establish a picture of the business drivers for agility of the enterprise, two questions need to be answered: What are the common changes in the environment of you enterprise that you need to deal with? And how often do these changes occur? The first question can partially be answered by looking at common changes over the last couple of years (depending on your industry). More frequent changes of course require a higher level of agility.

After these business drivers have been identified, it is important to know which types of changes are currently difficult to accommodate: the barriers to change. You should focus your attention in particular on those business drivers that are important or frequent but are difficult to accommodate.

To help you get a grip on this, we have developed an *agility scan*: an instrument to identify the situational factors of an organization, its strategy and business drivers, and barriers to agility. This scan uses a questionnaire intended for business managers and strategists. Based on the answers to the questions, the agility requirements for the enterprise can be determined.

The agility scan first assesses which elements of an organization are most likely to be affected by strategic and situational factors and shows what the relative importance of these influences is. This part of the scan is based on the drivers for agility described in Chap. 2. This results in a conclusion on the areas and aspects where business agility is required.

6.5 Step 1: Identify Situational Factors, Goals, and Practices

Example: AgiSurance Strategy and Business Drivers

AgiSurance's strategy is to be a product leader in niche insurance products, as described in Chap. 2. Interviews are held with the CEO, COO, and business line managers to determine which business drivers this strategy affects. The obvious answer is product/service dynamics, i.e. introducing new products or services.

All interview partners identify that the insurance product portfolio changes every month and they expect the frequency of changes to increase in the future. The CEO states: 'personalising products to specific customers and their demands will be our core competence. This will also lead to new products, but in particular the parameters and rules of existing products will change rapidly. In addition, the economic crisis will lead to an increased regulatory pressure, affecting the parameters, rules and maybe the processes behind our insurance products'. This gives us a second important business driver: continuous compliance.

From these two drivers, we derive that AgiSurance services must be agile in particular with respect to rules and parameters. Therefore, we define the following goals:

– Easy adaptation of product parameters
– Easy configuration of new products

In a second batch of interviews, the operational and IT managers are questioned, mainly to assess the barriers to agility. Combining the results of the interviews, we draw the following conclusions. First, it is difficult to change the IT implementation, a key resource of all insurance products, because product rules are hardcoded within the software application. It is also hard to change rules or parameters of products at the business level, because a proper overview of the portfolio of insurance products is missing.

To show the desired business agility of an enterprise, we use an extended version of the Business Model Canvas (Osterwalder and Pigneur 2009). The scan provides 'heat maps' of the aspects in which agility is required but lacking, helping you to focus your attention on the important points for improvement. Figures 6.3 and 6.4 show examples of these heat maps for our example insurance company AgiSurance. In these figures, darker colours imply a relatively higher importance. Note that these are not absolute values; they simply imply where we should focus most of our attention. In Fig. 6.3, we see that in particular, the Key Activities deserve our attention, which is in line with our analysis above. Other potentially important areas are Key Resources and Risk and Compliance.

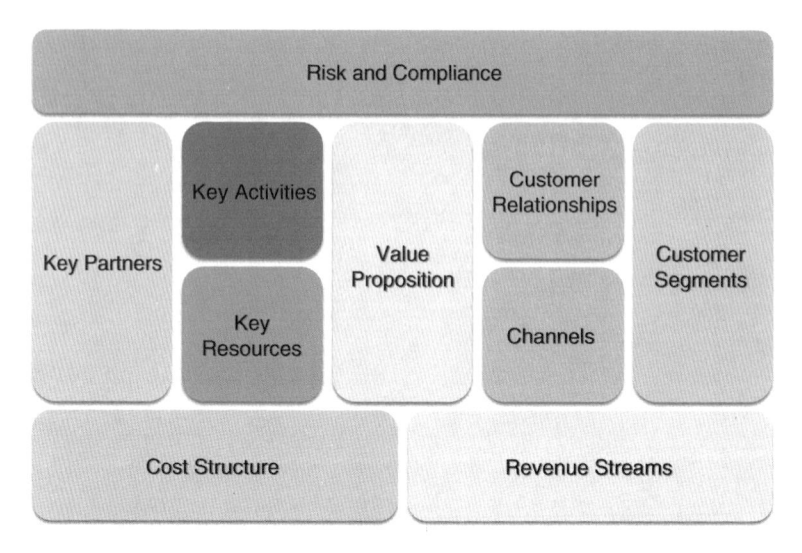

Fig. 6.3 Desired business agility of AgiSurance

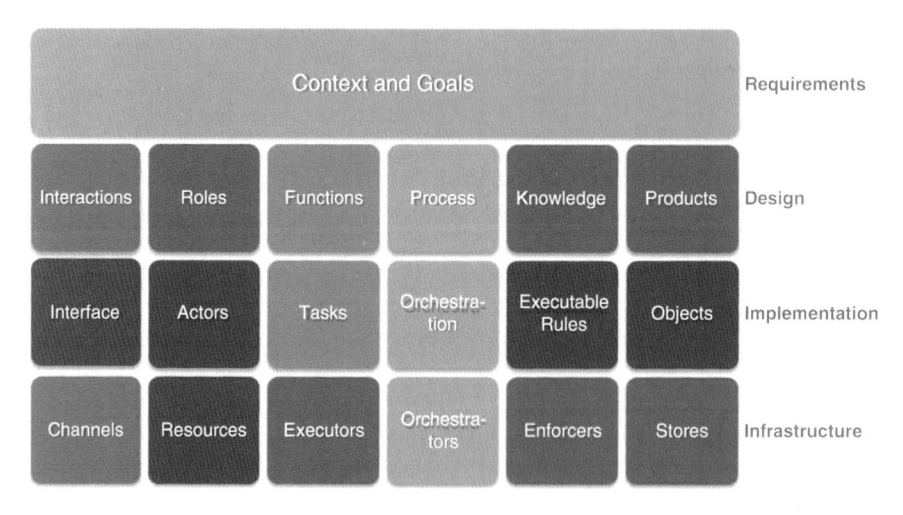

Fig. 6.4 AgiSurance's enabling agility

6.5.3 Situational Factors: Service

In addition to the business strategy, business drivers, and barriers to change, two additional sources of situational factors exist: the service requirements and development process requirements. The first will be discussed in this section, the second in the next.

6.5 Step 1: Identify Situational Factors, Goals, and Practices

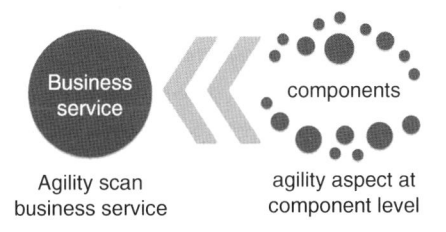

Fig. 6.5 Component breakdown of service

The previous section already introduced our agility scan. In addition to business strategy and business goals, this scan also supports assessing the service environment. Again, the scan provides a heat map aspects in which agility is required but lacking, in this case using the framework discussed in Chap. 4.

In Fig. 6.4, we observe the enabling agility of AgiSurance, i.e. how well the desired business agility (depicted in Fig. 6.3) is supported by the company's current structures and systems. It shows the relevant aspects that make up the enterprise's architecture, and the different abstraction levels we use in the design process, from requirements to infrastructure.

In this figure, we see that AgiSurance's processes are relatively stable. For example, the order of activities in approving an insurance claim hardly ever changes. However, the implementation of decisions (in executable rules) and information (objects) must be more flexible, given the frequent changes in insurance policies we mentioned before. Also, the resources needed (in particular scaling up the number of employees) and the way in which the company interacts with its customers may require more agility.

We should be aware that not all components and aspects of a business service need the same amount of agility, for example, because different business drivers and risks are involved. As you can see in the example, different parts of a service system may require different levels of agility. It is therefore a good practice to break down the components of the business service and assess both the required process agility and the required system agility at the individual component level (Fig. 6.5).

To this end, you should examine for each component:

- Which of the business drivers and goals of the business service as a whole are related to that component
- Which of the identified risks and uncertainties are applicable to the component, and what the impact of these risks might be
- Which of its aspects need frequent adaptation or maintenance

This step can be seen as a decomposition of the agility scan, and goals, drivers, and risks will be defined on more detailed scale. This decomposition also helps in defining sub-teams for the development of larger services in accordance with Conway's law, which states that '[...] organizations which design systems [...] are constrained to produce designs which are copies of the communication structures of these organizations' (Conway 1968). His reasoning is that in order for two system parts to be linked correctly, the designers and implementers of each part must communicate with each other. Therefore, the structure of a system (whether you use a component-based or feature-based decomposition) will be limited by the social structure of the organization that produces it; conversely, the envisaged structure of the system is an important input in setting up the organization that should build it. It is unwise to have two different teams working on system elements that are highly interdependent, because of the communication overhead this induces.

Example: AgiSurance's Service Architecture

AgiSurance's insurance products are realized by several software components and organizational elements. The business processes of these insurance products are relatively stable. The steps needed to approve an insurance application or to handle a claim are fixed; the knowledge, rules, and information used within these process steps need to be highly changeable, however. To this end, AgiSurance wants to employ a business rule management system, as outlined in Chaps. 3 and 4.

Another software component will handle the connection to an existing, well-documented back-office system. All requirements for this connection are clear and stable, it is fully known what needs to be built, and service users do not need to be involved. For this component, there is no particular need for an agile development method.

On the other hand, the development of the self-service portal for customers has to deal with a lot of uncertainty. New technology will be used (HTML 5, iPads), and most requirements for this portal are only known in general terms. Stakeholders such as the marketing and product development departments want an incremental development approach, to help them discover the exact needs, functionalities, and possibilities, with direct user feedback. This component needs to be developed in an agile way, with very short iterations (1 week).

Another component will take care of risk assessment. Risk assessment policies are known and well documented, but the business is uncertain whether these policies are still adequate. Because of this need for validation, an iterative development process is needed, giving periodical insight into the quality of the implemented policies.

6.5.4 *Situational Factors: The Process*

The type of service development process you need is also determined by the situation. An agile development process is very useful in situations where you need to deal with uncertainty, for example, about goals, requirements, technology, and/or added value. Agile methods are also important when stakeholders should be kept involved by means of incremental development.

However, if you have a clear and stable set of requirements, no uncertainties about the technology, and an experienced team, an agile development process may not be necessary and could even be inefficient because of the overhead involved (multiple iteration demos, planning sessions, etc.). For example, in rebuilding a premium calculation component in another proven technology without changing the behaviour of that component, users and other stakeholders will not notice the replacement, and all requirements are known up front.

There are also other circumstances that influence the type and agility of the development process. For example, regulatory requirements may force you to create certain project results with a prescribed process. An example of high regulatory pressure is the health-care industry, where specific quality and risk management practices are mandatory, such as the ISO 13485 and ISO 14971 standards (ISO 2003, 2007).

6.6 Step 2: Select Agile Practices

Now that we have determined the goals (Sect. 6.5.1), strategy and business drivers (Sect. 6.5.2), service factors (Sect. 6.5.3), and process factors (Sect. 6.5.4), we can now select relevant practices. To this end, we have constructed an instrument that weighs the relevance of a set of some 80 practices, collected from various sources in the agile, architecture, and modelling communities. For each of these practices, we have identified:

- The *scope* in which the practice can be applied (e.g. strategy, business drivers, requirements, design, implementation, infrastructure)
- The *agility contribution* of that practice (e.g. speed, responsiveness, competency, flexibility, sustainability; see Sect. 2.3.2)
- The *activity* in which the practice can be used (e.g. communicating, strategizing, analysing, etc.; see also Sect. 5.3)
- The *artefacts* used or produced by the practice (e.g. analysis result, business knowledge, code)

The instrument is tied in with the agility scan described in Sect. 6.5. The input for heat maps described there is also used in selecting relevant practices. Other inputs are the activities performed, the artefacts used and produced, and the roles involved. The instrument merely provides a recommendation of potentially useful practices but does not mandate their use. The method engineer can still make his or her own choices regarding these practices, in order to construct a situational method.

6.7 Step 3: Combine Practices

The approach to select practices as described in the previous section does not automatically lead to a coherent, consistent, and complete set of practices, i.e. a full way of working. Sometimes, practices may overlap, complement, use, or conflict with

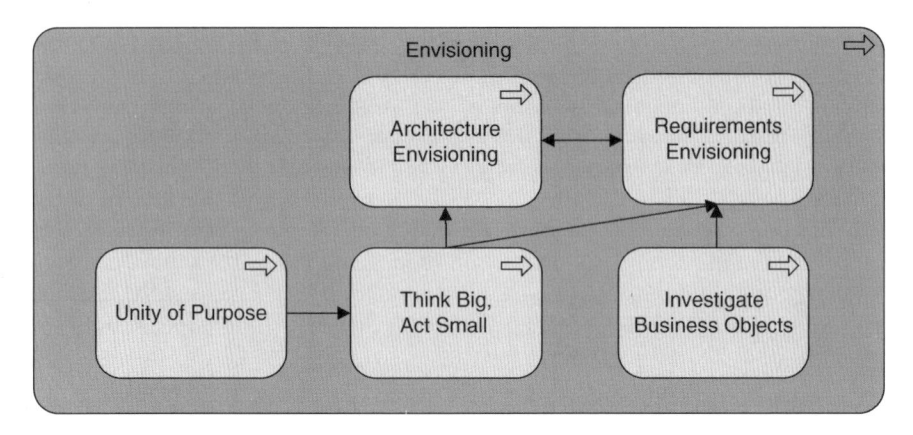

Fig. 6.6 Agile practices related to activity 'Envisioning'

other practices. And in many cases, practices depend on each other's outputs. To help us with this issue, we have modelled various relations between practices in ArchiMate (The Open Group 2012). Using these relations between practices helps in selecting a consistent set of practices for certain activities, practices that use or produce specific artefacts.

The next sections provide different guidelines on the assembly of practices in time based on activities, artefacts, preconditions, post-conditions, process increments, and iterations. It is too ambitious to expect that such assembly of practices will result in a full-fledged method. But it is feasible to partially relate practices, thereby inducing a temporal ordering in these practices.

6.7.1 Assembly Through Activities

In our model of interrelated practices, we have first aggregated all practices that belong to a certain activity, using the set of activities listed in Sect. 5.3.1. These practices have also been related to one other, indicating which practices use another as a sub-practice.

Take, for example, the activity 'Envisioning'. Figure 6.6 shows the practices (modelled in ArchiMate) that may be used in this activity and also how they use each other. For example, the practice 'Investigate Business Objectives', which focuses on the relevant business goals, is used by the practice 'Requirements Envisioning', which provides a high-level vision of the requirements for the service being developed.

These relations provide you with a hierarchy of practices that use other, 'smaller' practices. But this does not tell you the order in which to use various practices. That is addressed in the next sections.

6.7 Step 3: Combine Practices   131

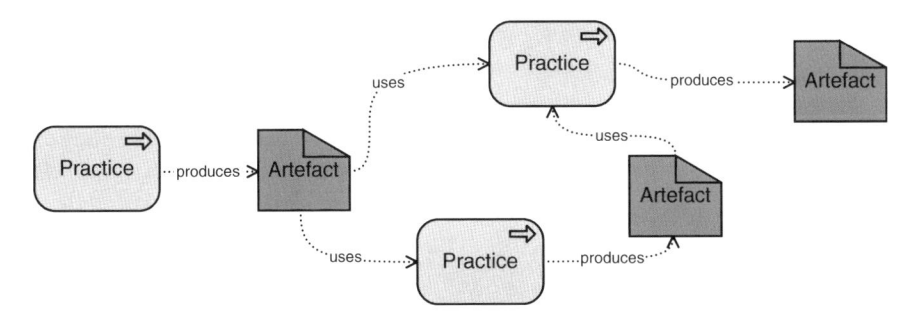

Fig. 6.7 Practice assembly through artefacts

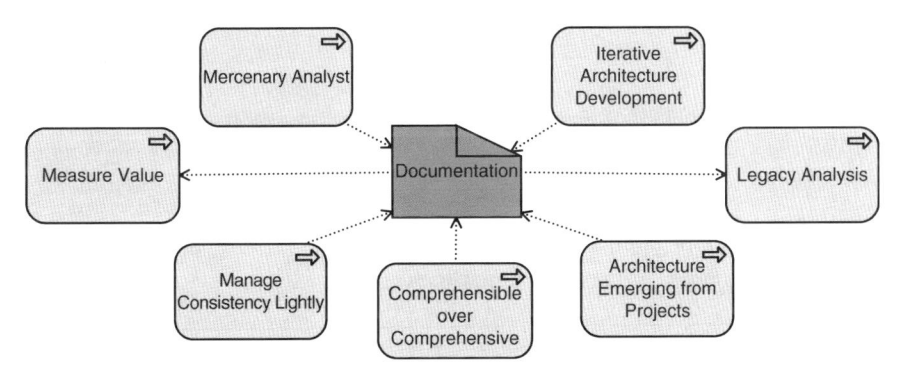

Fig. 6.8 Practices related to the 'Documentation' artefact

6.7.2 Assembly Through Artefacts

One way to combine and order practices is through the artefacts that they use and produce (Fig. 6.7). These artefacts serve as preconditions and post-conditions for practice selection. Both are documented in the artefact element of the practice template from Table 6.1.

To this end, we have modelled the relation of practices with the artefacts that they use or produce. For example, Fig. 6.8 illustrates the practices related to the artefact 'Documentation' and shows, for example, that 'Mercenary Analyst' produces documentation and 'Legacy Analysis' uses it. Based on these dependencies, causal relations between practices can be established. This is visualized in Fig. 6.7.

6.7.3 Assembly Through Conditions

Some practices can be only applied when certain conditions on their usage, resources, participants, or other aspects are met. An example of such a practice is

'Active Stakeholder Participation', which is of course conditional upon the availability of stakeholders.

> **Example: AgiSurance's Sales Channels as a Condition on Development**
>
> In order for AgiSurance to sell insurance products to music festival visitors, it decides to use the websites of ticket vendors as one of their sales channels. This requires participation of these vendors in the service development process, since they must extend their website with the option to buy an insurance.

6.7.4 Assembly Through Process Increments

The composition of a set of practices in a well-defined process is very ambitious and often impossible. However, it is feasible to relate practices by allocating them to various phases or steps of baseline processes. For example, in a waterfall-like process, requirements are usually gathered before the architecture and design activities. In a more agile, Scrum-like approach, requirements gathering, architecture, and design are interleaved on a per-feature basis.

Such an allocation induces a partial ordering of practices: which practice should be carried out before another practice, and which practices could be done in parallel? Here, we will take three baseline processes that vary in agility: the waterfall process baseline, a semi-agile process baseline, and a fully agile process baseline (Fig. 6.9):

- The waterfall process baseline is characterized by different phases that are separated in time, type of stakeholders involved, abstraction levels addressed, and artefacts produced. For example, a typical waterfall process usually starts with requirements gathering, followed by design, implementation, and testing. These phases are executed in sequence, and the transition between phases is usually formalized in some way. Once a phase has been completed, it is not common to return to this phase. In each phase, the service under design is made more concrete.
- The fully agile process baseline is characterized by several short iterations (called 'sprints' in Scrum) that cover all abstraction levels, stakeholders, artefacts, and other aspects. Instead of having clearly recognizable phases as in the waterfall process, in the fully agile process requirements, gathering, design, realization, and testing are done in a short time span on a per-feature basis.
- The semi-agile process combines some aspects of the phased approach of the waterfall process with the flexibility provided by the fully agile process. An example of a semi-agile process is the use of an initial requirements analysis phase and the creation of a project start architecture (PSA) or a separate deployment phase, whereas the development of the service itself is done in an agile manner.

6.7 Step 3: Combine Practices

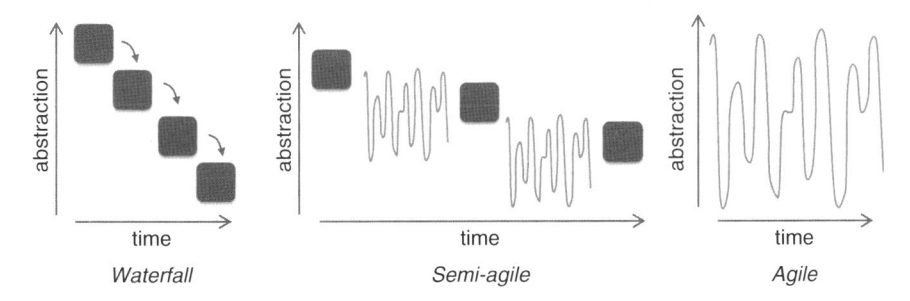

Fig. 6.9 Process baselines

6.7.5 Assembly Through Iteration Matching

Practices can be applied in different phases of service design and have different iteration cycles associated with them. For example, it is not likely that the enterprise's strategy will change very frequently, whereas design and implementation modifications for individual services occur much more frequently. Figure 6.10 illustrates this for different design levels of a service, corresponding to the levels discussed in Chap. 4.

Iteration cycles of practices are determined by two types of factors. First, there are external factors that cannot be influenced directly by an organization. Examples are the rate of change in laws that have to be implemented, the rate at which external infrastructure providers can scale up their resources to accommodate higher volumes, or the rate at which new external service distribution channels can be introduced. Second, there are internal factors that determine the iteration cycles of service development. For example, an organization can plan to create a service in a development process using iterations of its own choice.

An enterprise can be considered agile when it is able to modify its strategy, business, service, design, implementation, or infrastructure sufficiently quick to respond to the events that drive these modifications. The key to agile service design is to 'match' the iteration cycles of the practices that are needed in such a way that delays in carrying out changes to the service are minimized. For example, it is unlikely that practices used to create or change the enterprise strategy are used as frequently as those for the adaptation of a service's parameters. Given the differences between cycles (Fig. 6.10), this matching may not be easy. For example, a lower frequency of change of the infrastructure may be an obstacle to agility, if the higher layers depend on the changeability of that infrastructure.

> **Example: AgiSurance Project Resource Planning Process**
>
> As outlined before, the business of AgiSurance is to quickly create new insurance products for niche markets, such as for music festival visitors. Sometimes, such events come up on short notice, for example, when a tribute concert is organized when a famous pop star dies. Hence, there may be little
>
> *(continued)*

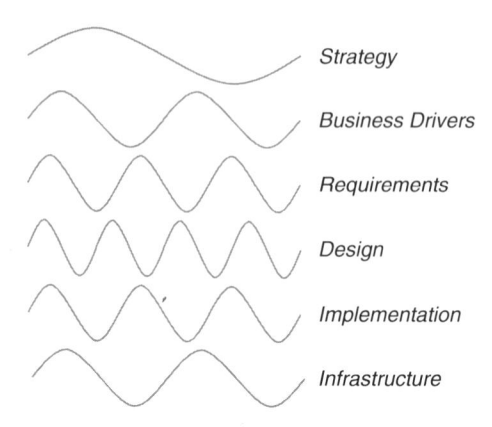

Fig. 6.10 Iteration cycles

> time to plan and execute the creation of these new products and services. AgiSurance needs to use a flexible human resource planning process to free up people from existing projects to create such a new insurance product and match the speed of change in the environment.

These iteration cycles also help us to order practices in time. This ordering depends on the nature of the practices. Some are typically applied on a regular basis (e.g. daily, weekly, or monthly, such as 'Daily Stand-up' or 'Sprint Planning Meeting'), others are only useful when certain conditions are met (e.g. making sure that the team possesses the right skills), and yet others may depend on the development state of the service (e.g. 'Definition of Done').

6.7.6 Activity Planning

To realize goals, various activities must be carried out. How do you plan these? Activities are concrete tasks to be done in order to achieve goals, with a time, a place, people involved and responsible, and possibly with methods, tools, and techniques chosen to help things along or to fit a greater whole (standardization, architecture, conventions, or compliance).

Every goal can have one or more activities specified to achieve it, but it is also possible that a goal is left without specific activities. Does this mean that nothing needs to be done to achieve that goal? Not at all: such a goal without an activity is either assumed to be covered by other goals, or it is simply left to team's powers of self-organization. This reason for 'leaving out an explicit activity' is particularly important for an agile way of working: do not specify more than needed, to keep your plans 'lean', but also to minimize the number of goals or activities you have to change explicitly if your plans are changed. If there is good reason to believe the team can cope on their own, leave them to it. Other goals do have one or more explicitly planned activities that can be linked to them.

Another important aspect of goals better left unspecified is that of their order in time: the order in which the goals are to be achieved. It pays to keep goals separate from planning: what you put in some order of execution should be the activities, not the goals. But of course, by planning activities one before the other, indirectly, you do order the achievement of goals; it is just that by separating activities and goals, you can keep your planning minimal and, therefore, as agile as possible. This is in line with the principles of declarative workflow (van der Aalst 2009) and allows for minimal specification.

As for activities, they usually have a goal they set out to achieve and possibly more than one. Yet, perhaps unexpectedly, sometimes it is smart to leave out explicit specification of the goal of some activity. This is not because such an activity is really 'without goal' (that would be rather unusual in a businesslike project), but in some cases, precisely defining the goal is simply useless: it is just not worth it, and it just adds to the complexity. To give an extreme example, if a detailed meeting agenda includes a coffee break, specifying why this is done is just not relevant.

Still, it is of course a good idea to at least think, for every single activity you plan: 'what goals drive this activity'? Also, from an agility point of view, it is often recommendable to use goals and sub-goals as the main structure for prioritizing and planning, minimizing details of time, place, resources, etc. However, we also recognize the practical needs to have specific planning possibilities. For this, we describe five planning instruments.

6.7.6.1 Determine Stakeholder Involvement

Forget the ideal role of the single Product Owner as advocated by Scrum (Schwaber and Beedle 2002). In practice, multiple stakeholders are involved with developing a business service, each having their own perspectives, knowledge, vision, and attitude. It is naïve to believe that one person within the organization can represent all those expertises and perspectives (and will get the mandate to do so!) If you are lucky, you may find a person who can help you to find the right stakeholders instead.

For each activity, the type and purpose of the artefact that is involved in the activity indicate which stakeholders should be involved and what should be their profile in terms of experience, attitude, ability to envision a future situation, etc. For this purpose, the communication situation templates described in Chap. 7 are a very useful aid.

Note that it is the purpose of the artefact and target quality of that artefact that indicate which stakeholders are important in the development process; this is more complicated that using a simple practice like 'Active Stakeholder Participation' suggests. User involvement when creating version 0.1 of a new service may even be counterproductive. Most users find it hard to imagine a not yet existing future situation. However, once version 0.1 is finished and version 0.2 has to be developed, users can be very good at telling you what needs to be changed. Of course, some user involvement may be useful in developing a first version of a service, but only by adopting a highly incremental development process; and even then, users might not manage to see the complete picture.

6.7.6.2 Discovery Iterations

At the start of a project, we advise you to determine whether the amount of certainty with regard to both requirements and architecture is enough to start an implementation iteration. Often, your stakeholders will have no idea what to expect and cannot provide you with enough useful requirements (user stories). If this is the case, we recommend you to schedule some preliminary discovery iterations (commonly two with a duration of 2 weeks each), aimed to get enough requirements to safely start the full implementation iterations.

Be careful! Do not aim for completeness in all levels of detail or the complete set of requirements ('Big Requirements Up Front') or the architecture ('Big Design Up Front'). Try to get just enough to run a short implementation iteration (1–2 weeks), and to gather the various stakeholders' feedback on this preliminary implementation of your service. This will help you to establish important requirements or to find out the really relevant architectural guidelines. See, for example, the agile practices 'Architecture Envisioning' and 'Requirements Envisioning' (Ambler 2003).

6.7.6.3 Setting the Duration of the (Next) Iteration

For those development tracks that are developed in an agile way, the duration of the iterations should be tuned to the amount of uncertainty and the need to keep stakeholders aligned. A general rule is that the higher the degree of risk or uncertainty is, the shorter an iteration should be. Examples from our own experience show this clearly.

For a car lease company, one of the authors was involved in developing a very complex self-service portal using rare state-of-the-art technology, while not knowing the requirements or functionality needed up front. The complete business service, including coupling to an SAP back-office service, was developed in seven sprints of 1 week each.

For a government organization, a system had to be implemented based on a set of available use cases. Stakeholders were not able to understand or validate these use cases in such depth that they could oversee the overall operation of the system and the added value of its functionality. Although requirements were 'known' as 'the set of use cases that must be implemented', for the sake of stakeholder involvement and their disbelief in the quality of the use cases, an agile development process was been chosen. However, sprints of 3–4 weeks were quite sufficient.

6.7 Step 3: Combine Practices

6.7.6.4 Parallel Development Tracks

As we already outlined in Chap. 4 and in other sections of the current chapter, a business service comprises many different aspects and elements, each of which may have its own development track. Often, these different development tracks can very well be executed in parallel by different teams, no matter if they are actually agile or not, or have a different iteration pace. Once development tracks are defined and configured, attention should be paid to their interrelationships in terms of:

- Dependencies in artefacts: an artefact in development track A may be a prerequisite for an activity in track B and this artefact might (economically) be impossible to stub or imitate.
- Risks: it has no use to start parallel development tracks A and B if during development of track A, it turns out that you cannot eliminate a risk that makes development of track B no longer useful.
- Shared resources: if two parallel tracks use the same resources, availability of resources might constraint parallel execution. Be very careful with the assumption of having one Product Owner available constantly. He/she will always need other constrained stakeholders to fulfil the Product Owner role.

Admittedly, keeping track of this, all this can be a bit of a pain, because the goals are interlinked, as are the activities, and then many goals are linked to activities and vice versa. Adequate tool support is a prerequisite for practical use of this approach.

6.7.6.5 Backlog Grooming

For the components in the development tracks, the requirements are prioritized and estimated on the project backlog in the form of 'user stories'. There are many ways to prioritize this backlog. Because agile development is meant to reduce risks on the one hand and on the other hand focus on the implementation of the most critical or high-value functionality, a very effective way to prioritize backlog stories is by:

1. The added value for the enterprise's business goals and strategy
2. The degree of risk introduced by uncertainty and the impact this will have on the business goals and strategy
3. The importance of the functionality for the stakeholders involved

Note that this means that each 'user story' or 'epic' should be related to the added value for the business goals and strategy. The term 'user story' commonly used in agile method is actual not quite well chosen (in analogy with 'use case' in UML). A user story tends to focus on what the service should do for the end user of the service. It does not describe the rationale: why it should do this, or what the contribution for the customers, goals, and mission of the enterprise will be. A good practice is to write business and strategic stories as well and to relate the 'user stories' to these business and strategic stories.

Moreover, many aspects of service development do not lend themselves to a user point of view. Having 'architecture stories' or 'technical stories' is often also necessary, for example, to investigate the impact and risks of using new technology by building a spike solution (see Sect. 3.3.1) or to reduce technical debt using refactoring techniques (see Sect. 3.3.2).

6.7.7 Tool Support

To assist the method engineering and execution process, we have developed an experimental prototype that supports the generation of 'goal trees', visualizing the goals and how they are related. Also, activities can be represented and linked to this goal tree (e.g. by using hyperlinks). So goals and activities can be represented in a number of ways that are helpful to the project manager and project workers. We have used a wiki for our prototype, but in principle, any form of digital documentation can be used here (though hyperlinks are extremely useful). Further integration of such functionality with mature development tool suites would be very useful to support agile teams in their choice of practices.

The structures described above aim at planning project activities, and such a plan can be changed relatively easily. But with such a structure in place, it is also very simple to keep track of goals achieved, by simply 'ticking them off'. In the prototype, we used a very simple mechanism in which an authorized person could change the state of any goal: 'not started', 'pending', or 'achieved'. We could even neatly visualize the achievement of goals and super-goals over time.

In full, as described in (Taufan 2011, pp. 38–39), goal entries included a 'goal description', a 'goal type' (e.g. product goal, communication goal), optionally a 'deadline', an indicator of 'top goal' (yes or no), 'achievement criteria' (optional), 'related activity', 'sister goal', and 'super goal'. Activities included a 'description', a 'goal to which it is allocated', a 'location', a 'person responsible to accomplish the activity', 'due date/time', and 'resources, tools, and information used'. Also, to allow for specification of repeated activities, an activity could be set to recur at some interval (daily, weekly, or monthly).

6.8 Step 4: Execute the Way of Working

In the previous sections, all preparations have been completed to actually start building the required service. First, the business drivers for agility were identified, which resulted in a set of relevant agile aspects that need to be addressed (Sect. 6.4). Next, agile practices were selected that support agility for these aspects (Sect. 6.6).

In Sect. 6.7, several ways to assemble the selected practices into a coherent way of working have been discussed. Now it is time to execute the way of working!

Many things can be said about the execution itself, but the bottom line is 'just do it!' In many cases, the execution itself will be timeboxed and budget-boxed to prevent that it will take unlimited resources (time and money wise). The bad thing is that at the end of the timebox, there is no guarantee that the service under development is finished and that all stakeholders are satisfied. But no project approach can give these guarantees for complex design projects like service development; there are simply too many unknowns to be factored in. You should therefore be wary of any methods that do promise you this holy grail of project management; no amount of process or documentation can force your stakeholders to come up with a coherent, consistent, and complete set of requirements in a domain that they simply do not fully understand yet. Iteratively and gradually building up this understanding is the only way forward. The good thing of such an approach is that the end of a timebox provides a natural point for reflection, and possibly adaption, of your way of working. This innate learning and feedback cycle is perhaps the strongest point of agile methods.

6.9 Step 5: Reflect on the Way of Working

Let us now reflect on what we have done so far and return to the big picture. We have collected the stakeholders' goals and business drivers and identified the relevant situational factors associated with these, selected corresponding practices, and combined these in a coherent way of working. In the previous section, we briefly discussed the execution of the way of working.

The key to agile service development is the ability to adapt the services being developed and the way of working when circumstances change. An iterative way of working allows you not only to incorporate new or changed requirements for the service ('system agility') but also to change the way of working itself ('process agility'). As we already argued in Chap. 2, true enterprise agility requires a combination of these.

Figure 6.10 sketches the basic iteration that includes feedback on system agility and process agility. Based on the stakeholder goals and situational factors, practices are selected and a way of working is constructed and executed. After the each iteration, the contribution of the way of working to the individual stakeholder goals is assessed. For some stakeholders, the previous execution may result in a positive contribution of their goals, and for others, it may result in a negative contribution. This may result in an adaptation of goals, and of course changing situational factors may also lead to new goals. Second, the suitability and effect of the individual practices are assessed: did they work well, should they be changed, should new practices be adopted? Based on these assessments, a new iteration is started: new goals are set, practices are selected, etc. (Fig. 6.11).

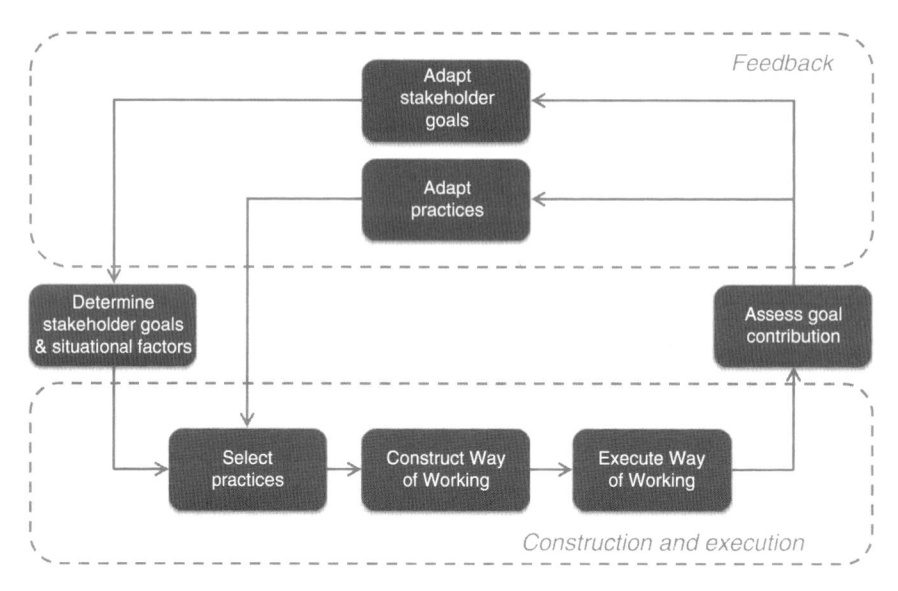

Fig. 6.11 Iterative way of working

Example: Feedback on AgiSurance's Security

The Chief Customer Operations (CCO) of AgiSurance wants to make it easy for customers to log in to their personal online environment 'MyAgiSurance', where they can manage their insurances online. He proposes to use a username/password authentication scheme with safety questions for authentication. The Chief Security Officer (CSO) believes that such an authentication scheme is vulnerable to fraud and proposes a better but more costly authentication mechanism, using a dedicated login device. To save costs, it is decided to have the IT department of AgiSurance build software that realizes authentication based on username/password. This positively contributes to the CCO goals but negatively to the CSO goals. However, when AgiSurance receives negative press attention due to fraud, the company quickly decides to change tack and to partner with national banks that already have a safe and reliable authentication solution for their customers.

Chapter 7
Stakeholder Communication

S.J.B.A. Hoppenbrouwers, W. van Stokkum, M.E. Iacob, I. Wilmont,
D.J.T. van der Linden, C. Amrit, and M. Joosen

In this chapter, we address the issue of communication with stakeholders in agile development projects. Our approach pivots round 'communication situations' that occur in such communication; we do not cover all communication that may occur in projects but focus mainly on the model-oriented kind and on situations in which stakeholders (apart from developers) play an important role. We provide some context and background but also concrete ways of analysing and guiding communication situations using some dedicated instruments. We illustrate this with examples from practice.

7.1 Introduction

Why include a whole chapter on communication in a book on agile service development? Communication is important in any project, but in agile service development, it is especially important. As mentioned in Sect. 2.1, the Manifesto for Agile Development (Beck et al. 2001) states right away that 'we have come to value individuals and interactions over processes and tools'. This implies that communication is a primary factor rather than one of many 'enabling aspects' in an agile way of working.

Agile service development projects have some things in common when it concerns communication:

- **Intensive:** Communication with stakeholders and others involved is intensive and remains intensive throughout the project's time span, and possibly even after (maintenance).
- **Non-technical:** Disregarding professional developers, such communication involves people who are not able or willing to talk in 'technical terms' unfamiliar to them and not able or willing to use technical 'tools of the trade' like detailed specifications or models. Moreover, these terms and tools may be not so adequate in capturing the essence of what stakeholders talk about.

- **Diverse**: There is much diversity between stakeholders involved concerning their background, knowledge, skills, concerns, focus, interests, language (jargon, terminology), and so on.

Communication is always a challenge, especially when it occurs between people with different backgrounds, outlooks, and goals. Generic communication skills are vital in daily work for most professionals, if not for every human being. Some quite general rules of communication have long ago been observed and laid down in a nutshell by Paul Grice in the form of his famous maxims (Grice 1975), reinterpreted here with modelling in mind (Lankhorst et al. 2009):

- Make your model as informative as necessary.
- Do not make your model more informative than necessary.
- Do not model what you believe to be false.
- Do not model that for which you lack adequate argumentation.
- Be relevant.
- Avoid obscurity in expression.
- Avoid ambiguity.
- Be brief (keep your model or view small).
- Be orderly (structure your model well).

Much can be said about general human communication and how to excel in it, and elaborate communication courses of many sorts are given throughout the professional world, covering both authoring and more direct interpersonal communication, both online and offline. However, we do not cover any such generic ground in this chapter. Instead, we focus on *communication with and about models* and specifications (both in verbal and diagrammatic form).

So what is special about 'communication with and about models'? In many 'technical' models, rational demands are reflected in strict rules on the way such models and other artefacts are put together, using specific languages with specific concepts and a specific syntax, for example, UML, BPMN, ArchiMate, ultimately, also SQL or Java. Such languages are central in many branches of computer science and IT. We believe, however, that if you think about how models are made and used by people, it is useful to realize that all models are *also* 'texts'. Besides providing focused and well-structured information on some domain or system (usually just of some limited aspect thereof), these texts are then *also* subject to quite strict demands stemming from the practices of rational analysis and design: they have to be expressed in modelling languages. So the obligation to use rational, artificial languages comes from the world of engineering rather than from the usual way of communicating in or about 'business', 'management', or 'organization', let alone 'HRM', 'mortgages', or 'our unique selling points'. How to deal with this is often a bit of a struggle: it means respecting human-oriented communication demands but also the demands set by rational engineering.

Now, as long as the people involved in model-oriented communication are trained in, or at least sufficiently familiar with, the modelling languages and concepts used, the challenge is reasonable. Developers with a technical analysis and design background generally have few problems dealing with models—nothing that reading a good textbook or doing a 2-day course cannot remedy. However, as we have seen, in an agile service development context, we simply cannot assume that all people involved have received even the most basic technical training. For many 'business people' (to use a gross generalization), as opposed to 'technical people' (likewise), creating or even just understanding and evaluating models are either very hard indeed or something they really do not want to do, and often both. This is not just a matter of 'using modelling languages'; despite all laudable efforts to achieve 'business-IT alignment', the mindset and *way of thinking* of the business community are seriously different from that of the IT community (Hoppenbrouwers 2008). Creating information systems is simply a very different occupation than that of creating and running businesses, and quite likely, this will remain so forever. *Abstraction* is at the core of the skills required to deal with models and modelling (Wilmont et al. 2012); we return to this in Sect. 7.4.2.

In many cases, the lurking communicational conflict underlying the necessary use of models is solved or avoided by keeping the models out of view of 'the business'. Specialists with an IT background talk to relevant people from the business, interpret what they hear, conceive models (e.g. business process models, domain models, business rules, and so on), and present them to the business stakeholders for validation. Unfortunately, this practice has some important disadvantages, in particular in agile service development contexts. To mention just the most important ones, first, it tends to create a false sense of achievement. Stakeholders too readily assume they sufficiently understand the details, meanings, and implications of the models to pass valid judgments about them. Analysts and modellers often make the same mistake and too easily consider a model to be 'properly communicated or validated'. A stakeholder simply saying 'yes' when asked whether a model is understood and agreed does not equal proper validation.

Second, models that are conceived and validated this way fail to create the 'sense of ownership' among all stakeholders which is much wanted in any participatory approach. The model is not 'theirs', and when push comes to shove, they may not back up the model or commit to it after all.

Working together in a heterogeneous group, possibly involving people with not only different backgrounds but also different concerns and interests, requires a serious investment in *having people talk to each other*. Resources simply have to be allocated for this. Some managers may perceive this as a waste of time; they are wrong. Investment in talking, as long as it is focused and serves a clear communicational purpose, will pay itself back. People just *have* to get to know one another and their various points of view, concerns, and vocabulary. Based on a common understanding, they can then go on to construct a shared view of whatever domain or aspect it is they need to describe or agree or decide about, and only then they can safely move on to commit to what they came up with (e.g. accept it as 'official state of affairs' or build it). So working on models typically involves three basic levels of agreement (Hoppenbrouwers et al. 2005):

- Shared **understanding** of each other's situation, concepts (words), viewpoints, concerns, and interests
- Shared **consensus** on current situations and future plans, based on shared understanding of each other's thoughts and viewpoints
- Shared **commitment** about taking action, based on shared consensus.

Importantly, each consecutive level requires the previous level to be taken care of, so *understanding* of what is said in the model or specification is extremely important. If one level fails, the level built upon it also collapses. In addition, to really communicate and validate models, it is vital not just to produce the models as such, which are often rather abstract (i.e. hide much information), but also to talk *about* them, preferably in a focused and systematic way so as to cover all important concepts and, in particular, *the argumentation behind them* (Hoppenbrouwers 2008).

In addition, the most basic level of understanding is closely connected to investing in *people understanding each other's language*. Note we do not even include differences between national languages here: we talk about vocabulary and jargon that differ between professional groups, domains, companies, departments, and so on. To mention a simple example, the definition of what 'week' means is not as straightforward as it may seem. When does a week begin? Does it have 5 days (working week) or 7? Such parameters in meaning are known and are even reflected in advanced calendar software, but the different understandings *still* have to be communicated, understood, and agreed among collaborating parties. Terminological differences are a major cause of misunderstanding and often cause fierce debate in meetings and reviews. Yet such debate (or negotiation) is very much preferable over *hidden* differences in what words mean to different people or groups of people. A specific instrument for finding out what people and communities really mean by particular words and concepts, especially meta-model concepts (van der Linden et al. 2011), is discussed in Sect. 7.4.1.

At this point, it is necessary to say something about the related terms 'model' and 'view'. In the definition of (Lankhorst et al. 2009, pp. 56–57), a model is 'a purposely abstracted and unambiguous conception of a domain', while a view is 'a representation of a system from the perspective of a related set of concerns'. These definitions do not draw a sharp line between models and views, but it is clear that a view on a large model gives a restricted focus on certain aspects of that model. A view is meant to focus on providing information about a system or domain, while a model *may* provide more elaborate information that can become very complex and may not focus on a particular set of concerns (and associated stakeholders). This makes the view a typical instrument of communication: better fit for achieving some specific communication goal than a complex model that meets a number of such goals all bunched together. Not surprisingly, then, if we talk about 'communication with and about models', views play a key role. However, it is not important to always keep a strict distinction between 'views' and 'models' as long as it is clear that it is possible to 'zoom in' on some aspect of a model and single it out for focused communication. For example, it is not all that interesting to establish whether some process diagram in BPMN is a 'model' or a 'view' on a larger, more complex model

7.1 Introduction

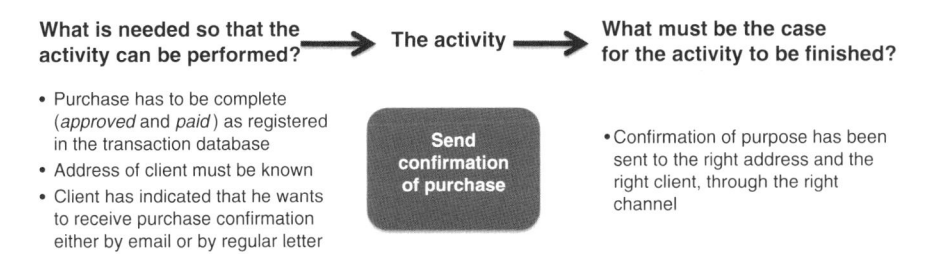

What is needed so that the activity can be performed? → **The activity** → **What must be the case for the activity to be finished?**

- Purchase has to be complete (*approved* and *paid*) as registered in the transaction database
- Address of client must be known
- Client has indicated that he wants to receive purchase confirmation either by email or by regular letter

Send confirmation of purchase

- Confirmation of purpose has been sent to the right address and the right client, through the right channel

Fig. 7.1 Example of a focused view for validation purposes

(perhaps of the entire enterprise). What is important is whether it helps achieve the specific communication goals its creators and users set out to fulfil.

Focused communication lies at the core of our approach to 'stakeholder communication with and about models'. By identifying communication goals and abilities and then selecting and applying certain practices or techniques to meet them, you can better cope with the many diverse communication challenges you might face.

In Fig. 7.1, a simple view is shown for describing pre- and post-conditions for an activity in some process model. The information gathered in the view goes beyond the typical information represented in a flow chart, even if it includes business or data objects. The extra information contributes to the validation of the main (process) model by business experts, as it implies that certain activities have to be finished before this one and some will have to come after it. While this may not be terribly urgent from a analysis point of view, the example serves to highlight that for one main process model, a number of specialized, focused views can help greatly in systematically 'talking through' a model.

We cannot possibly give a complete overview of all communication situations and possible set-ups to deal with them. Therefore, we will give some examples of situations and recommendable practices and show you how you can analyse and deal with communication situations in general.

The chapter is structured as follows. In Sect. 7.2, we will explain what communication situations are, give an overview of the aspects involved, and in general, provide a backbone for talking about and organizing communication in service development projects. In Sect. 7.3, we turn towards more operational ways of bringing insights in communication into practice: how to embed the creation of communication set-ups for specific situations in a general agile way of working. After this generic part, we spend some time elaborating on certain key points. In Sect. 7.4, we consider various aspects concerning individual stakeholders. In particular, we explore two sources of differences between stakeholders important in working with them: their languages (Sect. 7.4.1) and their cognitive and abstraction skills (Sect. 7.4.2). In Sect. 7.5, we elaborate on how visualization can be applied effectively through using visualization patterns so that the result is optimally fit for human consumption. The chapter is rounded off in Sect. 7.6 with an overview of a number of newly formulated 'communication practices' summarizing the communication-related results of the ASD project in an applied context; we illustrate them with examples from practice.

7.2 Communication Situations

With a lot of communication going on all the time, it pays to think about what a particular situation that you may encounter demands in terms of communication and, of course, to use this insight in organizing the communication so that it is both effective and efficient. This is why we introduce the following notion.

> *Communication Situation* (CS): An interactive session between people involved in service development, during which a structured, meaningful, purposeful exchange of information takes place.

People involved may be stakeholders, users, developers, or others. The situation may or may not be part of an explicit project planning method, and it may, in itself, also be guided by a predefined method/technique, or not. Interaction may be online or face to face. We focus on 'model-oriented communication situations', but this includes CSs that only *indirectly* involve models (e.g. they could concern only a textual representation of some specialized view of a model). In principle, anything goes, but we will try to help you make sense of it.

Communication situations typically have a *goal*, the achievement of which results in progress for the project. A *series* of operational CSs will often be required to fulfil the larger project goals. For example, if a goal in the project is to 'create and validate a domain model', then it is to be expected that more than one CS (i.e. several *sessions*) will be needed to achieve this. There will be *tangible outcomes*, such as a model or a structured description of knowledge elicited during a session, and *social outcomes*, such as shared vision, shared understanding, and model acceptance (understanding, consensus, commitment). Sessions in which such results are worked towards may require careful preparation, possibly even including the selection and assessment of participants and, in any case, some thinking about the documentation, knowledge, and skills required to run the session: its 'input', which includes both artefacts and people.

We will first take a look at how to identify and describe CSs. This starts with a practical way of identifying and 'naming' CSs. There are very many possible CSs, and they are very diverse. We recommend to label them using a combination of two aspects: the *basic communication activity* performed in the situation and the *main artefact* on which this activity focuses.

The main activities you can expect to encounter are (A stands for any 'artefact'):

- Create A.
- Change A.
- Comment on A.
- Inform about A.
- Evaluate A.
- Prioritize/scope A.

7.2 Communication Situations

This may seem to be a very limited list; surely, you might think of many, many more activities. You are free to choose and name activities any way you like, and the list can certainly be added to, but we do point out that the short list above covers the main, concrete activities normally encountered in view of 'handling an artefact'. Other, more refined activity names can usually be seen as either very similar or a combination. For example, what about 'Review A'? Surely that is done a lot? Well, a review may be just an opportunity for people to *comment*, but it may (also) include and *evaluation*. In addition, it may include suggestions for *change*. So a review can be any one of the following combinations of activities:

- Comment.
- Evaluate.
- Comment and evaluate.
- Comment and change.
- Evaluate and change.
- Comment and evaluate and change.

So you can safely use the term 'review', but it pays to at least make clear what you mean by this in terms of the basic activities we listed. Also, it is quite possible to combine various basic activities in one session or CS, but it may be a good idea to see whether the activity can be broken up in successive smaller ones (e.g. first comment, then change) to increase the focus of the single activities.

As for artefacts, there is really no sensible way to be comprehensive here. The list is virtually endless. Just to give some examples: process models, domain models, business rule specifications, requirements, use cases, product inventories, application architectures, architecture principles, transformation models, business goals, and service signatures. And this is a fairly random list that could have easily been ten times as long. So we do not even try to categorize the deliverables in any definitive way here. Still, there are some ways of looking at them that might be helpful, and one good way of sorting them out would be using the reference framework for service modelling introduced in Chap. 4 of this book, which provides an overview of the different subjects, conceptual foci, and uses of the main model-oriented artefacts relevant in service development.

In the end, however, the most important bit from a communication perspective is that for everyone involved, the artefact label you use is clear and well understood: people know what artefact you mean and preferably also what purpose(s) it serves in project context. Artefacts take many shapes and may involve many different media: they can be digital or paper, draft or highly official, highly specialized or meant for a wide audience, confidential or public, external or internal, and so on and so forth. We cannot tell you what they are like and what they are for: only you, as a 'user', can. We just point out that you can ask some simple questions concerning every artefact you encounter, work with or work on, for example:

- What is it used for?
- What is it about?
- Who is it for?

- What is it based on?
- Who produced it (or will produce it), and what do they (have to) know for that?
- What terminology, concepts, or modelling languages are used in it?
- How was/is it made: what was/is the process or set-up leading to its creation?

It is important to see that it may be risky to assume that 'a model' always concerns the same single artefact and the same way of dealing with it in communication. There are at least three reasons why 'the same model' may need to be approached differently in a different communication situation and possibly also as a different artefact:

- Depending on the phase of the project, the 'same' model may be created or used for different *purposes*.
- Depending on the purpose, the *focus*, *scope*, *level of detail*, and *level of agreement* on the model that may be quite different.
- Also depending on the purpose, but even more on the people/stakeholders involved in dealing with the model, different *representations* of the model (or parts of it) may be used.

As described in Chap. 6, based on the goals set, risks involved, and further situational factors present, suggestions can be derived for the use of agile *practices* as well as *activities* in some project. Once it is sufficiently clear, in enough detail, what the goals and practices and activities are that need to be taken up, it is time to move to operational planning of meetings or other types of interaction that should lead to realization of the goals. Part of these activities concerns the type of communication situations we focus on: model-oriented communication with and among stakeholders. You can proactively look at communication situations you are planning and try to organize them in an effective way. This will not only save time and money, but, usually, it also reassures people involved that someone knows what is needed and how to get the job done.

This does not mean that every CS can be planned, nor that a plan or set-up, once conceived, cannot be changed (even radically). However, even if trouble strikes or unexpected things happen in a session, a structured way of looking at the communication situation will help a lot in dealing with the issues at hand.

The main instruments we offer to view CSs in a structured way are two 'communication situation templates' (CSTs): the *intentional* CST (covering goals, and the given situation) and the *operational* CST (covering the CS set-up: how it is to be organized). In the current section, we will introduce the intentional CST; the operational CST will be covered in the next section (7.3). The templates show some overlap in content, but their *use* is what really sets them apart (*situational analysis* versus *operational planning*).

As we have seen, communication-intensive activities of the kind we are looking at here typically involve artefacts (models, software, documentation) as well as more immaterial, social results like consensus, commitment, enthusiasm, etc. Which artefacts have to be created in the activity and, more importantly, which *quality requirements* are involved with the artefact (completeness, level of detail,

7.2 Communication Situations

level of commitment/validation) are mostly determined by the goal of the activity. For example, a goal could be 'reducing the risks of which the severity and impact currently are unknown'.

Analogous to situational method engineering (see Chap. 6), but at a more operational, interactive level, practices for model-oriented communication situations can be used for driving successful communication situations in agile service development. Some such practices (sometimes represented as patterns) have been suggested as part of existing methods or textbooks, some new ones are resented in this chapter, and plenty could be added or refined by you or your organization. Listing them exhaustively is almost impossible. Just becoming aware of them, and generally of the fact that such patterns exist and can be used, is a good start. Illustrative examples of existing communication practices are discussed in Sect. 7.3.2.

Moving from practices to a way of matching specific sets of practices to specific communication situation, the following structure can be used. A communication situation is meant to realize some **activity** (*create, change, comment on, inform about, evaluate, prioritize, scope*) concerning some **artefact**. The artefact is to capture a specific **state** (*as is, to be*, or both) for a specific **purpose** (achieving a *project goal*) by involving a particular **role in the organization** with a specific **profile** (*background, knowledge, competences*). The actual **domain** about which communication will take place is also an important input variable for the pattern, concerning 'content' rather than 'action'. It is likely to play an important role in determining the structure or language (topics, concepts; semantics) that are to be used and covered in the artefact under consideration. Also, it may determine which design patterns may be used in the creation of the artefact (see Chap. 5).

> **Example: AgiSurance Product Model**
>
> In the context of our AgiSurance case, *how well the complexity of a certain insurance product is understood* is a risk factor. The risk can be managed by creating a *product model*. The intentional communication situation template (I-CST) described in Fig. 7.2 applies here. Such a description provides a very useful and workable overview of the communication situation at hand, from a 'demand' point of view.

The distinction between 'intentional' (goal-oriented, sorting out the context and the high-level pre- and post-conditions of what needs to be done) and 'operational' (active shaping of the set-up of the situation: getting the goals realized) seems simple enough, but experience shows that some confusion lurks. In particular, it is not always clear whether to put something under 'intentions' or 'operations', i.e. whether to put it in the I-CST or the O-CST, or even in both. In many cases, the choice is simple. For example, if the project approaches demands that a domain model is created of some domain because various stakeholders need to agree on basic concepts on which a service is based, then creation of that domain model,

Goal	Activity and artifact	Creating a product model for insurance products
	Purpose	Understanding product complexity
	State	As-is situation
Stakeholder	Role	Product developers
	Profile	Having overview of products
		Having overview of product characteristics
		Ability to abstract over instances of products
		Ability to identify relations between products
		Ability to identify discriminating characteristics between products
Domain		Life insurances

Fig. 7.2 Instantiated intentional communication situation template (I-CST)

involving a certain level of agreement (social goal) among participants, clearly belongs in the intentional template.

The operational template is where operational (practical, concrete) choices need to be made aimed at realization. This often requires making some goals (even rather concrete ones) even more concrete. For example, actual people who will participate need to be selected, invited, and briefed. In the intentional template, these people *may* have been named explicitly (in which case they are probably mentioned in both the intentional and the operational CST). But in many cases, only stakeholder *types* will have been mentioned in the intentional template (e.g. 'legal expert' or 'product owner'). In such cases, the operational CST will refine the intentional CST by naming actual people fitting the types. It is also possible that in the I-CST, no specific thought is given to stakeholders. In that case, people will still have to be assigned: domain models do not appear out of thin air. In such cases, only the O-CST and not the I-CST will cover stakeholders involved. For quite a few other aspects, only the O-CST will be relevant. For example, spatial set-up (how to organize the room some session takes place in) normally does not belong in the intentional template.

> **Example: AgiSurance Product Development**
>
> To create better insight in its product portfolio, AgiSurance decides to use an online card sorting game, in which cards with various product characteristics and relations are used to group products into useful categories, by domain experts supported by a facilitator.
>
> In Fig. 7.3, we present the operational communication situation template (O-CST). In the example, the filled-in template matches the example I-CST (Fig. 7.2), demonstrating a possible way to realize the goals set there.

7.2 Communication Situations

Artefact creation pattern		Fragments-to-networks
Technique		Card sorting game
Structure	Language/concepts	Product, relations between products, characteristics of products
	Headings	Product categories
Representation	Verbalization	Natural language
	Visualization	Lists of category groups
Artefact		Set of categorized products with similar and discriminating product characteristics
Level of detail		All products, global description of product characteristics, full validated description of discriminating product characteristics
Practices		Comprehensible over Comprehensive
Facilitator	Name	Jane Doe
	Role in activity	Introducing scenarios for grouping products/product characteristics
	Profile: expertise, skills	Domain knowledge not too detailed (open mind for new concepts). Ability to abstract and ability to capture the reason why stakeholder will group certain characteristics.
	Attitude	Open minded
Participant(s)	Name	John Smith
	Role in organization	Chief Product Manager
	Role in activity	Domain expert
	Profile: expertise, skills	Detailed knowledge of products; no advanced analytical skills required
	Attitude	Collaborative; critical attitude to correct specification
Media		Cardsort tool on iPad; whiteboard
Space		Room 3.2; seats grouped around table.
Time		Synchronous; Feb 31, 2012, 10.00-16.00h

Fig. 7.3 Instantiated operational communication situation template (O-CST)

One special source of confusion about whether to include some aspect in the I-CST or the O-CST is the adoption of communication practices as part of the *generic* project approach instead of just for a particular CS. For example, the approach chosen for a project may explicitly include the 'model storming' practice. In such a case, even some operational aspects of organizing that type of communication situation are known at the start of project: the general way of working imposes method choices (practices). If in such a case you use the I-CST as well as the O-CST, we recommend that you put clear goal-oriented aspects in the I-CST (encouraging situational reflection on the usefulness of model storming in the project communication context) but still put clearly operational matters (like spatial planning or specific people assigned) in the O-CST.

7.3 Communication Set-Ups

Having discussed various aspects and contexts of communication situations, we have now arrived at the question how we can organize such situations at an operational level: get together the people, and structure and guide activities. In this section, we will give you some advice on how to approach this challenge.

7.3.1 Artefact Creation Patterns and Communication Practices

Not every model-oriented CS requires the same way of dealing with sources (documents or people) and combining them or evolving them into an end product. This is of considerable influence to how you arrange your set-up (one CS or a series of CSs; which goals and foci to set for each session). At the 'Collaborative Usage and Development of Models and Visualizations' (CollViz) workshop (part of the ECSCW conference in Aarhus, Denmark, Sept 2011), the participants defined six 'artefact creation patterns' (Fig. 7.4). They are:

1. Merging (negotiating your way from some similar but different artefacts to a single common artefact)
2. Combination (piecing together an artefact from various given parts)
3. Growth (starting with a central item and systematically adding items)
4. Linking (taking artefacts for what they are, but defining relations between them)
5. Fragments-to-networks (starting with a bunch of ill-defined, isolated items and gradually refining and relating them)
6. Reuse (selecting existing items and putting them together into a new artefact; note that the selection sets this one apart from 2).

Clearly, such patterns may be combined and refined. Mostly, they can help you in determining how to organize the steps to be taken in your CS or CSs.

Many existing practices are documented in the professional and academic literature that refer to or directly describe 'ways of communicating'. Such 'communication practices' can always be used to help fill in the O-CST, and if they are described in problem-context-solution format, they may even be used to select a practice based on the I-CST. In particular, if your organization or project is keen on using standards (internal or external), it is worthwhile to explicitly document the practices you use or even describe any newly developed or refined practices you find useful to 'keep for posterity'.

7.3 Communication Set-Ups

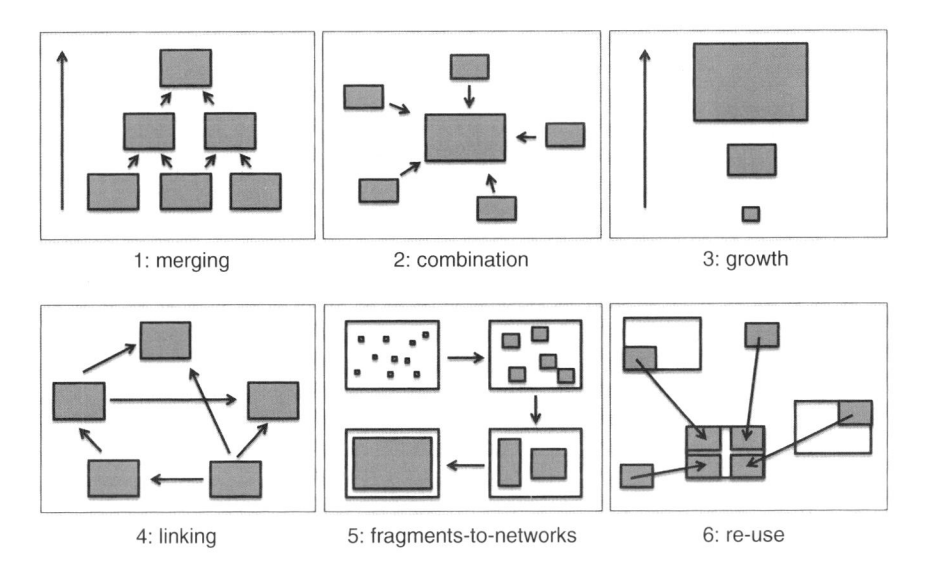

Fig. 7.4 Visualizations of six common artefact creation patterns

So let us consider just five examples of existing communication practices taken from the literature and how they fit our framework:

7.3.1.1 Communicate Powerfully

'A team needs to have effective means of communicating, both amongst team members and also to stakeholders. To communicate powerfully, a team needs to prefer in-person communication over distributed communication. Synchronous over asynchronous communication. High-bandwidth over low-bandwidth communication. Multi-mode communication over single-mode communication' (Agile Advice 2006). This quite generic practice bundles a lot of advice on how to communicate in an agile context. However, it should not be blindly applied in every CS! For example, in-person communication has much to say for it, but in many situations, distributed communication is either the only option available or has significant advantages. We prefer more diversity and situational nuance in dealing with communication situations.

7.3.1.2 Comprehensible Over Comprehensive

'To create documentation that will actually be read, we have to take the audience into account. Documentation needs to be comprehensible for the targeted audience, or it will become TAGRI (They Aren't Gonna Read It) documentation.' (Xebia 2010). This is a practice that we wholeheartedly subscribe to. We would replace 'documentation' with 'artefacts', but that hardly changes anything. The practice is a variation on our approach to let clear communication goals drive your communication set-ups.

7.3.1.3 Daily Stand-Up

'Each day during the sprint, a project status meeting occurs. This is called a 'daily scrum', or 'daily stand-up'. The meeting is usually time-boxed to around 15 min and held at the same time and place every working day. All team members are encouraged to attend, but the meetings are not postponed if some of the team members are not present'. This practice is a neat example of a quite comprehensively prescribed 'communication set-up'. It is a key part of the Scrum approach (Schwaber and Beedle 2002). However, if you choose to apply it, do spend some time thinking about the project goals and communication goals you want to achieve by that, so you know it *really* fits your project, and why.

7.3.1.4 Plan (and Conduct) Interviews

This widely applied practice just suggests the use of a technique, which is one way of realizing a score if information needs. The practice as formulated by Graham aims (2007) at answering a clear question, 'How do you discover relevant but implicit business knowledge?'

7.3.1.5 Ten-Minute Rule a.k.a. Two-Minute Rule

This is a nicely detailed practice by Graham (2007) that sets a cut-off point for discussion of a detailed issue in a group session: if after ten (or two) minutes of discussion the issue remains unresolved, 'park' it until later to avoid getting bogged down. This sort of practice can be used in many different CSs, applying different set times, and has a very concrete impact on how a CS set-up is realized: it helps maintain sufficient focus. It is a typical guideline for *facilitation*.

7.3.2 Structures, Languages, Representations; Topics

If they are not given in the I-CST (and this will often be the case), you will have to decide on which representations, structures, views, or even model types you want to actually work within your CS. Much advice in this area can be found in Chap. 4. You may be choosing a model type (e.g. 'process model') and a language (e.g. 'BPMN'), but note that in this category, it may also be enough to simply devise a table of contents or some headings for a document. In any case, think

7.3 Communication Set-Ups

through your choices in view of what you want to achieve, and whether your representation directly contributes to this. 'KISS' (Keep It Simple, Stupid) applies here.

Furthermore, always consider who you will involve in the CS and whether they will be able to cope with the type of representation used. Which visualizations or verbalizations work best for your stakeholders/participants? If you need to involve various consecutive representations to achieve your communication goals, how do they map to each other, and does the mapping require extra information or further abstraction?

Thinking up a CS set-up (or a set of closely related ones) will usually require some creative goals—means thinking. For example, you may need some representation that does not go down well with the intended participants (e.g. they don't know BPMN). In such a case, there are two main ways out: either involve other participants or (more likely) find an alternative way of talking about the concepts covered by the BPMN diagram you want to eventually arrive at. This will often mean that you have to extend the communication activities and split them up: perhaps first perform a 'walk-through' and develop some scenarios; then develop a first BPMN diagram 'offline' and create a verbalization of it; then validate this verbalization with your stakeholders. Alternatively, you may use simplified versions of BPMN. In some cases, you will just have to discuss every inch of the diagram with the stakeholders, but whether this is needed pretty much depends on the *social goal*: how deep does the understanding, consensus, or commitment have to be? It is up to you, but *keep your eye on the goals* and do not ignore signs that people cannot cope or get annoyed with what they are asked to do.

This relates to a rather difficult issue: the level of detail of your discussion and representation. On the one hand, this very much depends on your goals, but on the other hand, you need to keep things efficient and feasible. Primarily, you have to watch out for activities in which people keep adding detail just for its own sake. If you miss out on detail, you can usually go back and refine. If you give too much detail, however, this may not only be a waste of time but also cause confusion: people may have to abstract again from your detail. However, in certain cases a high level of detail *is*, of course, needed. In such cases, be prepared to take all the time needed. Just do not simply *assume* some generic level of detail for a certain type of artefact: choose your level of detail according to the situation at hand. This is, of course, completely in line with the general Agility Principle.

Importantly, never forget that concepts, structures, modelling languages, etc. are less important than simply *knowing what you want to know* and *why you want to know it*. These pragmatic goals, leading to a pragmatic focus (or simply put, the setting of a clear *topic*), are what should drive your CS; at the end of the day, conceptual 'lenses' like modelling languages are just semantic and syntactic means to help achieve clear *pragmatic focus* (Hoppenbrouwers and Wilmont 2010). If you master a language, but do not know what to talk about using it, you make for poor, unfocused modelling.

7.3.3 Participants and Facilitation

No communication without participants; no participants without communication. Participants in communication situations may be selected to fulfil project goals (as reflected in the O-CST), but their participation may also be *part* of the project goals (I-CST); thirdly, participations may be actively involved in *setting* the goals. Participants may well act on individual motives, which may be hidden or out in the open; they may represent larger groups or organizations; and they may have some degree of power or authority, and certain expertise (e.g. domain knowledge) and skills (applied capabilities, apart from domain knowledge). They will have a certain set of concepts, words, and languages they are familiar with, and which they may like or dislike. They will display a positive or a negative attitude towards the goals and the way of working in the project; they may have doubts, biases, convictions; they may be heroes; they may be diplomatic; they may be warriors; and they may be bloody mindedly vindictive. They may even be stupid or geniuses. The point is you will have to work with them. If you can select them, do so with an eye on the I-CST and the O-CST; if they are simply there, in project context, work with them in the best configuration possible, and take their individual characteristics and goals seriously insofar you know them. It may be necessary to try and find out more about them first.

This is not the place to discuss matters of group dynamics and social skills. However, in practice, social factors (including inter-human relationships and politics) are so important that denying or ignoring them is downright silly. We may declare them 'out of scope', and engineering-oriented perspectives tend to do so, with good reason. However, from a communication and interaction perspective, we have to emphasize the importance of the people factor. In Sect. 7.4, we will have some more to say on some specific aspects: abstraction and psychological skills, and terminology/language.

One particular aspect in selecting participants cannot be left unmentioned here: make sure you do not accidentally leave out key people in the knowledge sharing or decision process. These may be figures of authority, but they may just as well be lower ranking people with a specific responsibility or expertise. Some sessions can be rendered totally useless if the right people don't show up. Whether they do this deliberately (sabotaging the process) or for very mundane reasons (having a bad cold) does not matter; the result is the same. Reschedule a session if necessary, despite the trouble this may take.

The typical person that is responsible for dealing with 'the human factor' in communication situations is the facilitator: the person leading the session, usually in a neutral and supporting role (but with some authority with respect to procedure and matters of order). However, the work of the facilitator also involves planning and organization of interactive sessions, and this, of course, heavily involves the O-CST and its project context. Professional, even certified facilitators exist but are not cheap; in most cases, it is just a fact of life that project members will take up the role of facilitator. In principle, this has the disadvantage that the facilitator may not

7.3 Communication Set-Ups 157

be as neutral and 'objective' as we might wish and that she might even have a stake in the project. On the other hand, a facilitator who knows the participants and what they are dealing with may actually be more effective. It is all a matter of balance; just try not to cross the boundaries of the acceptable.

A further disadvantage of using non-professional facilitators is simply that their level of experience and professional skills may be insufficient to do the job properly. As a middle way, it may be worthwhile investing in some basic facilitation training for certain members of your organization.

7.3.4 Space and Time; Media, Tools, and Technologies

Finally, there are the quite concrete matters of space, time, and 'tooling'. Choose your space wisely; do not stuff too many people in small, poorly ventilated spaces; make sure the set-up of tables, chairs, and media like flip overs, whiteboards, or projectors is adequate. This also holds for digital media, if you use them: availability and positioning of screens, laptops, etc. In some cases, recording devices (audio or video; smart screens) may also require spatial planning. Alternatively, the whole spatial factor may be less relevant because you work in 'virtual space': online, via individual screens or through projection. This may take place with everyone in a different room (even on a different continent), but some people may also be physically together while others 'call in' or 'beam in'. Note that even in virtual space (i.e. on individual screens), spatial thinking can play a role; for example, advanced set-ups for video conferencing often emulate 'physical' meeting rooms by projecting images in fixed, familiar positions, even 'at a virtual table'.

As for time, for regular meetings, this boils down to planning (setting a date and a time; not having too much time pass between sessions) and pacing (when to have breaks, how long to continue). Estimating how long some activity will take is always a challenge, and you do not want to waste people's time (in particular if senior staff is involved).

Another temporal matter to take into consideration is that of working *synchronously* (in direct and immediate interaction, in 'real time') or *asynchronously* (with longer intervals between interactions, preventing immediate replies in interaction). Note that these notions do not apply to digital media only: sending a document for review via good old snail mail concerns asynchronous communication just as well as sending an email. Also note that, in particular, when using digital media, the distinction between synchronous and asynchronous is blurring. After all, if you send emails as immediate replies, this hardly counts as 'asynchronous', and a 'chat' (typically synchronous) may now be recorded and maintained almost infinitely. All this just means you have an increasing liberty to *choose* your temporal mode of interaction instead of having it imposed by the medium you use.

And then there are the media used, the physical means carrying the communications. Media cover everything from no tech (the air between two people talking) via low tech (a whiteboard) to high tech (smartboards, electronic meeting software, modelling tools, groupware, videoconferencing). Low tech often works fine; only use high tech if you are sure it contributes something besides a high gadget factor, and make very sure you *test* stuff before you use it. Mr. Murphy really enjoys high tech.

Despite our advice to use high tech media wisely and perhaps conservatively, we do not want to take a position that is adverse to high tech, in particular to asynchronous and distributed (online) communication. Technology has advanced tremendously, and, for example, chat, video conferencing, and groupware have become truly available to almost every professional now. Many people still feel such new media are 'second choice': you only use them if there is no 'real-life', face-to-face alternative; the 'communicate powerfully' practice mentioned in Sect. 7.3.1.1 is a case in point. While indeed face-to-face communication is most natural and provides optimal information on nuances like non-verbal expression, body language, and so on, virtual forms of communication also have great advantages. Tricky negotiations with people you don't trust should of course only be conducted face to face. However, collaborative work in context of global collaboration has become standard in some branches of industry, and younger generations are *quite* used to communicating intensively through mobile devices like laptops and smartphones. Digital media just take a certain amount of getting used to. Choose your medium objectively, and do not let cultural prejudice or conservatism deprive you of good opportunities to improve your communication through using either low tech or high tech means as best match your communication situation.

7.4 Communication Needs and Capabilities of Stakeholders

In this section, we take a closer look at the many different people that may be involved in communication about model-related artefacts. Though our main focus is on 'stakeholders', i.e. typically people from 'the business' somehow involved in service development (so not the group called 'developers'), it is worth emphasizing that some of the developers (or 'IT people') are involved in most communication with stakeholders in one way or another.

As we already pointed out, even to refer to 'the business' or 'stakeholders' in general is an enormous generalization, even worse than referring to 'IT people'. Similarly, some quite general terms are sometimes used to label roles for stakeholders, often in method textbooks on modelling: 'domain expert' or 'informant'. Clearly, this represents a very limited viewpoint. There are many different roles to play for stakeholders, and their backgrounds, insights, interests, concerns, vocabularies, attitudes, knowledge, and skills may also vary greatly. What many of them share is that they are not of the 'engineering' persuasion (engineers usually share a specific view on organizations and systems that is rather different from that of 'business people'), but even this depends on the situation. For example, in highly technology-oriented enterprises, it is possible that your stakeholder is more technology minded than you are. The main point being: be aware of the worldviews and backgrounds of the people involved, and do not underestimate how different they may be compared to other people involved—including you.

Just to give some examples of the diverse nature of 'stakeholders': they could be sponsors, (end-)users, product managers, business analysts, product owners, product marketeers, legal specialists, and dozens things more. If you go and look in large companies, a whole range of company-specific terms to label different roles tends to buzz around.

This brings us to another important point that is often ignored by textbooks and organizational culture alike. Stakeholders do not primarily belong to some fixed 'type' or 'role'. First and foremost, they are individuals, who may or may not precisely 'fit' a general type. For example, if you enthusiastically start 'doing business modelling' with a bunch of lawyers, you may be in for a nasty surprise—and then again, you may not. Generally, lawyers will be 'text people' and they will not be happy about 'doing diagrams'. They will characterize business process models as 'technical', no matter if you agree with that or not. They will also typically refuse to be very specific and explicit about details that from their professional perspective are best left unspecified, so some room is left for interpretation. But then again, you may meet a lawyer who has somehow gained experience in working with process models, and who sees the need to strictly specify some workflow in view of automation of a decision process.

The two subsections below introduce some interesting and useful applications of research, looking at individual participants in communication situations from two rather different angles: one focusing on stakeholder language (in particular, how stakeholders interpret modelling concepts) and one focusing on basic skills of stakeholders and how they match their capability to deal with models, involving abstraction of some kind.

7.4.1 Measuring the Meaning of Concepts

One of the basic needs that stakeholders have in a communication situation is to *be understood*. While they have concrete goals to achieve (e.g. to have their interests properly represented in a model or product or to see certain requirements complied with), those goals cannot be reliably achieved unless others involved understand what they attempt to communicate. This depends not only on the ability of a stakeholder to formulate her opinions and needs clearly but also on a shared linguistic background so that the meaning of the words used by different stakeholders is compatible.

Meaning has two sides here: personal meaning (i.e. how a specific person understands things) and agreed-upon or shared meaning (i.e. how people have agreed to talk about things). Together, these sides determine whether stakeholders have 'compatible meaning systems' (or to use the technical term: compatible *semantics*). Personal meaning is important because most, if not all, people reason by using the semantics of their natural language and real-world experiences and not using formal specifications or agreements (Sowa 2000). Because of this, even if in some communication situations a relevant professional dictionary (covering some kind of 'jargon') is available and agreed upon, there will still be semantic influences from the personal understanding that an individual stakeholder has. Because of this, it is quite risky to just assume that every stakeholder means *exactly* the same with the jargon they use.

To exemplify this, take some of the common constructs used in conceptual modelling languages: actors, resources, restrictions, and so on. While most people will easily agree that an actor is 'something that acts', what exactly that *something* is can (and often should!) be a matter of discussion. Some people might immediately think of Hollywood actors, and from that perspective, actors must be *human beings that act*. Others might look at it from an industrial production line point of view and interpret actors as *machines that act*. Looking at this in more detail, there could be a discussion on whether actors are always easily singled out and identified (*singular things that act*) or whether, for instance, people working together as a group can be seen as a single actor—*composed things that act*. In most situations, these different interpretations cannot be simply represented by the exact same concept in a modelling language: for example, in some modelling languages, actors typically must be *human beings that act*, so a computer system that does something cannot be represented with that notation. So what is to be done when another stakeholder wants to include a computer system as an actor in some process model?

Clearly, in artefacts that require a high level of detail and precision, understanding the exact semantics used by people involved is necessary to make sure that the models created are an actual representation of what their creators mean. If we ignore such issues and just pretend everyone understands each other, misunderstandings may propagate through development stages and may eventually even lead to costly, but necessary, corrections in products that have already been implemented and deployed. For agility's sake, it is necessary to detect and resolve these kinds of misunderstandings as early as possible in the modelling phase.

Unfortunately, truly understanding what someone means by something is quite a challenge, even for communication situations involving rather narrow professional vocabularies. You might set out to explicitly define all terms, but all the possible details that contribute to describing the complete meaning someone has for a specific concept would add up to such an unwieldy nest of definitions that it rapidly becomes unworkable. This is reflected in the fact that the conceptual models that we produce are often quite incomplete specifications of our conceptualizations (Guarino 1998). We just cannot effectively 'gauge' someone's complete conceptualization of a domain from the models they produce or the verbalizations they utter without investigating the individual as such.

Characterizing people and their semantics by focusing on the details that matter is a feasible approach. Standardized *discriminants*, points on which people often differ in understanding, are a useful and manageable way of figuring out how different people understand terms. These discriminants can be properties that are often points of discussion, divide people into different groups, and so on. For example, the properties 'composed' and 'intentional' often come up in relevant distinctions between concepts. A possible method for discovering different understandings of words, assuming that the concepts and their discriminants are known, is called the *semantic differential* (Osgood et al. 1957). Pairs of words that have a meaning linked to a discriminant ('is it human', 'is it material', 'is it intentional', and so on) can be used to find out how strongly people feel about these factors and to determine whether someone would stereotypically understand concepts as being like them—actors being single human beings, resources being composed material resources, and so on.

You can build such semantic differentials for groups of people fairly easily if you know what discriminants you want to investigate. For instance, if you want to chart the different understandings people have whether something is human or not, all you need to do is figure out which words ring true and strong about that property, for instance, asking people whether something 'is self-aware', 'has feelings', and, the obvious, 'is human'. With enough of these adjectives, you can find a statistically significant score for any discriminant you want to investigate.

The results from such a semantic differential can be visualized as simple graphs (see Fig. 7.5) which show how someone thinks about different dimensions of a word. For example, Fig. 7.5 shows how two different people understand the concept *restriction*. The orange pattern has a decidedly neutral response to most dimensions—implying that person either has little experience or is simply completely neutral about the concept. The other person, represented by the blue line, has stronger responses to some of the dimensions. The scores for whether something is composed and whether it is vague are strongly negative, meaning this person understands restrictions as specifically detailed singular 'things'. The scores for whether something is necessary and intentional, on the other hand, are very positive, meaning that this person sees restrictions as things that are intentionally created and necessary to adhere to.

Patterns like these can be used to verify the semantic range of a model someone creates by indicating what this person would typically mean by common concepts like actor, restriction, and so on (van der Linden et al. 2011). The patterns in Fig. 7.5 are more than just assistants for model integration—they show how two specific people think about modelling concepts. Such individual-based understandings could also be used to match people and technology, both by matching those people who have similar understandings and by giving them the tools (e.g. modelling languages) that are closest to their common conceptual understanding(s). Furthermore, how you communicate to your stakeholders and users can be personalized by understanding them, effectively enabling you to create service versions aimed at specific user groups (Hoppenbrouwers 2003).

7.4.2 Abstraction Skills in Talking About Models

Most communication situations, in particular those involving models, concern rational thinking. They are typically problem-solving-oriented discussions, based on a logical argumentation and split-second decision making, requiring unambiguous

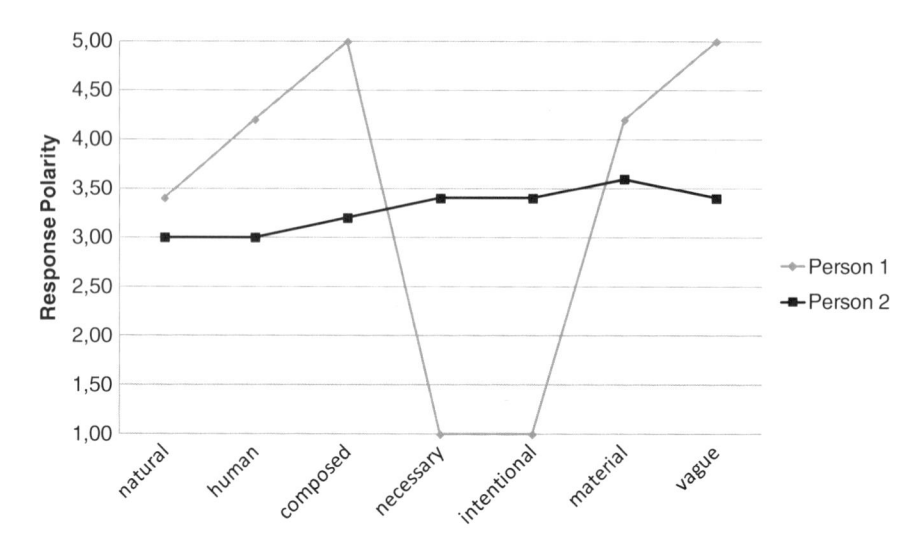

Fig. 7.5 A semantic differential graph for the conceptual understanding of 'restriction'

concepts. They will largely conform to the rules of proper discussion (van Eemeren and Grootendorst 2004).

But creating, discussing, evaluating, and changing models take the game to a higher level. A rational communication situation is characterized by a clear goal, towards which participants should continually work, which often involves structuring knowledge and information in a precise and unambiguous way. Communication in such a situation often concerns models, which can serve multiple purposes: ranging from a simple illustration of a complex point being made to representing a whole body of complex domain knowledge.

To get a stronger grip on all this rationality and abstraction stuff, let us look into some psychology. What capacities do participants in a model-oriented communication process need in order to successfully execute this highly specific type of task? One of the most important skills is the ability to fluently comprehend and reason with *abstractions*. This capacity heavily depends on one's background knowledge and cognitive capacities. Background knowledge and experience influence what participants consider to be 'abstract' and 'concrete'. Cognitive capacities influence the extent to which people can comprehend abstractions and how fast they can learn to make abstractions. Furthermore, individuals differ with respect to the level of abstraction to which people can take their reasoning.

Neuroscientific research shows that the brain responds to at least three different levels of abstraction: *concrete*, *first order* (a relation between two concrete objects), and *second order* (a relation between two first order concepts) Christoff and Keramatian (2007). Concrete talk is typically illustrated with a real-life scenario or a first-hand experience. A first-order abstraction could be, for instance, two different types of *signals* like a letter and a phone call, which both share the property 'signal' but require to be differentiated because they are associated with

7.4 Communication Needs and Capabilities of Stakeholders

a different physical action. An example of a second-order abstraction is, for instance, viewing two abstract concepts like 'signal' and 'end of a period' as 'process triggers', because they both trigger identical activities even though they come from different sources.

There are several key cognitive processes that deserve special attention when dealing with abstract reasoning. These are known as *executive functions.* They control and manage other cognitive processes, and conscious awareness of the executive functions is essential for successful modelling. An operational definition of the executive processes is given by (Ylvisaker et al. 1998):

- Knowing what is easy and what is difficult
- Goal setting
- Planning behaviour to achieve the goal
- Initiating behaviour towards achievement
- Inhibiting interfering behaviour
- Monitoring behaviour
- Strategic thinking
- Flexible problem-solving performance

As part of the ASD project, we observed over forty modelling sessions and specifically looked at the cognitive skills used and needed in them. These are some of our findings (Wilmont et al. 2012):

- Concrete illustrations are needed for shared comprehension. Without a shared concrete representation that both participants can visualize, reason with, and provide examples of, there can be no thorough understanding and no further formation of necessary abstractions; progress towards the goal of the communication situation stalls.
- If people talk at different levels of abstraction, several things can happen: either the necessary abstractions are not made because of one person lagging behind or the people who do tag along leave behind the people who cannot cope. In the latter case, the process gets stuck in an initial 'define and represent problem' phase as long as there is no match in abstraction level and understanding. This results in stalling of the process. Discussions then take an unnecessarily long time, with unnecessary details being covered.
- Modelling sessions that do proceed well involve a high level of so-called *monitoring behaviour.* These sessions typically start by stating explicitly what the goals of the session are, and during the course of interaction, attention is frequently turned to these goals and to whether the discussion is still relevant. If not, actions are taken to turn the discussion towards relevant issues again.
- We do find that some social behaviour plays a role in this process. For instance, if a participant perceives that others doubt the quality of his work, feelings of insecurity set in and negatively influence focus and motivation. Also, if a participant works with others who are less capable, and they keep veering off and do not comprehend the crux of the discussion, nor respond to attempts to get it on course again, then his motivation is negatively affected and participation dwindles.

So what can we do to make a modelling process a success?

1. Use concrete scenario illustrations and examples from the participants' daily experience and environment to make abstract concepts clear.
2. Carefully monitor the participants' basic understanding: does everyone perceive the abstraction level of concepts used in the discussion in the same way? Then tailor the concepts used in the session to suit this level. This becomes relevant when moving towards higher levels of abstraction: these still have to be tested and monitored for comprehension with concrete illustrations.
3. Be aware of the *learning process* that takes place as part of the project. With practice, executive processes can become reflexive, and perception of abstraction levels can change as people become familiar with concepts. As people become flexible with abstract reasoning, the process can proceed faster.
4. Monitor what level of conceptual change people can deal with, so that goals may be achieved more quickly and participants who have trouble can be helped, also depending on how crucial they are in the process.
5. Monitor people's progress. How many concrete explanations do they need in order to grasp a concept? How easily do they grasp relations between different concepts? Can they actively reason with these concepts and provide examples of possible scenarios? Or do they only tend towards passive understanding?
6. Carefully monitor the content of the interaction: is everything still relevant to the goals stated? Why have you deviated from focus?
7. Be aware of your own executive functions, as described above in the list by (Ylvisaker et al. 1998). What are you currently doing to ensure the structure of the modelling session is correct, that goals are being achieved, that everything is relevant?
8. After completing the model, explain it to others to verify whether your vision is coherent with those of other stakeholders. Ensure you have not missed important points or made erroneous assumptions. While explaining, make sure that the implicit relations in the model become clear to the stakeholder. These relations, and your thought processes which these relations are based on, are not directly visible to the stakeholder and should therefore be made explicit. Verification occurs as a consequence.

7.5 Model Visualization Guidelines

Visualization is a powerful and important means in communicating models; in fact, some people only call something a model if it is visualization (i.e. a diagram or graph of some sort). While we do not agree with this, we acknowledge that visualizations of models and views are crucial. However, visualization has its own rules, and creating visualizations that 'work' is not always easy, especially if what you visualize is large (i.e. contains many concepts or relations) or complex. In this subsection, we discuss generic rules for making visualizations work.

7.5 Model Visualization Guidelines

Such rules, guidelines, or principles are generally not formally structured and do not provide information on impact and application details. We try and overcome this by structuring these rules as *patterns* instead. This is in line with the general approach in this book and with Chap. 5 in particular. 'Visualization patterns' help practitioners understand the problems associated with using visual model notations and provide concise and precise solutions to those problems in a particular context.

Many of the patterns are based on the principles for visual notation as described by Moody (2009). However, we also draw on literature on aesthetics of graph and model visualization (Eichelberger and Schmid 2009). We try to come up with a comprehensive set of model communication patterns, which is what this subsection is about.

The patterns follow the template suggested by Meszaros and Doble (1998) and have the following constituent elements:

Context: the situations in which the pattern would apply
Problem: a statement of the problem to be solved
Forces: the factors which must be considered when applying the pattern
Solution: the proposed solution to the problem
Examples/Explanation: cases or explanation demonstrating the existence of the recurring problem and the application for the pattern

As the *Context* of all the patterns is designing, or using a modelling language, we will drop the Context from the pattern descriptions below. Let us first consider the semiotic clarity visualization pattern.

7.5.1 Semiotic Clarity

Problem: Lack of correspondence between symbols and concepts the symbols refer to.

Forces: Model symbol redundancy, excess, or overload can cause increase in complexity.

Solution: To limit diagrammatic complexity, it is preferable to have a symbol redundancy when mapping constructs to the language symbols.

Explanation: The semiotic clarity pattern refers to the relation between the shapes, symbols of any modelling language/notation, and the real-world concepts to which those shapes refer. Some modelling languages are simple and use relatively few shapes (circles, rectangles, lines) to represent a whole range of concepts. On the other hand, other more complex languages have a variety of shapes and symbols to represent slightly different concepts. To put this more precisely, when there is no one-to-one correspondence between constructs and symbols, one or more of the following anomalies can occur (Moody 2009):

- *Symbol redundancy* occurs when multiple graphical symbols can be used to represent the same semantic construct.
- *Symbol overload* occurs when two different constructs can be represented by the same graphical symbol.

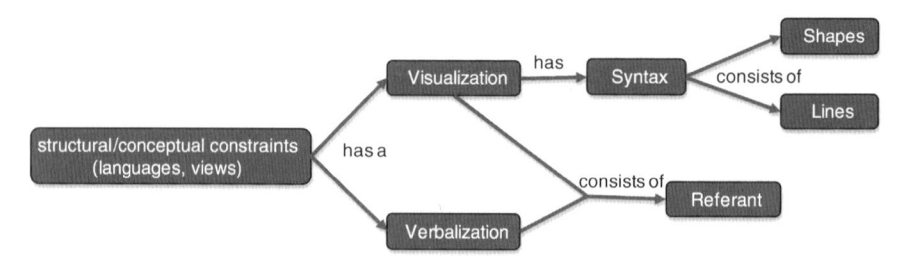

Fig. 7.6 Semiotic clarity pattern

- *Symbol excess* occurs when graphical symbols do not correspond to any semantic construct.
- *Symbol deficit* occurs when there are semantic constructs that are not represented by any graphical symbol.

When the model analyser finds a lack of correspondence between the symbols and the referent concepts, then if it is possible, one can try and reduce the number of symbols being used (as suggested in the pattern solution and, e.g. symbol deficit).

Example: A trivial example of symbol overload can be observed in the diagrams produced by c-map tool (Cañas et al. 2004).

Figure 7.6 represents a conceptual model of any generic modelling language. However, the symbol used for completely different concepts such as visualization, verbalization, shapes, and lines is all the same. In fact, this is a trivial example as c-map supports just one shape for any concept. A related pattern is called *graphic economy*, which suggests that one needs a balance between the numbers of different symbols provided by a modelling language and the expressiveness or effectiveness of the language to communicate to the reader, implying that if a language has too many symbols covering a range of concepts, then the understandability of the models created could be reduced, especially for novices.

7.5.2 Symbol/Edge Overlap

Problem: The model consists of many overlapping symbols and connecting lines/edges, placed randomly.

Forces: When symbols overlap, the symbols are difficult to understand. On the other hand when edges overlap, it could be construed that the edges are meant join and makes it difficult to discern the individual paths of the lines/edges.

Solution: It is best to avoid symbol–symbol, edge–edge, and edge–symbol overlap in models.

Example: In Fig. 7.7, the left represents how edge crossings reduce the aesthetic appeal of a graph/model. In the diagram on the right, the edge crossings are removed, while at the same time, the nodes have been placed in a grid to improve the aesthetic appeal (Bennett et al. 2007).

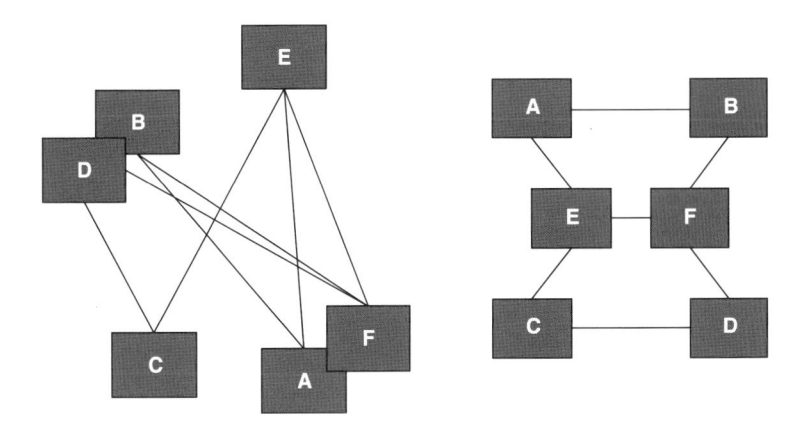

Fig. 7.7 Symbol/edge overlap

The symbol/edge overlap pattern is a typical sample pattern which helps the modeller with aesthetics of the design notation. The other patterns dealing with aesthetics of model visualization deal with the following *minimize edge bends* pattern.

7.5.3 Minimize Edge Bends

Problem: Too many edge bends in a model.

Forces: Edge bends make edges more difficult to follow, as an edge with a bend can be perceived as two edges.

Solution: It is better to try and reduce the number of edge bends in a model—especially in circuit diagrams where bent edges can be trouble spots.

Example: In Fig. 7.8, the graph on the left has two bent edges, while the same graph on the right has no bent edges. Quite clearly, the graph on the right is more elegant.

The *minimize edge bends* pattern is shown by recent empirical evidence to have a greater impact on the understandability of models/graphs compared to the *symbol/edge overlap* pattern (Eichelberger and Schmid 2009). Related patterns include *minimize drawing size,* which supports a homogenous symbol and edge distribution to reduce the need for scrolling the diagram. Similarly, *uniform appearance* pattern focuses on the similarity and homogeneity of the model, emphasizing on short edge lengths, high density of nodes, as well as the use of an underlying grid or symmetry of nodes and edges.

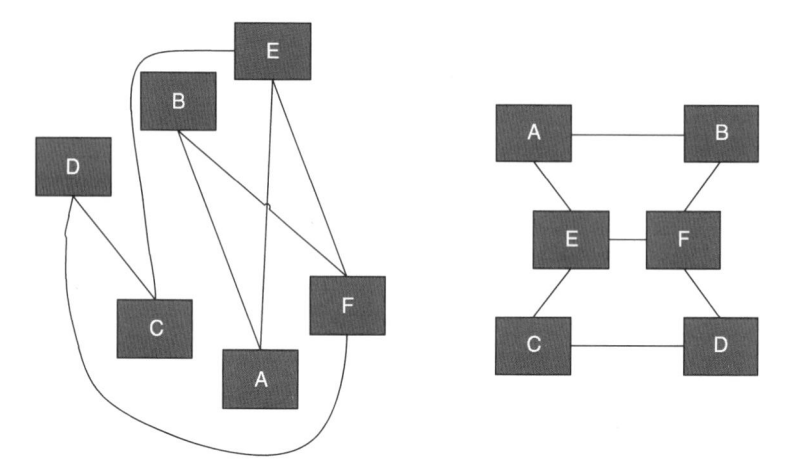

Fig. 7.8 Minimize edge bends

7.5.4 Semantic Transparency

Problem: If the semantic meaning (i.e. the concept referred to by the symbol(s)) of the symbols is different from their intuitive or natural meaning.

Forces: It is very hard for novices to understand symbols that are not intuitive and rather designed without keeping a novice reader in mind.

Solution: Symbols should provide clues to their meaning and need to be 'intuitive' or 'natural'.

Example: Arguably, the figure on the right in Fig. 7.9 provides a better idea of how a Customer: Person and Organization are related, that a customer could be a Person or an Organization and they could overlap.

7.5.5 Complexity Management

Problem: Excessive diagrammatic complexity—a diagram with too many symbols and links—is one of the major barriers to end user understanding of diagrams.

Forces: Complexity has a major effect on cognitive effectiveness as the amount of information that can be effectively conveyed by a single diagram is limited by human perceptual and cognitive abilities.

Solution: Modularization and hierarchy can significantly reduce the complexity of diagrams.

Explanation and Example: Hierarchical organization is seen as a way to manage diagrammatic complexity, while at the same time improving the diagram's aesthetics. In the example below, we show how both clustering and hierarchical representation can help in improving the understandability of a graph. Modularization works by

7.5 Model Visualization Guidelines

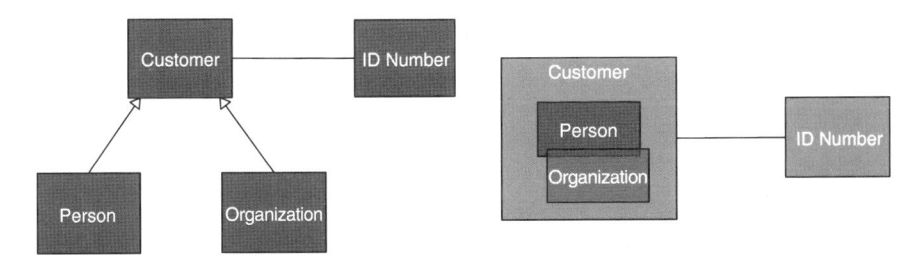

Fig. 7.9 Semantic transparency

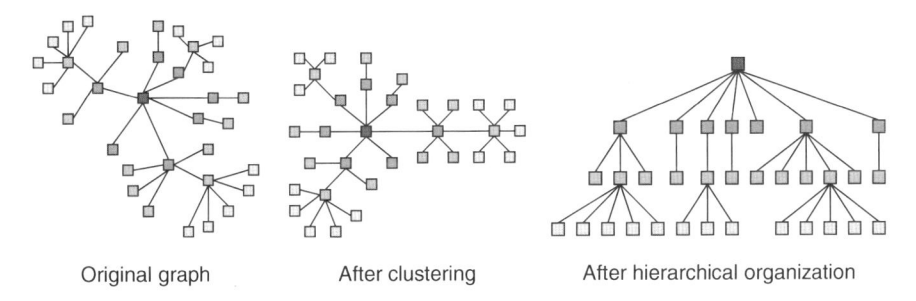

Fig. 7.10 Complexity management

dividing complex domains into smaller parts and, in models, leads to bunching common parts of the model together and represent a domain.

In the first graph of Fig. 7.10, we see the original graph; in the middle figure, we see the clustered version, and in the figure on the right, we see the same graph with a hierarchical layout. Clearly, the central and right figures improve the aesthetics and understandability of the graph by helping the reader navigate to the different sections of the graph. This effect of the application of this pattern would be more evident with a far more complex original graph/model.

Similar to the *hierarchical organization* pattern is the *cognitive integration* pattern that investigates the complexity of multiple models representing the same domain. The *cognitive integration* pattern determines if the different models 'belong together' and represent the domain.

7.5.6 Visual Expressiveness

Problem: Using a small range of visual variables (shapes, colours, line types etc.) reduces the understandability of the diagram.

Forces: The use of few (sometimes one) visual variables to encode information results in the possibility of sometimes only representing minimal data and is hence quite inefficient.

Solution: The visual notation should try to match properties of visual variables to the properties of the information to be represented; use of redundant visual variables is considered better for the notation.

A related pattern is called *perceptual discriminability*—the ability to distinguish between the shapes used to model different concepts. For example, the shapes representing a data store, process, and an entity (in a data flow diagram) should be distinguishable. A data flow diagram where all of them are represented as rectangles would not make them distinct, and hence, they would not be discriminable.

On the other hand, the *dual coding* pattern relates to a judicious combination of text and graphical notation. The pattern suggests that adding text to symbols whose inherent meaning is not evident improves the understandability of the notation.

The *cognitive fit* pattern refers to the problem representation and the strategies required to perform a specific task. Therefore, the *cognitive fit* pattern implies that the cognitive effectiveness of a model could be different for experts and for novices.

A key property of these visualization patterns (that is essential for its optimum usage) is that they are not all completely independent of each other. This is the case with the more cognitive patterns (Moody 2009), as well as the aesthetic model representation patterns (Eichelberger and Schmid 2009). An example of conflicting patterns is that *hierarchical organization* could conflict with *symbol/edge overlap* and *uniform appearance* patterns. Also, the proposed solution of the *graphic economy* pattern clearly conflicts with that of the *visual expressiveness* pattern. The way to handle these conflicting guidelines is to treat the patterns as broad guidelines and strive for a balance—in order to attain maximum model understandability.

7.6 Communication Practices

In this section, we discuss and illustrate a set of communication situation practices. They are the combined best communication practices (and lessons learned) resulting from years of practice and research, and of the recent focus provided by the Agile Service Development project. Please note that these practices are not all applicable in all situations: some apply in *some* situations, as indicated in their descriptions.

7.6.1 Apply Focused Conversations

Many models tend to capture multiple aspects from different perspectives. For example, process models concern roles, events, business processes, process steps, authorization aspects, artefacts, guidelines, SLA requirements, compliance rules, etc. Organizing a modelling session by inviting all stakeholders involved (compliance officers, product developers, process managers, architects) is very ineffective. In such sessions, the focus and perspective are constantly and often implicitly shifting, resulting in loss of the overview, variation in levels of detail concerning the aspects involved, and loss of effectiveness because much time is needed to manage the process. Furthermore, the individual participant will not feel useful and effective all the time and may experience difficulties in understanding aspects of the model outside their own expertise.

The use of chained focused conversations turns out to be much more effective. For each individual aspect and perspective, a focused conversation or mini session is organized. Only relevant stakeholders should be involved. In a focused conversation, only a limited set of techniques and model elements are used. These sessions can be tuned to fit the competences and perspectives of the stakeholders involved. Note that models of the business (e.g. a BPMN model) will not be the direct outcome of such a session. This is not a problem because such complex multidimensional models are not effective in communication with multiple stakeholders having different goals or perspectives. Let an experienced modeller construct the overall BPMN model based on the outcome of the focused conversations. Key ingredient here is that all participants trust the experienced modeller to adequately integrate the complete model.

7.6.2 If a Problem Cannot Be Modelled, Do Not Model the Problem

Some problems just cannot be modelled. For example, our AgiSurance organization will find out that it is very hard to model all possible claim situations that may occur. With respect to claims related to car accidents, almost every accident is unique. Weather conditions are different, road situations are different, injuries will be diverse, and police may or may not have been involved. *Modelling the complete problem is* like modelling the ants in an anthill. Communication sessions trying to model the problem in general turn out to be disastrous, because if you cannot model the solution, how would you expect your stakeholders to be able to describe it? This is directly linked to the 80/20 rule: 80% of the cases can be processed with 20% of the effort, so only model that (simple) 80%.

Again, applying focused conversations is a good practice to be applied in such situations. For example, in the context of claim handling, a library of limited focused conversations can be used to model the different aspects of the claim handling problem.

7.6.3 Do Not Communicate the Model, Communicate the Effects of the Model

Consider this real-life example. In a time span of 6 weeks, a very comprehensive portal was developed for a Dutch car lease company. It was extremely rich in functionality; by means of business rules and fuzzy matching, detailed advice was to be given for cars that would fit the customers need and interest. Complex tax and expense calculations were to be made, marketing information provided to engage new customers, and existing customers would find all information about their contract, their current leased car, and the way they would use the car. Based on rules and models, customized advice was to be provided to drill down operational expenses for the customers given their personal situation.

Many domain experts were involved on many different aspects. In six sprints, each with a duration of 1 week, the complete system was developed. Communicating the models before development would have had a huge negative impact on development speed. Furthermore, because of the complexity of the models, understanding them would have been a very hard job for the experts involved. Instead, not the models but *the system being developed* was validated on a weekly basis by using a set of representative cases. Executable models (like 5 GL's) or executable UML is a prerequisite for this kind of situation.

7.6.4 Collaboratively Model, But Not Just for the Model

Collaborative modelling sessions are very useful to foster other results than just the model created in these sessions. In some cases, it is the argumentation or reasoning of the stakeholders during the creation of the model that really counts. For example, in order to capture the relevant decisions to make in a claim handling process, AgiSurance organized a set of collaborative modelling sessions handling a set of representative claims. The assignment given in the session was to set up a model to assess a claim. It was not this outcome, however, that was the main result of the session: the arguments behind the reasoning steps were the real outcome because these were used to model the assessment policies of the individual experts in order to set up generic assessment policy guidelines as training material for novice claim handling agents.

7.6.5 Respect Stakeholders Perspectives During Modelling

In many projects, multiple stakeholders are involved, each with a different language, background, and perspective on the problem at hand. Instead of trying to find a new highly abstracted unified (modelling) language that can suit every stakeholder, just respect the differences of the stakeholder, leading to multiple domain and perspective-specific models. Then let facilitator/modelling expert monitor and model the relation of the different perspectives, and model the (often rule based) relations between the models. Such an approach has been successfully applied for the Dutch Child Care and Protection Board in view of the ministerial 'Youth & Family' programme. It executes tasks that offer support to families and takes action if the development and situation of a child is in danger. Challenge was to realize an improved information exchange within the criminal law system, youth care, and protection chains. The Child Care and Protection Board was in search of a business service that could achieve this goal. Screening minors, identifying needs, and creating risk assessments were important components of this goal. This should improve the information exchange in the youth chains using, for example, process steps that are not linked together. The aim was to achieve a current, correct, and complete insight concerning the children in the chain. In order to achieve this, the perspective of each stakeholder in the chain was modelled: police officers, child protection agents, teachers, psychologists, etc. Information about a child is delivered and communicated for each specific perspective. However, an underlying rule-based model is able to 'translate each perspective into each other perspective'. In order to organize, maintain, and guard consistency for these perspectives, automatic support is required to lower the human effort involved.

7.6.6 Do Not Organize Stakeholder Interaction Sessions Without a Concrete Purpose of the Model

Quite often, models are created just 'because the methodology or architecture dictates it'. A typical example is the creation of domain models. Many business architecture handbooks prescribe the development of a domain model. In many cases, this results in isolated sessions in which architects try hard to model all concepts in the business on a quite high level of abstraction. In hindsight, many such domain models are not useful because the perspective (goal) that was set/used for the (isolated) domain model did not meet the perspective (goal) of the stakeholders that will eventually use the model. A domain model used to develop working instructions for agents will be quite different from a domain model that is used in the creation of formal legal documents, which in turn will be different from a domain model that is used to explain the product/service complexity of an organization. Without having an explicit goal, it is almost infeasible to choose the right perspective. General models tend to be huge and, as such, inflexible. Most of the time, a lot of configuration (or drilling down) is required to get the entities needed for the job at hand. Model only what is needed for the goal is a cornerstone of agile development.

7.6.7 Avoid Collaborative Sessions with Polarized Stakeholders

When setting up a collaborative modelling session, try to avoid meetings in which domain experts with contradicting views participate at the same time. It is problematic to let experts confront each other and let them solve contradictions. This is hardly ever going to happen, leading to frustration and endless sessions. Organize sessions for each domain expert individually, and let the facilitator try to build bridges by playing the ignorant but interested third party. Such a facilitator can contact 'the other domain expert' by stating: 'I don't know anything of the problem at hand of course, so what I'm going to say will probably be ridiculous, but what I was thinking: what about … (the contradicting view of the other domain expert)….'. The facilitator will find that the opponent will be much more open to think about this and consider the contradictory point of view, because he does not feel threatened.

7.6.8 Communication Does Not Stop After the Service Has Been Created

When having developed a service, enable domain experts and/or users to continuously adapt the model by means of specialized focused conversations. For large financial institutions and health-care organizations, tailor-made maintenance facilities are developed, to be used by business stakeholders, enabling them to maintain the agile aspects of agile services without the need to involve the ICT department or specialized engineers. Such maintenance facilities use the domain-specific language of each stakeholder and take the stakeholder mental model and capabilities into account. This practice makes the business responsible and is vital for closing the business-IT gap. It results in *real* agile services. It is not only the *ability to change service* that counts but also *the person who is able to change the service*. In some situations, the time to market of changed business services can be reduced from weeks to hours.

7.6.9 Be Aware of Power and Hierarchies That Might Affect the Outcome

Be aware of how hierarchical and informal power relations may affect the outcome of a modelling session, which will be different if you model with stakeholders having different levels of power. An advantage is that both parties will learn about one another by modelling together. However, when it comes to making design decisions, it is authority that counts.

Good practice is to organize different interactions for different purposes: organize joint sessions for modelling the aspects relevant to the problem at hand, but perform individual sessions for making design decisions, and then organize further joint session(s) to sort out *conflicting* design decisions.

7.6.10 Apply User Involvement with Care, Not by Default

User involvement is a great thing. Nobody dares to contest this anymore. However, be careful *when* you involve users. During innovation, as in creating a completely new system (version 1.0) with a new approach, involving users is not always such a good idea because they might lack the ability to envision the new situation; unless you are able to directly communicate parts of the new system to them at the end of a sprint session. However, involving them in the creation of version 1.1. or 2.0 is very useful because they will tell you exactly what is wrong with the first version. This practice applies especially for situations where a (radical) new way of working is being introduced, for example, an agile business service that will automate decision-making process steps (automatic scheduling, automatic assessment of insurance risks, automatic configuration of customer-tailored advice).

7.6.11 Do Not Always Publish a Model Publicly

'The requirement of transparency is a proof of distrust'. Being transparent is a good practice in principle, but beware of being too transparent; publishing each and every model publicly can be counterproductive. Unknowledgeable stakeholders may see this as an invitation to meddle with other people's business, frustrating both the process and the quality of the outcome. Moreover, the volume of models may create unnecessary communication overload.

7.6.12 Use Visualization Wisely

'A picture says more than a thousand words'. This can be really true, but a bad picture can also create a lot of misunderstanding. For example, a large institution developed a quite complex architectural picture for their multichannel strategy, but in this picture, they used the same symbol for both technical channels (e.g. telephone, internet, postal mail) and distribution channels (e.g. sales by intermediaries, self service portals, or by local offices). This picture, presented as the project bible, led to numerous miscommunications, false interpretations, and, in the end, in developing the wrong software components. For guidelines, see Sect. 7.5.

7.6.13 Take into Account the Limitations of Your Domain Experts

If, during development of an agile service, the domain experts strongly indicate that the task is difficult and that they want support, reconsider the feasibility of the project. It is likely that you will find that no one can actually help you in creating the models or business rules for developing the agile service effectively.

This concludes the chapter. We realize that some readers may feel a bit overwhelmed by the many aspects, concepts, and practices presented. We would like to finish with an encouraging note: whatever your role in service development is, and however agile you work, you *already* communicate all the time. Probably, you are not doing such a bad job as it is. We suggest you take our advice if you think you can use it and invite you, most of all, to become (more) aware of goals and means in communication situations and act accordingly.

Chapter 8
Adopting Agile Service Development

M.M. Lankhorst

In this final chapter, we describe how organizations can adopt our approach to agile service development. This is not an easy task, and many barriers need to be overcome, but the benefits are real and important. To help you reap these benefits, we outline the main issues that you may need to overcome and describe a gradual path to improve your agile capabilities, in which the elements of our approach are positioned. Finally, we give our conclusions and outline the challenges in moving forward with our vision of enterprise agility.

8.1 Barriers to Agility

Nearly all organizations we come across would like to become more flexible in their response to changing circumstances. Some look even further and want to be proactive, adapting their way of working, processes, and technology even before their environment imposes change upon them. They see agility as a strategic factor in outsmarting the competition.

But to reach such a high level of competency and flexibility, you may have to overcome many barriers, both at an organizational level and in your IT applications and infrastructure. Broadly speaking, we can distinguish between social, cultural, and organizational barriers on the one hand and structural and technical barriers on the other.

8.1.1 Technical Barriers

Many enterprises feel that their IT applications and infrastructure are hampering their agility. By its very nature, the infrastructure of an organization's IT is difficult to change. Large, administrative organizations often have a long history of IT system development, spanning often three to four decades. Their legacy systems are often very robust and business critical, but they are built in outdated technology that is difficult to maintain (and even more modern technology causes problems, as witnessed, for example, by overly complex J2EE applications from the last 15 years). Moreover, these systems were often built for a limited type of use and tailored to the needs of specific parts of the organization, hence the familiar silo landscape that many enterprises have to deal with. Finally, the interoperability of these systems is often low and their use in a different context is therefore problematic. An example of this difficulty is the effort that many banks had to make over the last decade to facilitate Internet banking with their large, batch-oriented transactional systems; similarly, government organizations have to make enormous efforts in adapting their systems to changing legislation.

Integration, renovation, or replacement of these systems is a difficult task and beyond the scope of this book. Unfortunately, enterprise agility is doubly hampered by these inflexible systems: First, they are difficult to adapt to the current demands posed by an increasingly integrated and networked world, and they hinder organizations in offering innovative modern products that meet customer demands and provide them with a competitive value. Second, proactively changing them to be more flexible in accommodating possible future changes is very difficult. So not only is the current agility adversely affected, the efforts in becoming more agile are also hindered.

In Chap. 4, we advocated the use of standardized infrastructures and platforms, configured with models that capture the relevant business and implementation knowledge. Many examples show that this approach really works in practice. However, this type of architectures is not without its own teething problems. The technical complexity of the infrastructure, often consisting of a number of interlinked platforms, must be kept in check. Expertise with these new technologies and models is often scarce and needs to be built up. Managing these models is a specific point of attention: both a clear organization of these models and a considered management process are needed to avoid ending up with an unmanageable mess.

Moreover, having an agile platform itself proves not to be sufficient. Business stakeholders responsible for policies and rules should preferably be able to maintain these rules themselves. Complex, ICT-focused models and relatively long release cycles hinder these objectives. Finally, these new systems often have to live in the context of a pre-existing IT landscape, posing the usual interoperability challenges.

8.1.2 Organizational Barriers

From an organizational perspective, agile ways of working may sometimes be perceived as a radical change. Most conventional methods try to reduce various forms of uncertainty (e.g. functionality, time, etc.) as early as possible, but agile methods work differently: they keep their options open as long as possible and decide 'just in time', when the best possible information is available. Initially, this apparent uncertainty may be difficult to deal with for various management levels in the organization. This also addresses a belief issue: some managers, but also many architects, are still convinced that they can 'rule' complex organization with comprehensive and detailed regulations and policies. Other management styles adopt the vision that the organization is capable enough to cope with many uncertain situations and that you should not implement large numbers of detailed rules but rather provide guidance in the form of principles and boundaries.

Moreover, management at different levels has to deal with different kinds of uncertainty. Whereas middle managers have uncertainties about introducing a new service or the right functionality for a new IT system, C-level management deals with issues like market share, cost reduction, and compliance. Being aware of these different levels of uncertainty, and being able to interrelate these, is crucial for being successful in agile service development. Furthermore, agile processes may clash with other procedures within the organization. For example, compliance demands or security audits may require a lengthy evaluation and testing process before a new service is put into production. The role of architecture as a way of reducing or mitigating risk, as outlined in Chap. 3, is very important in this respect.

As we have described in Chap. 2, agile methods require a strong sense of responsibility, self-organization, and a collaborative attitude of all those involved. This requires more discipline from team members than in conventional methods; team members are all accountable for the results and cannot hide behind fixed procedures or responsibilities. Moreover, agility requires transparency, measuring various aspects of team and business performance and focusing on continuous improvement of the way of working. This may also be perceived as a threat by some.

Thus, agile service development may demand both a cultural and a technological change. This is a time-consuming process; some organizations may not be able to make such a change in time and instead choose to start a new company or business unit, sometimes even allowing it to compete with the original company. This new organization is equipped with new technology and a fresh team of employees who are flexible and open to change.

Conversely, agile teams will have to live within a larger context that has different rhythms. Many parts of the organization will keep their usual monthly, quarterly, or yearly business cycles, and agile teams will often need to match such cycles. The same may hold for technical cycles; in particular, in the context of large IT landscapes with many interdependencies, a thorough development, testing, acceptance, and production (DTAP) cycle will often be enforced. This requires striking a balance between the need for speed and managing risk, and tuning these cycles requires a thorough analysis of the particulars of an individual organization. Modern, model-based architectures such as those advocated in this book will at least reduce the effort spent in such DTAP processes. Moreover, agile technology has already proven to empower the business to publish new policies, business processes, or services in a controlled way, independent from IT, thereby reducing time to market from weeks to hours.

Finally, the complexity of these new technologies and the specialized knowledge needed to get this off the ground should not be underestimated. Retraining the current workforce of an organization to work within such a sophisticated environment may pose a serious obstacle. Conversely, young employees with an open mind and knowledge of modern agile development are hard to motivate to maintain old-fashioned legacy systems. This may motivate some enterprises to outsource parts of their (IT) operations, but the essential business capabilities that differentiate a company from its competitors should be kept close to the heart. And in particular, if an enterprise explicitly builds its strategy on its agile capabilities and wants to define the right infrastructure to face a volatile future, it should be well aware of these potential limitations.

8.2 Scaling Up Agile Processes

Agile processes may not easily fit with all environments and circumstances. Turk et al. (2002) describe classical agile methods as providing only limited support for distributed environments, subcontracting, building of reusable artefacts, large team management, or safety-critical developments. But these limitations can be overcome. For example, globally oriented organizations have distributed units, which is incompatible with the face-to-face communication advocated by agile processes. This requires other rich forms of communication, such as video conferencing. Subcontracting is often based on precisely formulated contracts that describe the deliverables extensively. In an agile context, different ways of specifying contractual conditions should be used. Although variable elements may be part of a contract, the clear specification of iterations and milestones is not required in agile settings.

In addition, the desire to produce reusable artefacts to yield long-term benefits may clash with classical agile methods that are often more concerned with getting short-term results. However, the model- and platform-oriented approach we have advocated in this book is specifically intended to provide reusable agile solutions.

Larger projects also require additional measures since effective communication in an agile manner (e.g. informal face-to-face chats and review meetings) may be more difficult in large team environments. The 'Scrum of Scrums' practice is one such measure. But more may be needed, in particular to control complexity when building large-scale systems.

Furthermore, safety-critical development may require additional quality control mechanisms to assure product safety; for example, even extensive testing cannot cover all possible cases for all but the simplest systems.

Scaling up agile methods to be usable in such complex, distributed, and large-scale environments is an explicit goal of the Agile Scaling Model of (Ambler 2010). This provides guidelines on adapting agile methods for such environments, based on eight scaling factors:

1. Team size
2. Geographical distribution
3. Regulatory compliance
4. Organizational distribution
5. Technical complexity
6. Domain complexity
7. Organizational complexity
8. Enterprise discipline

The scaling model outlines how these factors influence the choice of methods and tools. It also includes a disciplined agile delivery approach for such environments, encompassing not only software construction but the entire life cycle from inception of the first ideas to the release and operation, and feedback from usage to complete the cycle. Basically, this can be viewed as a set of larger-scale feedback loops around the smaller-scale iterations that form the core of agile processes.

8.3 A Capability Model for Agile Service Development

As we already stated, creating truly agile enterprises is not an easy task and something that may take several years. Where do you start? What are the quick wins and bottlenecks? To help organizations plot a course to enhance their agility, we have developed a capability model for agile service development based on common models from the literature. This model positions the approaches and instruments we have described in this book at different levels. A self-assessment helps you in determining where your organization currently stands and hence where to use elements of our approach and what next steps may be useful to improve your agility. Note that we explicitly avoid the term 'maturity' here: it is not our intention that all organizations should strive for the highest possible level in this capability model, but rather that they choose appropriate capabilities that fit with their specific strategy and circumstances.

The capability model combines the business, process, and system aspects of enterprise agility, as explained in Chap. 2. These are also interdependent:

- System agility is often hampered by a legacy IT landscape that is difficult to change, which impacts the business options of the enterprise, its business processes, and possibly even its organization structure. By its very nature, a low system agility is difficult to correct. Hence in many organizations, current system agility will score lower than process agility.
- Process agility is needed to establish ways of working that rapidly and competently deliver results that provide business value. This is often relatively easier to realize, but only taking care of process agility merely helps you to build better silos. Moreover, it requires management recognition and support and hence depends on business agility as well.

- Business agility concerns the importance of agility for the enterprise's business model and strategy. But the ability to execute such a strategy depends on both process and system agility and of course on the cultural and organizational aspects described in the previous section.

Thus, to achieve true enterprise agility, all three aspects of agility must therefore be addressed. Of course, changing the agility of your legacy IT landscape or the culture of your organization may take considerable time, whereas improving the way of working within a project is often a matter of months. Hence, your organization may have different levels of capability in different aspects. Furthermore, the type of scale is different, since the first aspect mainly addresses the agility of various *structures* in the enterprise, whereas the second and third focus on (management and design) *processes*. Therefore we use two different scales.

However, the Agile Manifesto's 'individuals and interactions over processes and tools' should not be forgotten. Within the agile community, the use of maturity models is highly contentious. It is certainly not our intention to prescribe specific processes or management practices in the way the CMMI is often used to assess software development organizations; there is no cookbook for adopting agile, and our capability model does not come near the CMMI's level of detail. Nevertheless, we think such a model can help organizations in assessing where they are and which actions might helpful in improving their agility from that level.

8.3.1 System Agility Capabilities

To gauge the (organizational and technical) system agility of enterprises, we use a set of levels or stages derived from The Open Group Service Integration Maturity Model (OSIMM) (The Open Group 2009a), the Business Decision Maturity Model (BDMM) (von Halle and Goldberg 2009), and the staged model of architecture development of Ross et al. (2006); we have also reused the latter's names for levels. We have adapted these to an agile process context and extended them with our view on models and architectures for facilitating system agility, as described elsewhere in this book.

8.3.1.1 Level 1: Silos

At the initial level, system agility is unknown and possibly quite low. There is no insight into the enterprise and IT architectures. Individual parts of the organization are developing their own services independently, with no integration of data, processes, standards, or technologies. This severely limits the ability of the organization to implement business processes that require co-operation between the different parts, and the IT systems cannot be integrated, reused, or changed without significant manual intervention. Business knowledge is only visible at the level of these silos or within specific projects. The use of models is non-existent or limited to the design of very specific aspects, for example, data models. The lack of an integral view of the customer hampers the development of customer-focused processes and systems.

8.3.1.2 Level 2: Standardized Technology

At level 2, system agility is addressed reactively, only at the level of individual systems, and focused on IT. Architecture and design models are used in an informal way and mainly for communication purposes, across various aspects of the application-level design process, and for some specific parts of the business, such as processes. Standardized technologies and platforms have been put in place to communicate between silos and to integrate the data and interconnections. Modularity and reuse are low, however, and point-to-point connections between systems dominate the landscape. Modifying processes or IT systems is still difficult, and analysis of the impact is done by hand.

8.3.1.3 Level 3: Optimized Core

At level 3, system agility is addressed across the organization's enterprise architecture, and it is known where the most pressing problems with flexibility are in both business and IT. The enterprise is subdivided into a set of independent business functions; the IT systems in the silos have been analysed and broken down into component parts, which can be used independent from any organization structure. Services are used as a design concept to identify business-relevant functionality and to stimulate reuse. Business knowledge, including a unified view of the enterprise's customers, is externalized and accessible to business users. Within the context of an overall architectural backbone (Chap. 3), models are used for the design of the business and IT operations and at the level of enterprise goals, drivers, and requirements (Chap. 4). The relationship between these two levels is used for tracing the impact of business drivers for agility (see Chap. 2) and relates changes to business goals. However, the focus is still on the internal operations of the enterprise, and individual business and IT components are often tightly coupled; IT integration still requires writing code and is not yet based on declarative models.

8.3.1.4 Level 4: Business Modularity

At level 4, system agility is measured regularly and used to define improvements to avoid future problems. Business drivers for agility are monitored continuously. Enterprise architecture (Chap. 3) is explicitly used to measure and manage agility and to optimize business modularity. Composite applications are built from loosely coupled software services, using technology and models for service composition and orchestration. Relevant business knowledge is managed explicitly across different processes, with a focus on alignment between various parts of the enterprise. Models are use at three levels: for requirements and design purposes; to obtain, aggregate, and analyse management information and relate this to the enterprise strategy; and in suitable domains also for direct implementation (interpretation/execution or code generation). Business services to the environment can quickly be realized across the enterprise by combining and configuring internal and external business services, often by business analysts instead of software developers.

8.3.1.5 Level 5: Dynamic Venturing

At level 5, the organization's strategy is based on its agility. Tools are used in an integrated way to support teams in optimizing their work. They provide management with sophisticated, model-based forecasting, and these predictive capabilities help the enterprise in proactively adapting to its environment. System agility is continuously monitored and proactively improved to accommodate predicted future business needs. Architecture is used as a core instrument to support this rapid adaptation, and business and IT are regarded as an integrated whole within the enterprise architecture. This extends beyond the borders of the individual organization and includes the networked enterprise level. Automated, run-time assembly of software services is used to dynamically create composite business services that respond to needs from the organization's ecosystem.

8.3.2 Business and Process Agility Capabilities

For assessing business and process agility, we base our capability model on the 'mother of all maturity models', the CMMI (SEI 2010), the Scrum maturity model of Yin et al. (2011), and the agility@scale model of Ambler (2010). The names of the levels are taken from the CMMI. Roughly speaking, at level 3 an organization is mature in using agile development processes at the project level, which is equivalent to Ambler's 'core agility'. Levels 4 and 5 go beyond that and extend agile practices to the full service life cycle, the entire enterprise, its strategy, and even its network of partners.

8.3.2.1 Level 1: Initial

At the initial level, the organization is starting to recognize that it has issues with respect to flexibility, time-to-market, or other aspects of agility. However, no formalized roles, procedures, measurements, or instruments are used yet to address these issues. Processes are unpredictable, poorly controlled, and reactive.

8.3 A Capability Model for Agile Service Development

Management, both at the level of the organization and at the project level, has an ad hoc character. The organization has no strategy on its agile capabilities. Stakeholders are involved in service development but often at a distance and mostly in defining requirements. No tool support is available to agile teams beyond basic desktop applications and development environments.

8.3.2.2 Level 2: Managed

At level 2, the organization has started explicitly to manage its agility. Management recognizes the value of agile over command-and-control approaches in an increasingly volatile environment. Agile ways of working (Chap. 6) are introduced at the project level; some development teams use agile methods, but in a patchy way. There is no formal training or communication on agile working. There is a high degree of reliance on the responsibility and expertise of individuals. Managers above the project level are not aligned with an agile way of working; they are involved as stakeholders in decision-making (sometimes causing delays), but not as part of the ongoing agile development processes. Agile teams mainly focus on communication, stakeholder involvement, requirements management (e.g. user stories), and planning. Some specific tool support may be used next to the usual development environments, for example, for requirements management or modelling.

8.3.2.3 Level 3: Defined

At level 3, management of enterprise agility progresses beyond the project level. Business drivers for agility are recognized, and the organizational strategy appreciates agility as an enabling factor (Chap. 2). Agile ways of working (Chap. 6) are used across the organization and communicated through training. Internal best practices are not sophisticated, but shared widely, and they have full support and active involvement from management. The workforce is well acquainted with agile practices and uses these across various business and IT functions.

Stakeholders are closely involved in agile development processes. Stakeholder communication (Chap. 7) is actively managed and supported. Self-organizing agile teams are focused on rapid delivery of business value, stakeholder management, iteration management, and product quality, for example, through test-driven development. Mature tool support for these aspects, for example, for requirements management, process design, software development, and automated testing of services, is used.

8.3.2.4 Level 4: Quantitatively Managed

At level 4, the full service life cycle is addressed, from the business drivers for a new or adapted service, through the managerial decision-making process of needs, wants, costs, impact (organizational, ICT, development, etc.) and returns on investment, up to development, realization, deployment, and use of that service. Value and risk management (Chap. 3) are integral parts of this service life cycle. Strategic and architectural choices are made based on the current and predicted agility of the organization.

The organization actively measures outcomes and guides its process and system agility using statistical and other quantitative techniques. Agile teams extend beyond mere development into the primary process and management. These teams are self-organizing and empowered with adequate tools and techniques to monitor their outcomes and take action where processes appear not to be working effectively. The contributions of agile practices are measured and used to improve team performance and to ensure a sustainable pace.

Sophisticated, model-based communication techniques (Chap. 7) are used to keep stakeholders closely involved throughout the service life cycle. Stakeholder satisfaction is proactively managed, and stakeholders are actively involved in helping agile teams improve their performance. Next to the tools of the previous levels, various collaboration, communication, and visualization tools and techniques are used to support, for example, larger and distributed teams as well as stakeholder involvement in the service development process.

8.3.2.5 Level 5: Optimizing

At level 5, the organization's strategy is based on its agility. Agile working is an integral part of the organizational culture, which is based on an attitude of collaboration and self-discipline instead of hierarchal leadership. This collaboration is strongly supported by applicable technologies. Scenario analyses are used for stress testing the strategy, which is developed and adapted conjointly with business partners. Stakeholder involvement in service development thus extends beyond the boundaries of the enterprise.

Agile delivery is used at a large scale, where one or more of Ambler's (2010) scaling factors apply: large team size, geographic distribution, regulatory compliance, domain complexity, organization distribution, technical complexity, organizational complexity, and enterprise discipline. The agile teams' performance has been highly optimized, based on the results of continuous improvement and sharing of experiences with other teams and other organizations. Agile teams need little guidance, and everyone in the organization is fully aware of his or her contribution to the business value that the enterprise delivers.

Example: AgiSurance's Agile Capabilities

When we apply this capability model to our example company AgiSurance, we see that it reaches level 3, 'Defined', in its business and process agility; its development teams use agile methods, Scrum in particular, sharing experiences and practices. This only concerns the development phase, however, and not the rest of the service life cycle.

In its system agility, AgiSurance scores around level 3, 'Optimized Core'. It makes extensive use of models in various service design activities. Moreover, it already uses a case management system with a model-based business process engine; it now wants to move to direct interpretation of models with a business rules engine, in which it wants to specify insurance policy decisions and computations. However, large parts of the business logic are embedded in various legacy systems. As a first step in phasing out these systems, AgiSurance already has externalized most of their data (e.g. with customer or policy information) and moved these to separate databases. Next, it has wrapped the business logic in a service layer, with the intention to gradually replace this logic by the aforementioned model-based business rules solution. It is also well under way in building a full-service Web portal, 'MyAgiSurance', which uses the same business logic for making, for example, pro forma calculations and offerings.

To profit fully from such a flexible infrastructure, we advise AgiSurance to extend its agile processes beyond the development phase. In particular, because the business-oriented modelling practice will decrease the development time for new services, its strategic focus on product leadership is further enhanced. AgiSurance can now explicitly start using its agility as a competitive advantage, but this requires a strong focus on the relationships between strategy, service design, and operation. The different models AgiSurance employs should therefore be kept coherent across the service life cycle, and adequate tools are required. Furthermore, an enterprise-level architecture owner role is advisable, who is explicitly assigned the responsibility for architectural coherence and consistency.

In an increasingly unstable and fragmented financial world, speed is essential to survival. Having such a flexible landscape allows AgiSurance rapidly to try out new online insurance services and to monitor their usage and effects. By creating a closed-loop innovation and monitoring cycle, AgiSurance can quickly respond and even proactively induce changes to the marketplace. Thus, AgiSurance is well positioned to achieve its vision of becoming the market leader in special-purpose insurance offerings, serving niches that other companies are too slow to exploit.

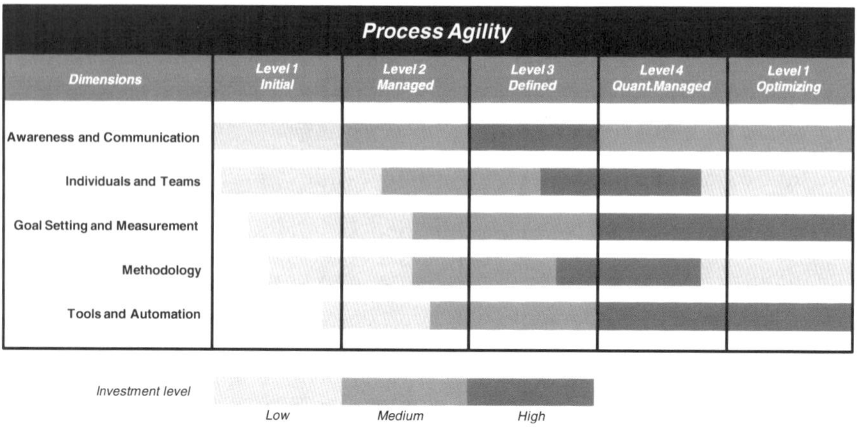

Process Agility					
Dimensions	Level 1 Initial	Level 2 Managed	Level 3 Defined	Level 4 Quant.Managed	Level 1 Optimizing
Awareness and Communication					
Individuals and Teams					
Goal Setting and Measurement					
Methodology					
Tools and Automation					
Investment level		Low	Medium	High	

Fig. 8.1 Investment pattern in process agility

8.3.3 Investing in Agility

One should be aware that each of these levels requires a certain investment on different aspects: awareness and communication, individuals and teams, goal setting and measurement, methodology, and tools and automation. A typical investment pattern (Fig. 8.1)—inspired by Gartner's model for the introduction of business process management (Sinur and Hill 2010)—shows that starting is easy, but significant investments are needed to reach level 4 or 5.

Making such investments is a strategic choice and should be supported by a thorough business case. Not all organizations need the same capability level. Moreover, agility is only one of the many considerations in investment decisions; many issues contend for the limited resources available in the enterprise, and a clear set of business goals is needed to decide on business priorities. As we have described in Chaps. 2 and 6, you should first investigate what the required agility of your enterprise is in the various aspects of its operation and innovation, given its strategy and business drivers. Only then can you make informed investment decisions.

8.4 Concluding Remarks

In investigating this field of agile service development and in developing and using our methods and techniques, we have observed a number of common themes we think will greatly influence the course of many enterprises in the years to come. First of all, we see that in an increasingly volatile business environment, successful enterprises embrace change as a positive factor. They deal with uncertainty and risk not by trying to reduce it, but by increasing their capabilities to respond adequately, and even proactively.

8.4 Concluding Remarks

What counts are proven business results. Examples from the authors' organizations include:

- Replacing four IT platforms by one uniform, flexible platform, cutting development effort by 75%, and reducing business support from 60 to 16 FTE
- Reducing time to market from weeks to hours for product variations, and from months to weeks for new, complex products in mortgages and insurances
- Improving customer satisfaction by pro-active interaction and the introduction of innovative customer-centred products and services, helping a Dutch financial institution move from a customer satisfaction level of 6.2 in 2009 to 8.3 in 2011 (on a 1–10 scale)
- Improving business alignment by giving business people a hands-on role in changing products, processes, and policies
- Improved employee satisfaction by giving them the ability to influence development processes, work with modern technology, and provide competitive products, resulting in a better retention of valuable employees and knowledge

But changing to agile ways of working does not come natural. A stable and predictable environment provides a form of security that is highly valued by many people. Agile ways of working may therefore be 'scary' to various levels within an organization, from management that does not get the comfort (or illusion) of exactly knowing at the start what a project will deliver at the end to the workforce that is confronted with rapidly changing processes and systems. This cultural change requires a high level of management commitment, and the nature of agile methods and their flat organizational models requires managers to be closely involved in a 'hands-on' style. Working with a clear business case for agility, which is constantly kept up to date in this changing environment, is a crucial instrument to show what the need and value of these changes is.

Secondly, agile enterprises strike a profitable balance between global, top-down, strategic guidance and local, bottom-up 'tinkering' and change. The classical business cycles, from strategy definition via various tactical design steps towards daily operations, are not flexible and quick enough to provide real agility. But neither can you determine the course of an enterprise by adding the directions of individual projects and local developments; that would result in a Brownian motion with no manner of control.

This brings us to another major issue: the culture clash between agilists ('localists') and architects ('globalists'). In agile software development circles, there is often a strong resistance against any form of structure or guidance from outside the project at hand. This is viewed as 'Big Design Up Front' or 'waste', and architects are often the representatives of this, sending down commandments from their ivory towers without knowing the daily life in the project's trenches. But individual projects cannot avoid the reality of the enterprise environment and questions like 'what will this project cost?' 'what value will it deliver?' 'how does it fit with the existing system landscape?' and 'how does it contribute to the business strategy?' will be asked. Conversely, many architects view the agile movement as a bunch of hackers, tinkering away without being aware of the grand scheme of things. They may quickly build something that works, but this may not always fit within the rest of the enterprise landscape. However, tightening controls, adding procedures, doing extensive reviews, or requiring building permits is not going to be the answer. Again, a clear business case, which relates critical business problems with the envisaged solutions, is essential in making the right decisions, locally and globally. Everyone should be focused on the overall business goals of the organization: the architecture should be aligned with these goals, as should the individual project priorities and results.

The best way to bring these two camps together is if architects work closely together with project teams to instil their larger-scale vision and directly add value to the team's results. Architects among themselves also collaborate in agile teams to resolve architectural issues beyond the project scope. Thus, they are the linking pins between the enterprise and project levels. The agile movement's focus on individuals and interactions also applies here: intensive communication between architects and other team members is essential; communicating architectures by throwing documents over the wall is not going to work.

This focus on communication is the next key point we take away from this work. Already in agile software development, the need for close communication with all stakeholders is stressed, but in service development, with its larger scope and associated stakeholder community, this is even more critical. Given the diverse backgrounds and skills of these stakeholders, we should pay close attention to the means and instruments we use to discuss service ideas, requirements, and designs. The closer we can get our designs to the business world and the concepts used there, the easier this conversation will be, not just during development but also, and perhaps even more importantly, during the entire lifetime of the agile service, to keep it aligned with a changing environment.

Furthermore, our ultimate goal is to use these business-level descriptions of services directly in the operational realization and execution. We advocate the use of appropriate models that capture this business essence and respect the different perspectives involved. We should not force IT-oriented models onto business stakeholders, but rather use domain-specific concepts and languages to capture and communicate relevant business knowledge. These models can then be targeted to suitable IT infrastructure, either by transforming them to technology-oriented models or software code or even by directly interpreting and executing these models. This requires intelligent software solutions that guard quality, reuse, and consistency of these business designs. Such systems should, for example, recognize reusable constructs such as policies and process fragments, identify conflicting business rules, and signal incompleteness of specifications.

This model-based vision is not without its own challenges. First of all, it requires a domain-specific approach. For example, the concepts and constructs used in an administrative organization are quite different from those in a chemical plant, and different models and infrastructures will be required. Traditional programming languages are of course much more general. Second, the use of models requires new skills, from both technical and business people involved. In particular, this

8.4 Concluding Remarks

demands a conceptual level of thinking and communicative skills that may require extensive training and experience.

Finally, our ideal is truly to bring service development to the business and let business experts do the design and modelling work. However, these experts are often completely involved in their business processes and are needed over there to do their jobs; involving them in agile teams as well requires a restructuring of the organization, breaking down the barriers between the primary business and the development and change organization. Moreover, people who can span this breadth of expertise and have the required skill set are still scarce. Both the professional and the academic community have an important task in communicating this vision; providing the right methods, tools, and techniques; and training the business service developers of the future.

References

Abrahamsson P, Warsta J, Siponen MT, Ronkainen J (2003) New directions on agile methods: a comparative analysis. Proceedings of the international conference on software engineering (ICSE'03), Portland, OR, 3–5 May 2003, pp 244–254

Agile Advice (2006) The seven core practices of agile work. http://www.agileadvice.com/archives/2006/09/practices_of_ag.html. Accessed 19 March 2012

Albani A, Hardjosumarto G, Terlouw L, Dietz JLG (2009) Enterprise ontology based service definition. In: Proceedings of 4th international workshop on value modeling and business ontologies, Amsterdam, The Netherlands

Alexander C (1979) The timeless way of building. Oxford University Press, New York

Alexander C, Ishikawa S, Silverstein M, Jacobson M, Fiksdahl-King I, Angel S (1977) A pattern language. Oxford University Press, New York

Ambler SW (2002) Agile modeling: effective practices for eXtreme programming and the unified process. Wiley, New York

Ambler SW (2003) Agile database techniques: effective strategies for the agile software developer. Wiley, New York

Ambler SW (2010) IBM agility@scale™: become as agile as you can be. IBM Global Services, Somers, NY

Amdahl GM, Blaauw GM, Brooks FP (1964) Architecture of the IBM System/360. IBM J Res Dev 8(2):87–101

Arnott D, Pervan G (2005) A critical analysis of decision support systems research. J Inform Technol 20(2):67–87

Annett J (2004) Hierarchical task analysis. In: Diaper D, Stanton NA (eds) The handbook of task analysis for human-computer interaction. Lawrence Erlbaum Associates, Mahwah, NJ, pp 67–82

Aquino N, Vanderdonckt J, Panach JI, Pastor O (2008) Conceptual modelling of interaction. Universitat Politecnica de Valencia, Spain. http://personales.upv.es/jopana/Files/Books/Conceptual_Modelling.pdf. Accessed 28 Sept 2011

Baida Z, Gordijn J, Omelayenko B (2004) A shared service terminology for online service provisioning. Proceedings of the 6th international conference on electronic commerce (ICEC'04), ACM Press, pp 1–10

Beck K (1999) Extreme programming explained: embrace change. Addison-Wesley, Boston, MA

Beck K et al (2001) Manifesto for agile software development. http://www.agilemanifesto.org. Accessed 19 March 2012

Bennett C, Ryall J, Spalteholz L, Gooch A (2007). The Aesthetics of Graph Visualization. In: Cunningham DW, Meyer G, Neumann L (eds) Proceedings of the computational aesthetics in graphics, visualization, and imaging, Banff, Canada, pp 1–8

Bossavit L (2002) The unbearable lightness of programming: a tale of two cultures. Cutter IT J 15 (9):5–11
Bouwman H, Haaker T, De Vos H (2008) Mobile service innovation and business models. Springer, Berlin
Breuker J, Van de Velde W (1994) The Common KADS Library. Technical report, University of Amsterdam and Free University of Brussels
Brinkkemper S (1996) Method engineering: engineering of information systems development methods and tools. Inform Software Tech 38(4):275–280
von Brocke J, Rosemann M (2010) Handbook on business process management. Springer, Berlin
Brown T (2009) Change by design. HarperCollins, New York
Bucher T, Winter R (2006) Classification of business process management approaches an exploratory analysis. Banking Inform Technol 7(3):9–20
Buschmann F, Henney K, Schmidt DC (2007a) Pattern-oriented software architecture, volume 4: a pattern language for distributed computing. Wiley, Hoboken, NJ
Buschmann F, Henney K, Schmidt DC (2007b) Pattern-oriented software architecture, volume 5: on patterns and pattern languages. Wiley, Hoboken, NJ
Buschmann F, Meunier R, Rohnert H, Sommerlad P, Stal M (1996) Pattern-oriented software architecture, volume 1: a system of patterns. Wiley, Hoboken, NJ
Calvary G, Coutaz J, Thevenin D, Limbourg Q, Bouillon L, Vanderdonckt J (2003) A unifying reference framework for multi-target user interfaces. Interact Comput 15(3):289–308
Cañas A J, Hill G, Carff R, Suri N, Lott J, Eskridge T, Gómez G, Arroyo M, Carvajal, R (2004). CmapTools: a knowledge modeling and sharing environment. In: Cañas AJ, Novak JD, González FM (eds) Concept maps: theory, methodology, technology. Proceedings of the first international conference on concept mapping, Pamplona, Spain
Chen P (1976) The entity-relationship model: toward a unified view of data. ACM Trans Database Syst 1:9–36
Christoff K, Keramatian K (2007) Abstraction of mental representations: theoretical considerations and neuroscientific evidence. In: Bunge SA, Wallis JD (eds) Perspectives on rule-guided behavior. Oxford University Press, New York, NY, pp 107–126
CIA (2011) CIA World Factbook—GDP composition per sector. https://www.cia.gov/library/publications/the-world-factbook/fields/2012.html
Ciborra C (1992) From thinking to tinkering: the grassroots of strategic information systems. Inform Soc 8:297–309
Cockburn A (2002) Agile software development. Addison Wesley
Cockburn A, Highsmith J (2001) Agile software development, the people factor. IEEE Software 34(11):131–133
Conklin J (2005) Dialogue mapping. Wiley, New York
Conway ME (1968) How do committees invent? Datamation 14(5):28–31
Coplien JO (1996) Software patterns. Lucent Technologies, Bell Labs Innovations, New York
Coplien JO, Harrison NB (2004) Organizational patterns of agile software development. Prentice Hall, Upper Saddle River, NJ, See also http://users.rcn.com/jcoplien/Patterns/Top10OrgPatterns.html
Cunningham W (1992) The WyCash portfolio management system. http://c2.com/doc/oopsla92.html. Retrieved 21 Jul 2011
De Caluwé L, Vermaak H (2008) Thinking about change in different colours. In: Boonstra JJ (ed) Dynamics of organizational change and learning. Wiley, Chicester
De Lara J, Vangheluwe H (2004) Meta-modelling and graph grammars for multi-paradigm modelling. Software Syst Model 3(3):194–209
Dietz JLG (1999) DEMO: towards a discipline of organisation engineering. Eur J Oper Res 128(2):351–363
Dietz JLG (2006) Enterprise ontology: theory and methodology. Springer, Berlin
Dietz JLG (ed) (2011) Enterprise engineering manifesto. http://www.ciaonetwork.org/publications/EEManifesto.pdf
Dividino R, Bicer V, Voigt K, Cardoso J (2009) Integrating business process and user interface models using a model-driven approach. 24th international symposium on computer and information sciences, Guzelyurt, Nothern Cyprus, 14–16 Sept

DSDM Consortium (2008) DSDM Atern handbook V2. DSDM Consortium, Ashford, UK
Dybå T, Dingsøyr T (2008) Empirical studies of agile software development: a systematic review. Inform Software Tech 50(9–10):833–859
van Eemeren FH, Grootendorst R (2004) A systematic theory of argumentation: the pragma-dialectical approach. Cambridge University Press, Cambridge
Eichelberger H, Schmid K (2009) Guidelines on the aesthetic quality of UML class diagrams. Inform Software Tech 51(12):1686–1698
Engelsman W, Quartel D, Jonkers H, van Sinderen M (2011) Extending enterprise architecture modelling with business goals and requirements. Enterprise Inform Syst 5(1):9–36
Enterprise Architecture Research Forum (2010) Enterprise architecture definition. http://samvak.tripod.com/earf.pdf. Accessed 19 March 2012
Erl T (2009) SOA design patterns. Prentice Hall, Upper Saddle River, NJ, See also http://www.soapatterns.org
Ernst AM (2008) Enterprise architecture management patterns. Proceedings of the PLoP '08, Nashville, TN, USA, Oct 18–20 2008. See also http://wwwmatthes.in.tum.de/wikis/eam-pattern-catalog/home
van Es RM, Post HA (eds) (1996) Dynamic enterprise modelling: a paradigm shift in software implementation. Kluwer, Deventer
European Commission (2010) Europe 2020—EU strategy for smart, sustainable and inclusive growth. http://ec.europa.eu/europe2020
Falkenberg ED, Verrijn-Stuart AA, Voss K, Hesse W, Lindgreen P, Nilsson BE, Oei JLH, Rolland C, Stamper RK (eds) (1998) A framework of information systems concepts. IFIP WG 8.1 Task Group FRISCO, IFIP, Laxenburg, Austria
Fehskens L (2008) Re-thinking architecture—the architecture of enterprise architecture. In: 20th Enterprise architecture practitioners conference, The Open Group, Reading, UK
Forrester (2009) From agile development to agile engagement. Forrester research, May 2009. http://www.forrester.com/research
Fowler M (1996) Analysis patterns: reusable object models. Addison-Wesley, Boston, MA
Fowler M (1999) Refactoring: improving the design of existing code. Addison-Wesley, Boston, MA
Fowler M (2002) Patterns of enterprise application architecture. Addison-Wesley, Boston, MA, See also http://martinfowler.com/eaaCatalog/
Gamma E, Helm R, Johnson R, Vlissides J (1994) Design patterns: elements of reusable object-oriented software. Addison-Wesley, Boston, MA
Gordijn J, Akkermans JM (2001) e3-value: design and evaluation of e-business models. IEEE Intelligent Systems, Vol. 16(4):11–17
Govers MJG (2003) Met ERP-systemen op weg naar moderne bureaucratieën? PhD Thesis, Radboud University Nijmegen
Govers MJG, Südmeier P (2011) De Sitter in het informatietijdperk. Management en Organisatie 65(2):31–45
Graham I (2007) Business rules management and service oriented architecture: a pattern language. Wiley, New York
Greefhorst D, Proper E (2011) Architecture principles—the cornerstones of enterprise architecture. Springer, Heidelberg
Grice HP (1975) Logic and conversation. In: Cole P, Morgan JL (eds) Syntax and semantics III: speech acts. Academic, New York, pp 41–58
Guarino N (1998) Formal ontology and information systems. In Guarino N (ed) Formal ontology in information systems. Proceedings of the FOIS'98, Trento, Italy. IOS Press, Amsterdam, 6–8 Jun 1998, pp 3–15
von Halle B, Goldberg L (2009) The Decision Model: a business logic framework linking business and technology. Auerbach Publications, Taylor and Francis
Halpin T, Morgan T (2008) Information modeling and relational databases, 2nd edn. Morgan Kaufmann, Waltham, MA

Harrison NB, Avgeriou P (2007), Leveraging architecture patterns to satisfy quality attributes. Proceedings of ECSA 2007, Springer, Berlin

Heitlager I, Kuipers T, Visser J (2007) A practical model for measuring maintainability, Proceedings of the 6th international conference on the quality of information and communications technology (QUATIC 2007), 12–14 Sept 2007, pp 30–39

Hevner AR, March ST, Park J, Ram S (2004) Design science in information systems research. MIS Quart 28(1):75–105

Hohpe G, Woolf B (2003) Enterprise integration patterns: designing, building, and deploying messaging solutions. Addison-Wesley, Boston, MA

Hoppenbrouwers SJBA (2003) Freezing language; Conceptualisation processes across ICT supported organisations. PhD Thesis, University of Nijmegen

Hoppenbrouwers SJBA (2008) Community-based ICT development as a multi-player game. In: Benoit-Barné C, Brummans BH, Cooren F, Giroux H, Létourneau A, Raymond D, Robichaud D (eds) What is an organization? Materiality, agency, and discourse: a tribute to the work of James R. Taylor. Department of Organizational Communication, University of Montreal, Montreal

Hoppenbrouwers SJBA, Proper HA, Weide TP van der (2005) Formal modeling as a grounded conversation. In: Goldkuhl G, Lind M, Haraldson S (eds) Proceedings of the 10th international working conference on the language action perspective on communication modelling (LAP'05). Kiruna, Sweden, Linköpings Universitet and Hogskolan I Boras, Linköping, Sweden, pp 139–155

Hoppenbrouwers SJBA, Stokkum W van (2011) Towards combining ThinkLets and Dialogue games in collaborative modeling: an explorative case. In: Proceedings of the collaborative usage and development of models and visualizations, part of the 13th European conference on computer supported cooperative work (ECSCW 2011), Aarhus, Denmark. Online publication: CEUR-WS proceedings, Sept 2011

Hoppenbrouwers SJBA, Wilmont I (2010) Focused conceptualisation: framing questioning and answering in model-oriented dialogue games. In: van Bommel P, Hoppenbrouwers S, Overbeek S, Proper E, Barjis J (eds) The practice of enterprise modeling. Springer, Berlin, pp 190–204

Iacocca Institute (1991) 21st Century manufacturing enterprise strategy. An industry-led view of agile manufacturing, vol 1 & 2. Iacocca Institute, Bethlehem, PA

IBM (2010) Patterns for e-business for new and enhanced IT solutions. IBM, Armonk, NY, http://www.ibm.com/developerworks/patterns/index-revised.html

IBM Research (2011) Services sciences, management and engineering. http://www.research.ibm.com/ssme/services.shtml. Retrieved 22 Jul 2011

IDEF (1981) ICAM Architecture Part II-Volume IV—function modeling manual (IDEF0), AFWAL-TR-81-4023. Materials Laboratory, Air Force Wright Aeronautical Laboratories, Air Force Systems Command, Wright-Patterson Air Force Base, OH

IEEE Computer Society (2000) IEEE recommended practice for architecture description of software-intensive systems, IEEE Std 1471-2000. IEEE, New York

ISO (2003) Medical devices—quality management systems—requirements for regulatory purposes, ISO 13485. International Organization for Standardization, Geneva

ISO (2007) Medical devices—application of risk management to medical devices, ISO 14971. International Organization for Standardization, Geneva

ISO/IEC (1991) Information technology – Software product evaluation – Quality characteristics and guidelines for their use, ISO/IEC 9126. International Organization for Standardization, International Electrotechnical Commission, Geneva

ISO/IEC (2005) Information technology—XML Metadata Interchange (XMI), ISO/IEC 19503:2005. International Organization for Standardization, Geneva

ISO/IEC (2008) Systems and software engineering—system life cycle processes, ISO/IEC 15288:2008. International Organization for Standardization, Geneva

ISO/IEC/IEEE (2011) Systems and software engineering—architecture description, ISO/IEC/IEEE FDIS 42010:2011. International Organization for Standardization, Geneva

ISPL (1999) Information services procurement for large-scale migrations. Information Services Procurement Library. Ten Hagen & Stam, The Hague, The Netherlands

ITGI (2009) COBIT 4.1. IT Governance Institute, Rolling Meadows, USA, http://www.isaca.org/Knowledge-Center/COBIT/

ITIL (2009) ITIL V3. Office of Government Commerce, United Kingdom, http://www.itil-officialsite.com

Jackson, M (1990) Some complexities in computer-based systems and their implications for system development. Proceedings of international conference on computer systems and software engineering (CompEuro '90), Tel-Aviv, Israel, IEEE Computer Society Press, 8–10 May 1990, pp 344–351

Jonkers H, Lankhorst M, van Buuren R, Hoppenbrouwers S, Bonsangue M, van der Torre L (2004) Concepts for modeling enterprise architectures. Int J Coop Inf Syst 13(3):257–288

Kendall S (2002) The unified process explained. Addison-Wesley, Boston, MA

Kircher M, Jain P (2004) Pattern-oriented software architecture, volume 3: patterns for resource management. Wiley, New York

Lagerström R, Johnson P, Höök D (2010) Architecture analysis of enterprise systems modifiability—models, analysis, and validation. J Syst Software 83(8):1387–1403

Lamsweerde A (2003) KAOS tutorial. Crediti, 5 Sept

Lankhorst M et al (2009) Enterprise architecture at work: modelling, communication and analysis, 2nd edn. Springer, Berling

Lankhorst M, Oude Luttighuis P (2009) Enterprise architecture patterns for multichannel management. Proceedings of the patterns in enterprise architecture management (PEAM2009), 2 Mar 2009, Kaiserslautern, Germany. See also http://www.telin.nl/Project/Kanalen/Kanaalpatronen.htm (in Dutch)

Lee G, Xia W (2010) Toward agile: an integrated analysis of quantitative and qualitative field data on software development agility. MIS Quart 34(1):87–114

Linden DJT van der, Hoppenbrouwers SJBA, Lartseva A, Proper HA (2011) Towards an investigation of the conceptual landscape of enterprise architecture. In: Halpin T, Nurcan S, Krogstie J, Soffer P, Proper E, Schmidt R, Bider I (eds) Enterprise, business-process and information systems modeling; 12th international conference, BPMDS 2011, and 16th international conference, EMMSAD 2011, held at CAiSE 2011, London, UK. LNBIP series vol 81, Part 8. Springer, Berlin, June 20–21 2011, pp 526–535

Lindvall M, Basili V, Boehm B, Costa P, Dangle K, Shull F, Tesoriero R, Williams L, Zelkowitz M (2002) Empirical findings in agile methods. In: Proceedings of the extreme programming and agile methods—XP/Agile Universe, Chicago, IL, USA, pp 197–207

Marca DA, McGowan CL (1987) SADT: structured analysis and design technique. McGraw-Hill, New York, NY

Martin J (1991) Rapid application development. Macmillan, New York

McGovern J, Ambler SW, Stevens M, Linn J, Sharan V, Jo E (2003) The practical guide to enterprise architecture. Prentice Hall, Upper Saddle River, NJ

Meszaros G, Doble J (1998) A pattern language for pattern writing. In: Coplien JO, Schmidt DC (eds) Pattern languages of program design. Addison-Wesley, Boston, MA, pp 529–574

Meyer B (1991) Design by contract. In: Mandrioli D, Meyer B (eds) Advances in object-oriented software engineering. Prentice Hall, Englewood Cliffs, NJ, pp 1–50

Misra S, Kumar V et al (2009) Identifying some important success factors in adopting agile software development practices. J Syst Software 8(11):1869–1890

Moody DL (2009) The "physics" of notations: toward a scientific basis for constructing visual notations in software engineering. IEEE Trans Software Eng 35(6):756–779

Nielsen J (1993) Usability engineering. Academic, New York

OASIS (2006) Reference model for service oriented architecture 1.0, OASIS standard. OASIS, Burlington, MA, http://docs.oasis-open.org/soa-rm/v1.0/soa-rm.pdf

OASIS (2011) Reference architecture foundation for service oriented architecture, version 1.0. OASIS, Burlington, MA, Public review draft 02, 06 Jul 2011. http://docs.oasis-open.org/soa-rm/soa-ra/v1.0/soa-ra.html

ODP (2010) Ontology design patterns. European Bioinformatics Institute, Hinxton, Cambridge, http://ontologydesignpatterns.org

OED (2009) Oxford English dictionary. Oxford University Press, Oxford, UK

OMG (2008) Semantics of Business Vocabulary and Business Rules (SBVR), version 1.0. formal/08-01-02. Object Management Group, Needham, MA, http://www.omg.org/spec/SBVR/

OMG (2009) Service oriented architecture Modeling Language (SoaML), version 1.0 beta 2. ptc/2009-12-09. Object Management Group, Needham, MA, http://www.omg.org/spec/SoaML/

OMG (2010) Object Constraint Language (OCL), version 2.3 beta 2. ptc/2010-11-42. Object Management Group, Needham, MA, http://www.omg.org/spec/UML/

OMG (2011a) OMG Unified Modeling Language (OMG UML), superstructure, version 2.4.1. Formal/2011-08-05. Object Management Group, Needham, MA, http://www.omg.org/spec/UML/

OMG (2011b) Meta-Object Facility (MOF) core specification, version 2.4.1. Formal/2011-08-07. Object Management Group, Needham, MA, http://www.omg.org/mof

OMG (2011c) Business Process Modeling Notation specification, version 2.0. Formal/2011-01-03. Object Management Group, Needham, MA, http://www.omg.org/spec/BPMN/

Op't Land M, Proper E, Waage M, Cloo J, Steghuis C (2009) Enterprise architecture: creating value by informed governance. Springer, Berlin

O'Reilly CA, Tushman ML (2004) The ambidextrous organization. Harvard Business Review, (April):74–81

Osgood CE, Suci GJ, Tannenbaum P (1957) The measurement of meaning. University of Illinois Press, Urbana, IL

Osterwalder A, Pigneur Y (2009) Business model generation: a handbook for visionaries, game changers, and challengers. Wiley, Hoboken, NJ

Papazoglou MP, van den Heuvel W-J (2007) Service oriented architectures: approaches, technologies and research issues. VLDB J 16:389–415

Pols R van der, Backer Y (2007) ASL - Application Services Library: a management guide. Van Haren Publishing

Poppendieck M, Poppendieck T (2003) Lean software development: an agile toolkit. Addison-Wesley, Boston, MA

Porter ME (1996) What is strategy? Harvard Bus Rev, Nov–Dec:61–78

Quartel DAC, Steen MWA, Pokraev S, van Sinderen MJ (2007) COSMO: a conceptual framework for service modelling and refinement. Inform Syst Front 9(2–3):225–244

Quartel DAC, Engelsman W, Jonkers H, van Sinderen M (2009) A goal-oriented requirements modelling language for enterprise architecture. In: Proceedings of the 13th IEEE international EDOC conference (EDOC 2009). Auckland, New Zealand, pp 3–13

Quinn JB, Baruch JJ, Cushman Paquette P (1987) Technology in services. Sci Am 257(6):50–58

Qumer A, Henderson-Sellers B (2008) An evaluation of the degree of agility in six agile methods and its applicability for method engineering. Inform Software Tech 50(4):280–295

Ralyté J, Brinkkemper S, Henderson-Sellers B (eds) (2007) Situational method engineering: fundamentals and experiences. Proceedings of IFIP WG 8.1 working conference (ME07), Geneva, Switzerland. Springer, 12–14 Sept 2007

Rittel H, Webber M (1973) Dilemmas in a general theory of planning. Pol Sci 4:155–169

Ross JW, Weill P, Robertson DC (2006) Enterprise architecture as strategy: creating a foundation for business execution. Harvard Business School Press, Boston, MA

Rowe GP (1987) Design thinking. The MIT Press, Cambridge, MA

Ruffa SA (2008) Going Lean: how the best companies apply lean manufacturing principles to shatter uncertainty, drive innovation, and maximize profits. Amacom, New York

Salvendy G, Karwowski W (2010) Introduction to service engineering. Wiley, New York

Sambhamurthy V, Bharadwadj A, Grover V (2003) Shaping agility through digital options: reconceptualizing the role of information technology in contemporary firms. MIS Quart 27(2):237–263

Sandhu R, Coyne EJ, Feinstein HL, Youman CE (1996) Role-based access control models. IEEE Comput 29(2):38–47

Schmidt DC, Stal M, Rohnert H, Buschmann F (2000) Pattern-oriented software architecture, volume 2: patterns for concurrent and networked objects. Wiley, New York

Schumacher M, Fernandez-Buglioni E, Hybertson D, Buschmann F, Sommerlad P (2005) Security patterns: integrating security and systems engineering. Wiley, New York

Schwaber K, Beedle M (2002) Agile software development with scrum. Prentice Hall, New Jersey

SEI (2010) Capability maturity model integration for services (CMMI-SVC), Version 1.3. Software Engineering Institute, Carnegie-Mellon, Pittsburgh, PA, http://www.sei.cmu.edu/cmmi/solutions/

Sharifi H, Zhang H (1999) A methodology for achieving agility in manufacturing organisations: An introduction. Int J Prod Econ 62:7–22

Sherehiy B, Karwowski W, Layer JK (2007) A review of enterprise agility: concepts, frameworks, and attributes. Int J Ind Ergonom 37:445–460

Simon HA (1996) The Sciences of the Artificial, 3rd ed. MIT Press

Sinur J, Hill JB (2010) ITScore overview for business process management. Gartner Research

Slot RG (2010) A method for valuing architecture-based business transformation and measuring the value of solutions architecture. Dissertation, University of Amsterdam

Sowa JF (2000) Ontology, metadata, and semiotics conceptual structures. In: Ganter B, Mineau GW (eds) Conceptual structures: logical, linguistic, and computational issues, vol 1867, LNAI series. Springer, Heidelberg, pp 55–81

Sowa JF, Zachman JA (1992) Extending and formalizing the framework for information systems architecture. IBM Syst J 31(3):590–616

Spohrer J, Maglio PP, Bailey J, Gruhl D (2007) Steps toward a science of service systems. IEEE Comput 40(1):71–77

Sprott D, Wilkes L (2004) Understanding service-oriented architecture. Microsoft Archit J 2004:10–17

Standish Group (2011) CHAOS manifesto. http://blog.standishgroup.com/cm2011

Stapleton J (1997) DSDM, Dynamic Systems Development Method: the method in practice. Addison-Wesley, Boston, MA

Steinberg D, Budinsky F, Paternostro M, Merks E (2008) EMF—Eclipse Modeling Framework, 2nd edn. Addison-Wesley, Boston, MA

Stevens W, Myers G, Constantine L (1974) Structured design. IBM Syst J 13(2):115–139

Taufan MD (2011) Method management system: rule-based method enactment using mediaWiki and semantic mediaWiki. Master's thesis, Radboud University Nijmegen

Terlouw, L (2011) Modularization and specification of service-oriented systems. PhD thesis, Delft Technical University, Delft, The Netherlands

The Open Group (2009a) The Open Group Service Integration Maturity Model (OSIMM), technical standard. The Open Group, Reading, UK, https://www.opengroup.org/projects/osimm/

The Open Group (2009b) Navigating the SOA open standards landscape around architecture. The Open Group, Reading, UK, http://www.opengroup.org/soa/source-book/stds/index.htm

The Open Group (2011) The Open Group Architectural Framework (TOGAF) version 9.1 'Enterprise edition'. The Open Group, Reading, UK, http://www.opengroup.org/togaf/

The Open Group (2012) ArchiMate 2.0 specification, technical standard. The Open Group, Reading, UK, http://www.opengroup.org/archimate/

Trætteberg H (2008) UI design without a task modeling language—using BPMN and Di-amodl for task modeling and dialog design. In: Forbrig P, Paterno F (eds) Proceedings of the 2nd conference on human-centered software engineering, HCSE 2008, and 7th international work-shop on task models and diagrams, TAMODIA 2008, Pisa, Italy, 25–26 Sept. LNCS 5247 Springer, Heidelberg, pp 110–117

Trætteberg H (2009) Integrating dialog modeling and domain modeling: the case of Diamodl and the eclipse modeling framework. J Univers Comput Sci 14(19):3265–3278

Turk D, France R, Rumpe B (2002) Limitations of agile software processes. 3rd International conference on eXtreme programming and agile processes in software engineering (XP2002), Alghero, Italy, pp 43–46

Van der Aalst W, Pesic M, Schonenberg H (2009) Declarative workflows: balancing between flexibility and support. Comp Sci Res Develop 23(2):99–113

Van Zeist RHJ, Hendriks PRH (1996) Specifying software quality with the extended ISO model. Software Qual J 5(4):273–284

Vanderdonckt J (2005) A MDA-compliant environment for developing user interfaces of information systems. In: Pastor O, e Cunha J F (eds) Advanced information systems engineering, 17th international conference, CAiSE 2005, Porto, Portugal, June 13–17. LNCS 3520, Springer, Heidelberg, pp 16–31

Vanthienen J, Snoeck M (1993) Knowledge factoring using normalization theory. In: International symposium on the management of industrial and corporate knowledge (ISMICK), DTEW Research Report 9306. pp 97–106

Van der Aalst W, Hofstede AHM, Kiepuszewski B, Barros AP (2003) Workflow patterns. Distrib Parallel Dat 14(1):5–51, See also http://www.workflowpatterns.com

Van der Veer G, Lenting BF, Bergevoet BAJ (1996) GTA: groupware task analysis—modeling complexity. Acta Psychol 91:297–322

Venkatraman N (1997) Beyond outsourcing: managing IT resources as a value center. MIT Sloan Manage Rev 38(3):51–64

Verhoef C (2002) Quantitative IT portfolio management. Sci Comput Program 45(1):12–96

Versendaal J (1991) Separation of the User Interface and Application. PhD thesis, Delft University of Technology

Vissers CA, Logrippo L (1986) The importance of the service concept in the design of data communications protocols. In: Diaz M (ed) Protocol specification, testing, and verification, V. North-Holland, Amsterdam, pp 13–17

W3C (2004) Web services glossary. World Wide Web Consortium. http://www.w3.org/TR/ws-gloss/

W3C (2009) OWL 2 web ontology language. W3C recommendation. World wide web consortium. http://www.w3.org/TR/owl2-overview/

Wagter R, van den Berg M, Luijpers J, van Steenbergen M (2005) Dynamic enterprise architecture—how to make it work. Wiley, Hoboken, NJ

Wells D (2009) Agile process. extreme programming: a gentle introduction. http://www.extremeprogramming.org

Weske M (2007) Business process management: concepts, languages, architectures. Springer, Heidelberg

Wilmont I, Barendsen E, Hoppenbrouwers S, Hengeveld S (2012) Abstract reasoning in collaborative modeling. Proceedings of the 45th Hawaiian international conference on the system sciences, HICSS-45; Collaborative systems track, Collaborative modeling minitrack. IEEE digital proceedings

Winter R (2011) Design of situational artefacts – Conceptual foundations and their application to IT/business alignment. In: Pokorny J, Repa V, Richta K, Wojtkowski W, Linger H, Barry C, Lang M (Eds) Proceedings of 19th international conference on information systems development. pp 35–49

Xebia (2010) Lean architecture principles. http://blog.xebia.com/2010/08/11/lean-architecture-principles-wrap-up/

Yahoo (2010) Yahoo! design pattern library. http://developer.yahoo.com/ypatterns/

Yin A, Figueiredo S, da Silva M (2011) Scrum maturity model. Proceedings of the 6th international conference on software engineering advances (ICSEA 2011), Barcelona, Spain, October 23–29 2011

Ylvisaker M, Szekeres SF, Feeney T (1998) Cognitive rehabilitation: executive functions. In: Ylvisaker M (ed) Traumatic brain injury rehabilitation: children and adolescents. Butterworth-Heinemann, Newton

Yu ESK (1997) Towards modelling and reasoning support for early-phase requirements engineering. In: Proceedings of the 3rd IEEE international symposium on requirements engineering, pp 226–235

Zachman JA (1987) A framework for information systems architecture. IBM Syst J 26(3):276–292

Zoet M, Ravesteyn P (2011) A structured analysis of business rules representation languages: defining a normalization form, Paper 20. In Seltsikas P, Bunker D, Dawson L, Indulska M (Eds), Proceedings of ACIS 2011, Sydney, Australia, 30 Nov–2 Dec 2011

Index

A
Abstraction, 143, 162
Action, 83
Active stakeholder participation, 117–118
Activity, 83
Actor, 79
Agile Manifesto. *See* Manifesto for agile development
Agile method. *See* Method, agile
Agile practice. *See* Practice, agile
Agile service. *See* Service, agile
Agile service development (ASD)
    conceptual model, 72–90
    framework, 64–72
Agility, 2, 18
    business, 9, 21, 23–25, 184–188
    drivers, 29–40
    process, 9, 21–22, 25–27, 112, 184–188
    system, 9, 22, 27–29, 182–184
Agility scan, 124
ArchiMate, 42, 44
Architecture, 42
    description, 42
    enterprise, 2, 43
    process, 56–57
    service-oriented, 44, 66
Artefact
    creation, 152–154
ASD. *See* Agile service development (ASD)
Attribute, 89

B
BDUF. *See* Big Design Up-Front (BDUF)
Big design up-front (BDUF), 44
BPMN. *See* Business process modelling notation (BPMN)
Bricolage, 8
Business agility, 125. *See also* Agility, business
Business driver, 124
Business Model Canvas, 24, 125
Business process management (BPM), 66
Business process modelling notation (BPMN), 83

C
Capability model, 181
Channel, 32
Collaboration, 78
Commitment, 144
Communication, 141
    participants, 156
    practices, 170–176
    situation, 146
    situation template (intentional), 149
    situation template (operational), 150
Communication activity, 146
Competency, 25–26
Compliance, 38–39
Concept, 74
Conclusion, 87
Condition, 87
Consensus, 144
Constraint, 74
Conway's law, 47
Coordination aspect, 67
Coupling and cohesion, 47

D
Daily standup, 20
Decision, 87

Decision aspect, 68, 85
Decision modeling notation (DMN), 92
Dependency, 84
Design and Engineering Methodology for Organizations (DEMO), 65
Design level, 69
Design thinking, 9
DMN. *See* Decision modeling notation (DMN)
DSDM. *See* Dynamic systems development method (DSDM)
Dynamic architecture (DyA), 56, 114
Dynamics
　product and service, 32–33
　revenue, 34
　volume, 35–36
Dynamic systems development method (DSDM), 19

E
Encapsulation, 47
Enterprise architecture. *See* Architecture, enterprise
Entity, 88
Entity relationship diagrams (ERD), 73
e^3value, 81
Event, 84
Execution capability, 46

F
Fact type, 87
Feedback, 139
Flexibility, 26
　channel, 36–37
　supply chain, 37–38
Flow, 81
Function, 81
Function aspect, 67

G
Gateway, 84
Goal, 76, 120, 123

I
Implementation level, 69
Infrastructure level, 69
Innovation capability, 46
Interaction, 84
Interaction aspect, 67

Interaction element, 78
Interface, 78
Item, 88

L
Learning, 139
Learning cycle, 20
Location, 79

M
Manifesto for agile development, 18
Meaning, 159
Method
　agile, 19–21, 113
　engineering, 113–114
　fragment, 114
Model, 61
Model-based development, 52–53
Model integration, 90–93
MoSCoW prioritization, 19

O
Object, 88
Object constraint language (OCL), 73
Object role modeling (ORM), 74
OCL. *See* Object constraint language (OCL)
Operating model, 49
ORM. See Object role modeling (ORM)
OWL. *See* Web ontology language (OWL)

P
Pattern
　classification, 98–101
　language, 96
Practice, 113
　agile, 114
Process, 83
Process agility. *See* Agility, process
Product, 88
Product aspect, 68
Property, 74

R
Refactoring, 55–56
Reference, 89
Relation, 74
Requirement, 76
Requirements level, 68–69

Responsiveness, 25
Retrospective. *See* Sprint, retrospective
Risk, 54–55
Role, 74, 79
Rule, 87
Rule set, 87

S
SBVR. *See* Semantics of Business Vocabulary and Business Rules (SBVR)
Scrum, 20
Scrum master, 20
Semantics, 159
Semantics of Business Vocabulary and Business Rules (SBVR), 74
Separation of concerns, 47
Service, 5, 6, 82
   agile, 10
   application, 6
   business, 6
   consumption, 7
   contract, 32
   delivery, 7
   economy, 1
   infrastructure, 7
   orientation, 4
   system, 7, 31–32
Situational factor, 118
SOA. *See* Architecture, service-oriented
Social complexity, 8
Spccd, 25
Sprint, 20
   planning, 20
   retrospective, 20
   review, 20
Stakeholder, 76, 120, 141

Standardization, 50
Strategy, 124
Structure aspect, 67
Sustainability, 26
System agility. *See* Agility, system

T
Technical debt, 55–56
The open group architecture framework (TOGAF), 41–42, 65
Triggering, 84

U
UML. *See* Unified Modeling Language (UML)
Understanding, 144
Unified modeling language (UML), 73, 83

V
Value type, 74
Visualization, 164

W
Waterfall process, 132
Web ontology language (OWL), 74
Wicked problem, 8

X
XMI, 93

Z
Zachman framework, 65